FORENSIC ACCOUNTING AND FRAUD INVESTIGATION FOR NON-EXPERTS

HOWARD SILVERSTONE

MICHAEL SHEETZ

WILEY

John Wiley & Sons. Inc.

This book is dedicated to my mother Coba and my late father Nat, who taught me to aim for the moon and only accept the rooftops as an alternative.

Howard Silverstone

This book is dedicated to Adam Sheetz, my son, who has blessed my life in so many ways.

Michael Sheetz

ACKNOWLEDGMENTS

I would like to thank all my colleagues and friends at Kroll, who have given me the platform to practice in the profession that was tailormade for me. Special thanks to Pat and Doug Adamson for helping dot all the "I's" and cross all the "T's".

Extra special thanks to my wife Debbie, for all the support anyone could ask for, and to my children Jonathan, Alec, and Emma for understanding why dad can't be at every soccer practice. Thanks also to my brother Phill, for setting the family media bar so high, and of course to my parents Coba and Nat, for their vision and encouragement of my life in the accounting world.

Howard Silverstone

I would like to thank Professors Michael Froomkin and Jonathan Simon of the University of Miami School of Law and the University of California at Berkley, respectively, without whose inspiration and guidance I would not have realized my goals of teaching and writing.

I would like to thank Captain Rick Facchine of the Palm Beach Gardens Police Department, whose friendship, guidance, and support have both guided my career and encouraged me to pursue my dreams.

Michael Sheetz

ABOUT THE AUTHORS

Howard Silverstone is a principal in the forensic and litigation services group of Kroll, Inc., a leading international risk consulting company. Based in Philadelphia, Mr. Silverstone has over 20 years' experience in the fields of accounting, auditing, and forensic accounting. Since moving from the United Kingdom in 1985, he has worked on hundreds of commercial litigation, fraud, due diligence, and insurance matters for lawyers, their clients, and governmental agencies. He regularly writes and speaks on the many facets of forensic accounting. Mr. Silverstone is a Certified Public Accountant in the United States, as well as a Chartered Accountant (England and Wales) and a Certified Fraud Examiner.

Michael Sheetz is a professor of Business, International Law, and Ethics and a graduate of the University of Miami School of Law. He formerly served as an appellate law clerk for the 4th District Court of Appeal in West Palm Beach, Florida, and has a combined 20 years as a criminal investigator pursuing economic and computer crime investigations for civilian and military law enforcement agencies. Mr. Sheetz is currently the President of American Forensic Associates, L.L.C., a south Florida consulting firm specializing in fraud and high-tech crime prevention and investigation.

CONTENTS

CONTENTS

CONTENTS

INTRODUCTION

This book is meant to make you, the business manager, the executive, the banker, the shareholder, the student, or any other "non-expert," more alert to what could be going on under the surface day-to-day at any enterprise in which you might be a stakeholder. Nothing can be taken for granted any more. Financial Statements cannot be assumed to be what they seem. And that goes for people too. We have all seen too many pictures of executives wearing $2,000 suits accessorized with handcuffs!

The world of accounting and therefore the world of business is changing in the wake of the Enron and other scandals that came to light after the dot-com bubble burst. The U.S. Congress, through the Sarbanes-Oxley Act of 2002, and the accounting industry, through its review of auditing practices, are trying to make financial reporting more transparent. But corporate financial statements can only be as good as the underlying accounts that support them. It is to the composition of these accounts, the possibility of their fraudulent manipulation, and the investigation of frauds that may arise that this book directs the reader.

Part One is designed to show you the historical, legal, accounting, and criminological ideas that define the world of white-collar crime. It goes on to introduce the basic accounting principles necessary to understand the accounting system in which the frauds occur. We hope this section makes you sufficiently familiar with accounting concepts and terminology to be able to follow discussions of financial fraud in your future reading. Part Two will take you through the actual process of forensic investigation, providing a foundation that will put the material in Part One into action.

Forensic accounting is the examination that takes place *after* the initial allegation or discovery of fraud; it is the deeper search to determine whether or not a fraud has occurred and to find the "how," "who," "what," "where," and "when." We want the book to serve the dual purpose of making you aware of where fraud *might* occur in order to prevent it and then to show you what to do if it has actually been committed. We hope to provide

1

you with enough knowledge not to conduct the whole investigation yourself but to know when to call in the experts to find the evidence, evaluate it, and preserve it for use in court or other public forum.

Fraud costs the American economy (and other national economies) hundreds of billions of dollars a year and is committed by the most seemingly respectable people. It is a disease that can infect any business with deadly results. We hope this book will make you aware that it could happen at your company or a company with which you are familiar, and be committed by a most trusted employee. We hope this book will assist you in becoming more aware of the risk of fraud to business and what you and others can do to prevent it or root it out.

PART ONE

FRAUD AND FORENSIC ACCOUNTING OVERVIEW

1

FRAUD IN SOCIETY

WHAT IS FRAUD?

Fraud is an activity that takes place in a social setting and has severe consequences for the economy, corporations, and individuals. It is an opportunistic infection that bursts forth when greed meets the possibility of deception. The fraud investigator is like the attending physician looking and listening for the signs and symptoms that reveal an outbreak.

Before dealing with the accounting details and the investigation itself, we introduce some attempts by the courts, law enforcement, and regulatory authorities to define fraud. Since the subject of this book is white-collar fraud, we then outline the nature of this type of fraud through a look at the accounting cycle. We complete the tour with a look at the motives of fraudsters and the consequences of their acts.

In the beginning were the words *fraus*, a Latin noun carrying a wide range of meanings clustered around the notions of harm, wrongdoing, and deceit, and its adjective *fraudulentus*. The modern definition of fraud is derived primarily from case and statute law, but many of the ancient elements remain. The contemporary definition inferred from case law focuses on the intent of the fraudster to separate the trusting victim from property or a legal right through deception for his or her own benefit. This deception involves any false or misleading words or actions or omissions or concealment of facts that will cause legal injury. Criminal prosecution of fraud must prove beyond a reasonable doubt that an act meeting the relevant legal definition of fraud has been committed by the accused. In civil cases, liability must be demonstrated on a balance of probabilities.

Although fraud and white-collar crime are similar in that the perpetrators deceive rather than use physical violence, white-collar crime should be viewed as a subclass of fraud. Fraud includes confidence schemes, art

5

forgery, falsified scientific research data, lying on a résumé, and so on. White-collar crime, however, is committed by individuals embezzling, manipulating accounts, taking bribes, and so on at their place of business. What they all have in common, however, is the intent to deceive. This book limits its discussion to the field of white-collar crimes committed against businesses and their accounting systems and will not discuss consumer and other types of fraud. The forensic accounting techniques discussed below are central to the discovery of fraud in the business environment.

U.S. Supreme Court Definition of Civil Fraud

Fraud takes many forms, and the courts and other institutions have had a hard time finding a definition broad, yet specific, enough to give anything beyond a working definition.

The U.S. Supreme Court in 1888 provided a definition of civil fraud as:

First: That the defendant has made a representation in regard to a material fact;

Second: That such a representation is false;

Third: That such representation was not actually believed by the defendant, on reasonable grounds, to be true;

Fourth: That it was made with intent that it should be acted on;

Fifth: That it was acted on by complainant to his damage; and

Sixth: That in so acting on it the complainant was ignorant of its falsity, and reasonably believed it to be true. The first of the foregoing requisites excludes such statements as consist merely in an expression of opinion of judgment, honestly entertained; and again excepting in peculiar cases, it excludes statements by the owner and vendor of property in respect of its value.[1]

Michigan Criminal Law Definition of Fraud

The difficulty of defining fraud is exemplified in the Michigan Criminal Law:

Fraud is a generic term, and embraces all the multifarious means which human ingenuity can devise, which are resorted to by one individual, to get an advantage over another by false representations. No definite and invariable rule can be laid down as a general proposition in defining fraud, as it includes surprise, trick, cunning and unfair ways by which another is cheated. The only boundaries defining it are those which limit human knavery.[2]

FBI Definition of Fraud

The Federal Bureau of Investigation (FBI) offers a broad but useful definition of fraud that incorporates the elements recognized over the centuries:

those illegal acts which are characterized by deceit, concealment, or violation of trust and which are not dependent upon the application or threat of physical force or violence. Individuals and organizations commit these acts to obtain money, property, or services; to avoid the payment or loss of money or services; or to secure personal or business advantage.[3]

Financial fraud, the subject of this book, is criminal fraud of the white-collar type. It is committed against corporations by both employees and outsiders such as vendors and contractors.

SEC Definition of Fraud

The U.S. Securities and Exchange Commission (SEC) has its own definition of fraud as it applies to transactions involving securities. Although the law governs securities, the principles invoked reiterate the constellation of ideas central to definitions of fraud with broader application. The Securities Exchange Act of 1934, Section 10b-5, states:

It shall be unlawful for any person, directly or indirectly, by the use of any means or instrumentality of interstate commerce, or the mails, or of any facility of any national securities exchange,
a) to employ any device, scheme, or artifice to defraud,
b) to make any untrue statement of a material fact or to omit to state a material fact necessary in order to make the statements made, in the light of the circumstances under which they were made, not misleading, or
c) to engage in any act, practice, or course of business which operates or would operate as a fraud or deceit upon any person, in connection with the purchase or sale of any security.

7

TYPES OF FRAUD

White-collar fraud involves an intentional deception by employees, management, vendors, and customers to obtain money or other assets or services from a business. Some frauds are perpetrated by individuals and some in collusion across the management-employee social boundaries or between insiders and outsiders. The most useful way to classify the activity of the fraudster is by locating it within the five accounting cycles of any business where it will likely leave some kind of audit trail. The five cycles follow:

1. Sales and Collections
2. Purchases and Payments
3. Payroll and Personnel
4. Inventory and Warehousing
5. Capital Acquisition and Repayment

Sales and Collections Cycle

The sales and collections cycle bills clients for sales of goods and services and collects the money. This is the most cash-intensive of the five cycles. The most common frauds in this cycle are:

- Outright cash thefts
- Theft of other assets
- Kickbacks to customers
- Front-end frauds

Outright Cash Thefts

Cash thefts are the easiest and most common type of fraud to perpetrate in this cycle and are usually carried out through unrecorded sales, under-ringing of sales, lapping schemes, and over-billing, among others.

Theft of Other Assets

Assets can be stolen by ordering and shipping goods to an address other than that of the business.

Kickbacks to Customers

In customer kickback schemes, the fraudster under-bills the customer for merchandise and they split the difference, or receivables are written off as uncollectible for a fee.

Front-End Frauds

Front-end frauds are committed by the fraudster directing customers to take their business elsewhere or misappropriating a rebate.

Purchases and Payments Cycle

This cycle includes noncapital procurements and payments for goods, equipment, and services used in company operations. The buyer may act alone by setting up shell companies to receive goods misdirected from his company by false invoices. These schemes are often extremely complex and involve bank accounts, mail drops, and even corporate filings for the dummy entities. Procurement fraud is frequently a collusive employee–vendor fraud. The vendor will typically provide a bribe or kickback in return for business or, in the case of tendered contracts, for the employee to rig the bidding in favor of the fraudulent vendor. In another scheme, which may or may not be related to the original procurement scheme, once the vendor has been awarded the contract, the cost of the bribe may be recovered and profits increased by substituting products inferior to contract specifications, billing for work not done, shipping less than ordered, padding overhead expenses, and so on. Collusive fraud is the most common form of acquisition-and-payment fraud.

Payroll and Personnel Cycle

This cycle deals with hiring and termination, salaries, timekeeping, expense account reimbursements, and health and other types of employee insurance coverage. Common forms of fraud in this cycle are paying ghost employees, overstating hours worked, overstating expenses, and filing false medical claims. Employee and management fraud can overlap in this cycle, especially in the area of false expense account reports. An important but often overlooked area of personnel fraud is the improper vetting of job applicants. Collusion between a personnel department employee and a fraudster applicant could install a fraudster within the company with untold consequences.

Inventory and Warehousing Cycle

This cycle controls the purchase and storage of goods for later processing and sale or just for sale. The most common frauds in this cycle are ordering unneeded inventory and then stealing it for personal use; committing outright theft; and charging embezzlements occurring elsewhere in the company to inventory losses. These schemes can often become extremely complex and involve loading-dock workers, inventory accounting personnel, truck drivers, and receivers of stolen goods in other parts of the state or country.

Capital Acquisition and Repayment Cycle

This cycle accounts for debt and equity financing, interest, and dividend payments. The results of these transactions are reflected on the financial statements of the company. Because these accounts are developed at the executive level, this type of fraud is committed almost exclusively by management. The usual frauds are borrowing company money for personal use, misuse of interest income, and misuse of proceeds from financings.

Other Types of Financial Fraud

Some frauds that affect business often occur outside the typical accounting cycle. Customer fraud, for example, can severely affect insurance companies through filing of false applications and fraudulent claims, especially those for personal injury. Banks and other financial institutions suffer customer fraud through submission of false financial information on loan applications.

Management fraud deserves special mention in these days of corporate scandals. In addition to theft through the capital acquisition and repayment cycle, management can commit fraud through the manipulation of earnings reported on the financial statements prepared for shareholders and creditors. This type of fraud can affect the stock price, management bonuses, and the availability and terms of debt financing. Enron Inc. is a particularly egregious example of management manipulation of the financial statements that enriched a few but caused the collapse of the company pension plan, enormous losses to innocent shareholders, and unemployment for thousands of Enron staff.

Recent Events in Perspective

It is sometimes suggested that the size and complexity of the Enron, WorldCom, Adelphia, and other cases mean we are living in a new era of fraud. What should we make of this suggestion? Actually, rather than being trend-setting events, these scandals are merely the latest in a history of revelations that have always followed market excesses since the Dutch Tulip Mania of the 1630s[4]. The dot-com bubble of the late 1990s was no exception. The English polymath Walter Bagehot captured all the elements of excess in the following passage from *Lombard Street*, his 1873 critique of the English banking system:

> The mercantile community will have been unusually fortunate if during the period of rising prices it has not made great mistakes. Such a period naturally excites the sanguine and the ardent; they fancy that the prosperity they see will last always, that it is only the beginning of a greater prosperity. They altogether over-estimate the demand for the article they deal in, or the work they do. They all in their degree—and the ablest and the cleverest the most—work much more than they should and trade far above their means. Every great crisis reveals the excessive speculations of many houses which no one before suspected, and which commonly indeed had not begun or had not carried very far those speculations, till they were tempted by the daily rising price and the surrounding fever.[5]

Rather than seeing Enron as an exception, one should say it would have been surprising if no Enron or WorldCom or Adelphia or Tyco had appeared after the extraordinary period of economic growth in the 1990s. The picture presented throughout this book could well continue to be the reality met by fraud investigators into the foreseeable future.

A Bit of Background

The great bull markets of the twentieth century were all followed by revelations of malfeasance that only came to light after equity values had declined from heights unjustified by earnings growth rates and historical price-earnings multiples. When the Jazz Age ended in October 1929, the reputation of business executives was in just as much trouble as it is today. The shenanigans of the bigger players were ultimately exposed when the investigations of the Senate Committee on Banking and Currency in 1933–1934 revealed the true behavior and ethics of the bankers and brokers in the previous decade. The practices of the great financiers of the day as presented in 12,000 pages of testimony were so shocking that the government felt it necessary to establish the Securities and Exchange Commission in 1934 to regulate the financial industry.

Richard Whitney, head of his own investment firm and five times president of the New York Stock Exchange, proved to be an exceptionally poor businessman. He borrowed $30 million from his friends, relatives, and accounts in his trust and owed $6.5 million at the time he declared bankruptcy. He served three years and four months of a five-to-ten-year sentence for misusing funds from his father-in-law's estate.

The More Things Change. . . .

The go-go market of the late 1960s experienced a similar collapse, followed by revelations of what had really been going on during the frenzy. This time conglomerates, a corporate structure similar to the investment trust favored by investors in the 1920s, became the entity overvalued by the accountants. Creative accounting produced wildly overstated values that were soon proven false by actual performance. The inevitable result was, once again, a catastrophic collapse of stock prices and total destruction of the value of the debentures and bonds. As in the case of Arthur Andersen's work with Enron, accountants in the 1960s lost their definition of themselves as independent critics of corporate financial behavior.

The bull market of the mid-1980s was also a time of merger mania and the heyday of the junk bond market. The *crime du jour* was insider trading. The investment banker Drexel Burnham Lambert collapsed, and Denis Levine, Ivan Boesky, Michael Milken, and others went to jail.

The most recent exemplar of overvaluation and greed is, of course, the Enron case. Enron commoditized energy, bandwidth on optical fiber networks, newsprint, and many other assets into commodities contracts to be traded in the futures market and hedged them with derivatives. To show strong growth on its published financial statements, the company resorted to aggressive accounting practices and extensive use of off-balance-sheet instruments called Special Purpose Entities (SPEs) to provide the dynamism rewarded by Wall Street with a healthy price-earnings multiple.

The company liberally interpreted GAAP (Generally Accepted Accounting Principles) and sometimes acted in violation of GAAP by, for instance, booking income immediately that would only be earned in the future on contracts that could take as long as 10 years to complete. Debts were shifted to SPEs controlled by the company, despite a requirement that such an entity must be at least 3-percent owned by an external party that also exercises control.

The screaming headlines concerning the Enron case should not be allowed to deafen us to the call of history. People become less vigilant when markets are soaring, and they are not in the mood for the cold water of reality. It is only when they return to looking more closely at their investments in the difficult times that inevitably follow that they, like Walter Bagehot, see what was going on while they weren't paying attention.

Sarbanes-Oxley

The purpose of the Sarbanes-Oxley Act of 2002 is to provide investors with greater confidence in American corporations and allow them to rely on financial statements as an accurate representation of the financial condition of the companies in which they are stakeholders. The Act is a response to the revelations of lax auditing practices and conflicts of interest between auditors and their clients.

The instrument of the Act is the five-member Public Company Accounting Oversight Board to be administered by the SEC. Accounting firms that audit publicly traded companies must register with the Board, and those issuing more than 100 audit reports a year must be inspected annually for compliance with Board regulations. Registered firms must retain audit working papers for not less than seven years after the engagement and must have all audits reviewed by a second partner.

Perhaps the most dramatic section is Section 302, which makes the CEO and CFO certify the "appropriateness of the financial statements and disclosures contained in the periodic report, and that those financial statements and disclosures fairly present, in all material respects, the operation and financial condition of the issuer." Maximum penalties for willful and knowing violations of this section are a fine of not more than $5,000,000 and/or imprisonment of up to 20 years.

Another key section (201) prevents an accounting firm from creating possible conflicts of interest by prohibiting it from performing other services, including financial systems design, appraisal or valuation services, investment banking services, or other nonaudit services "contemporaneously with the audit."

The lead and reviewing partners must rotate off the audit every five years. The General Accounting Office will study the consequences of requiring the rotation of the audit firms themselves (207).

The SEC intends to study Special Purpose Entities (401c) to see how widely they are used and to determine whether GAAP as currently constituted is capable of reporting SPEs in a transparent fashion.

It will be unlawful for audited corporations to extend credit to directors or officers (402a). A report on the existence and effectiveness of internal controls for financial reporting will be attested to by the auditor and included in the company annual report (404).

Title VIII of Sarbanes-Oxley, known as the Corporate and Criminal Fraud Accountability Act of 2002, makes it a felony to interfere with any federal investigation into the records of a public company. Auditors must retain all working papers for five years. The statute of limitations on securities fraud claims is extended to the earlier of five years (formerly three years) from the fraud, or two years (formerly one year) after the discovery of the fraud. Whistleblowers are protected from reprisals by employers and can be awarded damages and attorney's fees.

Title IX, known as the White Collar Crime Penalty Enhancements Act of 2002, increases the maximum penalty for mail and wire fraud to 10 years from 5. Tampering with records or impeding official proceedings is now a crime.

Even though the high-profile examples to which Sarbanes-Oxley is a response are extremely rare, the Act is a timely corrective to the whole issue of misleading accounting that has been a concern of the SEC for many years. These new laws will affect the fraud investigator by assuring that corporate records are accurate and that internal controls are in place which will assure a movement of information along an assured audit trail

WHAT THE NUMBERS TELL US ABOUT FRAUD

Comprehensive official fraud statistics are hard to come by because government agencies and industry groups tend to keep records only of those frauds that affect their area(s) of interest. The problem is compounded by the discovery of new frauds such as Internet "cramming" and recategorization of "old" frauds, for example, in the FBI's designation of frauds perpetrated against identifiable groups such as scams of the elderly as "association" fraud.

We must also remember that all fraud statistics are based on known frauds. What is most unnerving is the fact that the numbers quoted are considered to be only the tip of the iceberg. Aside from the many undetected frauds are those frauds not reported by the harmed company for fear of embarrassment

Many of the figures bandied about in discussions of fraud are educated guesses or extrapolations from the few figures that are gathered. As a result, the best we can hope for is to get a broad picture of fraud from focused studies.

Study: Association of Certified Fraud Examiners

For purposes of this book, the best overview of financial fraud comes from studies done by the Association of Certified Fraud Examiners (ACFE). In 1996, the ACFE published *Report to the Nation on Occupational Fraud and Abuse* based on occupational fraud cases reported by its members. Its second report, the *2002 Report to the Nation on Occupational Fraud and Abuse*, is based on a study of the $7 billion lost in 663 cases reported by the Certified Fraud Examiners (CFE) who investigated them.[6]

The ACFE estimates that occupational fraud alone costs the U.S. economy about 6 percent of its revenues—or about $600 billion, or $4,500 per employee in 2002. This is a 50 percent increase over the $400 million estimated to have been lost in 1996 when the first report was written. Large as these figures are, it must be remembered that they do not include money lost through the infinite variety of consumer scams, tax evasion, and other personal frauds. The U.S. Congress estimates that telemarketing scams alone are a multibillion dollar annual business.[7]

Small-Business Fraud

Most frauds occur at small businesses where the average scheme causes $127,500 in losses compared to $97,000 in the largest corporations. Fraud is most likely to occur at small businesses simply because there are more of them and their control of the accounting cycle is weaker than at large corporations. According to statistics derived from Internal Revenue Service (IRS) income tax returns, just over 24 million businesses in the United States file returns, of which 72 percent are sole proprietorships and 8 percent are partnerships. In other words, 80 percent of U.S. business is done at small businesses, even though they generate only 13 percent of the taxable revenue. (Corporations of all sizes account for the remaining 20 percent of businesses and 87 percent of taxable revenue.)[8]

One should keep in mind that, although the billion-dollar scandals at Enron, WorldCom, and other corporations have splashed onto the front pages in recent times, it is the slow, steady drip, drip, drip of fraudulent activity at small businesses that is larger in aggregate and potentially does the greater damage to the economy over the long run.

Statistics also show that one-third of business failures arise as a result of internal fraud. One of the perpetrator's most often heard rationalizations is: "I'm not hurting anyone . . . it's just money." Clearly, this statistic takes us well beyond the belief that fraud hurts no one.

Categories of Occupational Fraud

The ACFE divides occupational fraud into three broad categories[9]:

1. Asset misappropriations
2. Corruption
3. Fraudulent statements

Asset Misappropriations

Asset misappropriations are the theft or misuse of assets and account for 80 percent of all occupational fraud. This category includes theft of cash, which is the asset misappropriation committed 90 percent of the time. Thus, based on the foregoing, cash thefts account for 72 percent of all occupational fraud.

Cash thefts usually occur in three different ways:

1. Fraudulent disbursements
2. Skimming
3. Cash larceny

Fraudulent Disbursements

Fraudulent disbursements use some device such as false invoices or time-cards to create a false payment obligation for a company. It is the most common type of cash fraud, accounting for 71 percent of the studied cases and creating a mean loss of $100,000.

Fraudulent disbursements break down into five principal types:

1. *Billing*: Fraudulent billing schemes accounted for 46 percent of fraudulent disbursements and created a median loss of $160,000.

2. *Check tampering*: Check tampering made up 30 percent, with a median loss of $140,000.

3. *Expense reimbursement*: Expense reimbursements comprised 22 percent of schemes and caused a median loss of $60,000.

4. *Payroll*: Payroll schemes represented only 18 percent of cases studied, but the median loss was as big as that for check tampering at $140,000.

5. *Register disbursement*: Register disbursements made up only 3 percent, with the smallest median loss of the group at $18,000.

Skimming

Skimming is the theft of cash during its collection but *before* it is recorded on the company books. Skimming occurred in 32 percent of the cash frauds and showed a $70,000 mean loss.

Cash Larceny

Cash larceny is the theft of cash *after* it has been recorded. This form of fraud accounted for only 9 percent of the cases, with a mean loss of $25,000.

Extrapolating these numbers, one can see that 23 percent of occupational fraud is perpetrated through fraudulent billing schemes. Frauds of this type are not the largest occupational frauds in dollar terms, but they are the most frequently occurring. This statistic, together with the fact that 72 percent of all occupational fraud is attributable to the appropriation of cash, explains the emphasis on knowing basic accounting principles in Chapters Two and Three. Most of the frauds you will encounter will likely be a diversion of cash for personal use through exploitation of some weakness in the operation of the accounting cycle at the victim company.

Corruption

Corruption is a crime of fiduciary abuse in which an employee uses a position of trust and authority to gain a benefit. Corruption accounted for 13 percent of the occupational frauds tracked by the ACFE. The acceptance of kickbacks and engagement in conflict of interest are typical corruption frauds.

Fraudulent Statements

Fraudulent statements accounted for only 7 percent of frauds, but they were much larger than in either of the other two classes. The median loss through fraudulent financial statements was $4,250,000 compared with $530,000 in corruption schemes and $80,000 in asset misappropriations.

Drawing Conclusions

To put these figures into perspective as they might affect a small company, consider the following calculation. In the year before it became the victim of a fraud, a company had $5 million in revenues, gross profits of $500,000 on a gross margin of 10 percent, and 12 employees. In the following year, revenues increased by 8 percent to $5.4 million, and a fraud of the average amount was committed, that is, a fraud of $54,000 (12 × $4500) based on the ACFE figures of an average loss of $4500 per employee. At a 10 percent gross margin, $540,000 of the $5.4 million in total revenues was used to generate the $54,000 stolen in the fraud. Gross profits without the fraud would have been $540,000 but were actually $486,000 ($540,000 – $54,000) instead. The profit margin was thus reduced to 9 percent ($486,000 ÷ $5,400,000). An additional $54,000 was stolen in year three. To pay for this without affecting the traditional 10 percent gross profit margin, revenues would have had to be increased by $540,000. Unfortunately, this was a tough year in the industry, and revenues grew by only 5 percent, or $267,000, to $5.67 million. Without the fraud, a 10 percent margin would have produced gross profits of $567,000; with the fraud, gross profits were reduced to $513,000 ($567,000 – $54,000) to produce a gross profit margin of only 9.05 percent.

From this small example, we can see and infer many of the important consequences of financial fraud. For example, much of the company sales force's efforts were wasted since $540,000, or approximately 10 percent of total revenues, had to be generated solely to pay for the $54,000 fraud. The reduction in gross profits meant less money for paying down debt, reinvestment, or distribution to shareholders. The slowdown in gross profit growth and the reduction in margins could affect share values and the ability to borrow money or to remain within the terms of existing covenants.

Society's Perception of Fraud

Fraud is often perceived as a victimless crime. Governments and businesses are seen as so wealthy that the money taken by fraud won't be missed. "They can afford it," is the classic rationalization heard in confessions. Fraud is also viewed as an easy way to get money without running the risk of severe punishment. Dismissal is certainly a possibility, but many employers will, in fact, try to hush up news that they have been defrauded for fear of adverse publicity with their customers, vendors, bankers, and insurers. Fraud is also seen as benign. Nobody is told at the point of a gun to lie on the floor of the bank; nobody is waiting for you in the dark when you come home. There is little risk of being caught. It's the kind of crime a respectable person can commit and still not feel like a criminal.

The truth is quite otherwise. If, as noted above (see "What the Numbers Tell Us about Fraud" section above), $600 billion in revenues is diverted annually by fraudsters, then $600 billion will never work its way through to shareholders' equity and increase the wealth of the national industrial base. Since most fraud occurs at small, and thus more vulnerable, businesses, the risk is greater that it can cause bankruptcy with its consequent costs to vendors and lenders and unemployment for company staff. A lifetime of building respect in business, in the community, and with the family can be destroyed when a trusted employee who felt protected by a reputation for honesty is exposed as a fraudster.

Fraud is far from benign. As fraudsters take advantage of technology, fraud becomes more sophisticated. It can no longer be characterized solely as employee theft for personal benefit. It is international. An American businessman who was the victim of a Nigerian letter scam went to Lagos to check on his "investment" and was murdered for his troubles.[10] The line between individuals stealing for themselves and fraud as part of organized crime is getting harder and harder to draw. Ruthless gangs have been discovered behind corporations boasting respectable boards of directors which are actually set up to launder money and create stock frauds. As regulators close the traditional charities and other fronts used to raise money, terrorists are turning to identity, mortgage, and other types of fraud to raise the money needed to attack U.S. interests. Today the occupational fraud uncovered at a small company could be part of something much larger.

Who Commits Fraud?—Profile of the Typical Fraudster

Early academic research on white-collar crime includes the paper "White-Collar Criminality," which Edwin H. Sutherland presented as his presidential address to the American Sociological Association in 1939.[11] He was writing in the aftermath of an era that had been characterized by crimes committed among the middle and upper classes. The Senate investigations of the stock market scandals of the 1920s revealed the ethical shortcomings of the country's business leaders. Many prominent public figures, including Richard Whitney, former five-term president of the New York Stock Exchange, were jailed. The repeal of the Volstead Act in 1933 that ended Prohibition closed a period that had seen the widespread corruption of public officials and turned virtually the entire population of the United States into lawbreakers in their desire to celebrate the boom times with alcoholic beverages.

Up to this time, crime had been explained as a phenomenon of the lower classes "caused by poverty or by personal and social characteristics believed to be associated statistically with poverty, including feeblemindedness, psychopathic deviations, slum neighborhoods, and 'deteriorated' families."[12] Sutherland argued that any theory of crime rooted in poverty was not a true picture of crime in society, for it failed to explain many other types of criminal behavior, including that of business and professional men.

Sutherland's paper raised the profile of middle and upper class criminal activity by extending the definition of "criminal" to include statistics other than those of conviction for violations of the criminal code since "a large proportion of those who commit crimes are not convicted in criminal courts."[13] He pointed to violations of federal agency regulations such as those of the Federal Trade Commission which were met only with cease and desist orders, license revocations, or fines. Many otherwise criminal cases were settled in civil suits because the plaintiff was more interested in restitution and damages than in seeking punishment. He also felt white-collar criminals were sometimes immune from conviction because of what he called "the class bias of the courts and the power of their class to influence the implementation and administration of the law."[14] Crime was also underreported when, for example, a politician was convicted of accepting a bribe but the person paying the bride escaped prosecution.

Sutherland recognized what subsequent research has confirmed. The white-collar criminal was not usually a product of poverty or dysfunctional families and was not feebleminded or psychopathic. "They were seldom problem children in their earlier years and did not appear in juvenile courts or child guidance clinics."[15]

By 1949, Sutherland had reached what he called an "approximate" definition of white-collar crime as "a crime committed by a person of respectability and high social status in the course of his occupation."[16] Such language probably bespeaks the sharp business practices of the important persons paraded through the courts in the 1930s after their fall from prominence. In fact, every word cries out for greater definition and has raised controversy among scholars ever since.

Nevertheless, the sense that white-collar crime is a distinct class of crime distinguished by the social qualities of its perpetrators has stood the test of time. Around this central idea, however, additional research has recognized other aspects of the problem. One of the most important is the role played by organizational structures and the positions of authority held by the offenders in facilitating the crimes. Notice was also taken of the enormous harm such activity could have on the business environment and individuals. Though not directly related to recent financial shenanigans, books such as Rachel Carson's *Silent Spring* and Ralph Nader's *Unsafe at Any Speed* published in 1962 and 1965, respectively, raised public awareness that respectable people could conduct business in ways that should be criminalized and, in many areas, later were.

Unfortunately, despite enormous scandals such as Watergate, the Iran-Contra Affair, the Savings and Loan debacle, the Wall Street insider trading exposé, the collapse of the Bank of Credit and Commerce International (BCCI), and Barings Bank, white-collar crime has not been subjected to as much research as other types of crime.[17] The lack of research on crimes of this type has resulted in a paucity of research on the criminals. The small number of prosecutions and subsequent convictions further hampers such research. In this respect, corporations work against their own best interests when they refuse to prosecute employees because of a fear of adverse publicity. The result is a lack of the raw material for academic study that could lead to a better understanding of the white-collar criminal and development of better hiring and prevention policies.

Despite the deficiencies in gathering evidence and developing theory, several studies have been done that show some consistency. The spectrum of persons committing white-collar crime is much broader than that suggested by the respectability and high-social-status criteria of Sutherland's definition. Even in class-conscious Britain, a company survey showed that managers committed one-third of employee fraud, accounting personnel one-fifth, and directors or partners only one-tenth. The more socially elevated directors and partners committed *less* fraud than sales and shopfloor personnel.[18]

A 1980 study showed that fraudsters are indistinguishable from their fellow employees by any demographic or psychological criteria.[19] The researchers compared a group of white-collar criminals with a group of prisoners held for other property offenses and a group of noncriminal college students. The white-collar prisoners were better educated, more devout, and less likely to have criminal records or alcohol or drug problems. They were also more likely to be married and in good psychological health as measured by self-esteem, achievement, and family well-being. In other words, they had the very qualities human resources departments look for in new hires. This research could not find any features that would predict future fraudulent behavior.

Perhaps the most important recent analysis of fraud and fraudsters is a U.S. study using pre-sentence investigation reports (PSIs). The researchers analyzed the PSIs for 1,094 people, predominantly white males, convicted of any one of eight classes of white-collar crime in the federal districts centered on Los Angeles, Atlanta, Chicago, Baltimore, Manhattan and the Bronx, Dallas, and Seattle in the three-year period 1977–1979 inclusive. The classes of crime analyzed were: antitrust violations, securities frauds, mail and wire fraud, lending- and credit-institution fraud, false claims, bribery, tax violations, and bank embezzlement.[20] In order to compare these offenders with nonviolent common criminals convicted of federal offenses of a financial character, the researchers studied 15 persons convicted of postal theft and postal forgery in each of the seven districts.

What the study revealed was a large third class of criminal behavior lying between the street crime identified by Sutherland as only part of the criminal population and the high-status criminal he defined as a new group needing study. Weisburd et al. recognized that the number of white-collar occupations has increased significantly since the 1920s and 1930s when some of the groundbreaking studies of criminal activity were made. More people than ever are engaged in processing financial and other information that can be fraudulently manipulated for personal gain. Much of this manipulation requires very little education or skill. Credit applications requiring a statement of income and assets, job applications requiring a statement of credentials, tax forms and applications to government for all kinds of grants, medical care, and welfare payments can all be manipulated by almost anyone. Criminal opportunity has been democratized. The spread of computer technology alone has opened vast new opportunities to defraud for persons of both limited and highly sophisticated technical knowledge.

Socialization to succeed both in terms of increased status and greater affluence can create self-perceptions of failure and poverty that can become hidden motivators to commit fraud. People seeking to better themselves need the opportunities provided by good credentials and access to credit. Even people who are successful by every conventional measure may still perceive themselves as poor and seek to increase their net worth through fraud.

Securities and antitrust offenders had the highest social standing (67.4 and 61.1, respectively) of all the groups studied by Weisburd et al., as measured by the Duncan Socioeconomic Index, but measured far below the highest score (96.0) assigned to doctors and the only slightly lower 92.3 for lawyers. Antitrust offenders were stable family men still married to their first wives, had median assets of $613,000, and debts of only $7,000, usually owned their own homes, had good reputations in their communities, had no drug or alcohol problems, and possessed good employment records. SEC violators were better educated because their jobs required a sophisticated knowledge of finance, while several antitrust offenders had started with nothing and had worked their way up. The SEC violators tended to have more debts, less stable marriages, and worse employment records. They were also younger, with a mean age of 44 compared with 53 for the antitrust offenders. The lawyers in these two as well as the other categories of crimes worked on the margins of the profession in small firms or partnerships and had graduated from the less prestigious law schools.

Tax and bribery offenders were farther down the social scale. They were mostly white males in their 40s, employed, often sole proprietors, or business owners. Several were lawyers, doctors, or certified public accountants (CPAs) with troubled personal lives.

People convicted of perpetrating credit or mail fraud, or of making false claims were yet lower in social status, less likely to be male or white, and with a lower median age in the late 30s. Their work histories were less stable, substance abuse was more common among them, and their median net worth was zero. A full quarter of these offenders were unmarried parents; another quarter was unemployed, and financial, personal, and family troubles were common among them. The level of unemployment at the time the crime was committed was the highest of all the crime categories studied. About half those convicted of these offenses had prior records, the highest rate of all the categories.

Bank embezzlers were still predominantly white, but women accounted for about 45 percent of those convicted. The median age here was low at 31. Most were bank employees; the men were mainly managers, and the women were tellers or clerks. This group included the smallest number of college graduates and the smallest number of homeowners. These offenders were usually from stable working families of modest means.

One of the study's central findings was that "white-collar criminals are generally much closer in background to average Americans than to those who occupy positions of great power and prestige."[21] In other words, the white-collar criminal is not Sutherland's person of "high social status" but a person of the middle class as measured by the usual standards of income, education, assets, and the like. On the other hand, the white-collar criminal is sharply distinguishable from the common property criminal by the same criteria.

Looked at as a group, the offenders in this study had an unemployment rate at the time of the commission of their crimes similar to that of the general population in the seven federal districts. This contrasts sharply with the more than 50 percent rate typical of common crime defendants. White-collar offenders are better educated than the average American and tend to hold jobs with higher-than-average prestige but, with the exception of the few doctors and lawyers in the group, not the highest. Eighty percent of the white-collar criminals had high school diplomas compared with 69 percent in the general population and less than 50 percent among common criminals. About a quarter of the subjects in the Weisburd et al. study had college degrees compared with 19 percent in the general population and only 3 percent of common criminals. The white-collar offenders were quite different from the general criminal population by having a mean age of 40 compared with the mean age of 27 for offenders in the criminal justice system overall in 1977, the first year of the study.

Since crime in general is primarily a male phenomenon, it is not surprising to find that men committed 83 percent of the white-collar crimes committed in the eight categories. The crimes committed by women were usually less complex and less harmful.

White-collar criminals are more likely to be better off financially than common criminals but have more debt than the average American, despite giving the appearance of being well off. They are more likely to own their own homes than common offenders but less likely to be homeowners than the average American.

About 43 percent of the white-collar offenders in this study had had prior arrests, and about 35 percent had been convicted of a serious crime. This contrasts sharply with the fact that most people convicted of felonies have had prior arrests and convictions. There seems, however, to be little evidence of white-collar criminal careers among the study subjects since only about one in five had had a previous conviction for a white-collar offense.

Weisburd and Waring did a followup study in 1990 on the same subject population but this time supplemented the information on the PSIs with the arrest histories from the FBI "rap sheets," adjusted for a 14 percent mortality rate among the original subjects. By examining the subjects' arrest histories before the arrest for the crimes studied for the 1977–1979 period *and* for the period 1979–1990, Weisburd and Waring found that 48 percent had been arrested at least once. They found that 38.5 percent had been arrested before and 31.3 percent in the second period. The highest number of prior *and subsequent* arrests occurred among those committing mail fraud, credit fraud, and making false claims.[22]

The picture of the white-collar criminal with an arrest record for other crimes is quite different than that of the street criminal with a record. Even though a few white-collar criminals had 10 or more arrests, this number is still significantly below that for common street offenders who may be arrested 10 or more times in a single year. Street offenders are usually arrested for the first time in their teens; the white-collar criminals in this study were booked for the first time at an average age of 35. For 40 percent of the sample, the first offense was a white-collar crime.

There seems to be some inconclusive evidence that white-collar criminals as well as street criminals stop their criminal activity as they age. Street criminals stop because they lose the required agility and change the direction of their lives. On the other hand, an individual wanting to commit a white-collar crime actually gains knowledge with age and has increased opportunities through advancement up the corporate ladder into positions that control larger sums of money. These potential opportunities may, however, be put out of reach by an arrest! The reason for stopping also may be explained by something as simple as the recognition that "[g]oals and aspirations change for these offenders as for other people as they get older."[23]

Any attempt to draw the profile of the white-collar criminal, including the fraudster, must deal with the important fact that they are low-frequency offenders. As shown above, white-collar criminals are rarely career criminals, and, in fact the white-collar offense is often the only arrest on their record. The typical subjects of this study were in fact the very picture of middle-class respectability: a well-educated male achiever, a homeowner married to his first wife and without a substance abuse problem.

The ACFE study is by and large consistent with the findings of Weisburd et al. Men in the 40–50 age group with high school or less education and working alone committed most frauds. The largest amounts, however, were stolen by university-educated older men with no criminal records who were in positions of financial responsibility and perpetrating the frauds in collusion. Dishonest managers and executives working alone caused median losses of $250,000, or about 4.2 times the $60,000 stolen by lower-level employees operating by themselves. When executives and managers colluded with employees, however, the median loss jumped to $500,000, or double what executives and managers stole on their own and 8.3 times what employees stole on *their* own. Since management is responsible for the application of controls to detect fraud, the involvement of management makes detection more difficult and the fraud potentially more devastating for the company.

Women commit just about as many frauds as men, but the median amount is smaller. Fraud, too, has its "glass ceiling"! Most executive and managerial positions are still held by men, and their opportunities to steal large sums are greater. Fraudulent acts by women seem to increase as one descends the occupational hierarchy. The activity of women is especially marked at the clerical levels of the financial industry.[24] One can reasonably expect that the admission of greater numbers of women to positions of power will result in a more equitable balance in the gender statistics.[25]

Men over 60 also stole more than 27 times the median $18,000 taken by persons under 26 years of age, despite the fact that the older group accounted for only 2.5 percent of the cases studied, while the younger group accounted for 6.0 percent. In fact, one can conclude from this study that the median amounts taken vary directly with age.

Frauds by persons with university education are less frequent but involve larger median amounts than those committed by persons with only high school or below. Once again, this reflects the fact that educated people tend to rise to higher levels of responsibility and thus control larger amounts of money.

Perhaps the most disturbing statistic in the ACFE study is the one showing that 68.8 percent of the frauds were committed by persons who had never been charged or convicted of any previous crime. This is consistent with Romney et al. and Weisburd et al. who discovered no sociopathic behavior patterns in the fraudsters studied in their research.

Crisis Responders and Opportunity Takers

What, then, makes a person commit that one act that turns a respectable citizen into a criminal? How does a person who does not have the statistical profile of the common criminal form the intent to break the law? Weisburd and Waring identify two broad classes of offender: crisis responders and opportunity takers. The crimes of the crisis responders "seem to be situational responses to real stress or crisis in their professional or personal lives." The crimes of the opportunity takers seem to be "linked strongly to some unusual or special set of opportunities that suddenly materialize for the offender."[26]

The crisis responders were people in positions of trust who saw a criminal act as the way out of a perceived financial crisis. These events were anomalies in their social histories. The women acted to pay family bills, and the men stepped over the line for a variety of reasons, such as financial troubles at the company they owned or to reduce their income taxes payable.

The opportunity takers were not driven to commit a crime by financial pressures; they were drawn in by the temptation created by an unusual opportunity. Many of these events were isolated wrong choices. This group, however, also includes those recruited into conspiracies operating in permissive environments. Once involved, these offenders become socialized into criminal activity that can last for years or even decades. The offense for which they suffered their one arrest was, in fact, often one long, systematic criminal activity.

The commission of a crime requires a place that connects opportunity and victim. The most harm is done by officers and managers colluding with others in ways that exploit an organization for which they work. This is the quintessential middle-class crime. Owners and sole proprietors may be from a higher social class, but the businesses they control are usually too small to permit the magnitude of the thefts possible from large corporations. Others of high social status, such as doctors and lawyers, rarely commit large complex crimes. Exceptions are those doctors who open clinics to exploit Medicaid.

It is the officers and managers who hold their positions in large companies through education and hard work rather than birth who have the opportunities to commit the big frauds, This is because they command the accounting systems as well as the controls that should safeguard those same systems. These crimes are most frequently collusive because their commission requires an assembly of skills capable of exploiting the complexity of the corporate structure.

The largest frauds in dollar terms and the most complex are committed in the securities and insurance industries as well as in the service sector. Government is, of course, also large but the constant auditing leaves little opportunity for major internal frauds to develop through collusion. Instead, government is victimized from the outside through fraudulent contracts and claims for services. The banking industry, despite the constant presence of cash and other forms of money, is rarely the victim of a large complex internal fraud.

Detection

White-collar crime in general is usually detected by reports from the victim, routine audits, or informants. Since the victims of white-collar crime rarely know anything has happened at the time the money is actually taken, often a long lag develops between the commission of a crime and its discovery and report. Three quarters of all bank embezzlements and more than half of all credit card and mail frauds are typically reported by victims. These frauds are, in effect, self-detecting, and institutions spend relatively little on trying to discover it themselves. About 80 percent of tax fraud is, on the other hand, discovered through routine audits or investigations. Routine audits in the banking industry also discover many of the common internal employee frauds.

The discovery of collusive crimes is almost entirely dependent on informants. Antitrust crimes require the participants to communicate or meet in order to fix prices and carry the attendant risk that someone might break rank and inform. The more people involved, the greater the risk. Bribery is still a collusive crime, even though only two persons are required for its commission.

Motivations for Fraud

Put in the broadest possible terms, the history of criminology has been an attempt to identify the characteristics that distinguish criminals from noncriminals and then to find a theory that explains and predicts criminal behavior. After more than a century of investigation, there is much information on criminal behavior but still no general theory of why crime exists that has won wide acceptance. This is especially true of white-collar crime, which seems a statistical exception to what is known about common street crime. The central question of white-collar crime, namely, why people who are so typically upstanding and so unlike street criminals, commit the crimes they do, remains unanswered despite much theorizing.

Some theorists have taken a "big-picture" approach and argued that white-collar crime is the inevitable outcome of the competitive ethic of capitalism. According to this theory, competition is the field on which egotism and recklessness can have full play.[27] We are constantly bombarded by images of the wealth and success that can be achieved through winning in the great experiment in social Darwinism in which we live. The inevitable result of such competition is the recognition of the economic inequality of winners and losers, which can be internalized as the constant fear of failing. This discontent may be sufficient to make a person see white-collar crime as the great equalizing act. The drive for money and the trappings of success are, therefore, the motivators of the act.[28]

Recent theorizing has shifted the focus to the situation in which the crime is committed. This newer thinking does not dismiss the role of personal history, which is so important in the creation of the street criminal, but questions its explanatory power. It raises the question of why certain people commit certain crimes in certain situations. This is a useful line of theorizing since it allows the criminal act to be conceptually distinguished from the criminal's life story and explained as the pursuit of short-term gratification and not the culmination of a long history of personal disadvantage.

The situation in which the potential white-collar offender finds him- or herself plays a most significant role in determining whether or not a crime will be committed. The corporate culture lived daily at the workplace can often create enormous pressures to commit criminal acts. Examples are common in the famous cases of price-fixing, bribery, and manufacture of dangerous products that occurred throughout the last century.[29] A corrupt corporate culture can lead to the inversion of all values. The comfort of conformity then becomes the Achilles' heel of the middle-class person under pressure to "go along to get along." Loyalty can easily slip into complicity. Criminal behavior becomes normal. Team-playing becomes conspiracy. Fear of dismissal, ostracism, or losing the favor of superiors can be compelling forces in the world of a department or small company. In such an atmosphere, one learns criminal behavior "in association with those who define such behavior favorably," as Sutherland contended.[30]

These acts cannot be explained by a personal history of instability and deviance since stability and conformity are the principal characteristics of these criminals' lives. Even while committing the crimes, white-collar offenders are able to lead their conventional lives, which are, indeed, their camouflage. Their conventionality and stability are the foundation of the trustworthiness that gives them the opportunity to commit the crime in the first place. It is this life of conventionality that gives the criminal act the character of an aberration.

It is, however, the white-collar criminals' power of rationalization that is one of the most amazing aspects of their behavior. They are able to behave normally and aberrantly at the same time without feeling conflict. This behavior is possible through the use of techniques of "neutralization."[31] These are acts of mental deftness that allow persons to violate behavioral norms without simultaneously seeing themselves as deviant or criminal. Such self-exculpating explanations can occur both before and after the commission of a criminal act.

The most common rationalization is that financial crimes do not hurt other people. Embezzlers commonly tell themselves they are merely "borrowing" the money and intend to return it later without anyone else being affected. Many embezzlers justify it because they had to do it to pay mounting family bills. "Everybody's doing it" is frequently heard as an argument for systematic wrongful company behavior. Corporate offenders often consider laws as an unjust or unnecessary form of government interference disrupting free market forces. They may even argue that breaking the law was necessary for the survival of the company.

Employees frequently offer a moral justification for their thefts with the argument that their employer "owed" them the money. Fraud simply expressed their grievance. For example, they feel exploited and underpaid or hurt after receiving a smaller-than-expected bonus. Many feel justified after being passed over for promotion; others feel they can do the job just as well as, if not better than, the person with the higher education. Personal antipathies, anger after a reprimand from the boss, and the like can all be self-serving explanations for fraud. Such a sense of being wronged, whether justified or not, can fester for years before developing into a plan to defraud.

In rare cases, mental illness can drive a person to commit fraud through a wish to damage the company. Others can be motivated by pure egotism; they commit fraud just to show how smart they are. Yet others are driven by anticapitalist ideologies and think they are destroying the system from within.

Summary

With our present state of knowledge and theorizing, we can only say that we still know relatively little about white-collar crime after many years of research. All we can say for sure is that the white-collar criminal is more like Mr. and Ms. Citizen than like the common street criminal. It remains a mystery why these outwardly normal and respectable people commit white-collar crimes. We still cannot answer the question why the bank clerk with too much personal debt decides to embezzle instead of seeking credit counseling. No one can say why the opportunity taker decides to commit and rationalize a crime when he or she has never before sought out criminal opportunities to better themselves. What tips these people in the one direction rather than the other? No one knows. Perhaps the last word should be left to two of the field's leading and prolific researchers:

> Such causes (of the white-collar criminal's actions) may be so individualistic, and varied and found in such different places over the life course, that it is virtually impossible for scholars to identify them or for public policy makers to use them to develop crime prevention policies. The causes of criminality in this context may be similar to the causes of changes in our weather or other phenomena for which long-range forecasts are difficult. The chain of causal events involves so many factors that can have such varied effect that reliable long-term prediction at the individual level becomes virtually impossible.[32]

THE SOCIAL CONSEQUENCES OF ECONOMIC CRIME

Economic crime is an enormous social problem whose consequences are often not fully realized by the public at large. The *2002 Report to the Nation: Occupational Fraud and Abuse* of the Association of Certified Fraud Examiners estimated that fraud would cost the American economy $600 billion in 2002, or 6 percent of gross domestic production (GDP). This translates into an incredible $4,500 for each employee. These figures represent only the amounts stolen directly by the fraudsters and do not measure the ripple effect that can engulf whole companies, employees, vendors, suppliers, and banks. Even when the company survives the fraud, the energies of the sales staff have been wasted generating revenues that got siphoned off by the fraudster. Earnings are reduced, dividends are not increased, shareholders' equity does not grow, important financial ratios are jeopardized, bonuses are curtailed or eliminated, and so on.

Information about the many small but destructive frauds are buried in company or court records, and their consequences can only be surmised. Three well-documented frauds whose effects can, however, be measured illustrate the consequences where others cannot: the Equity Funding insurance and mutual fund scandal, the collapse of the savings and loan industry, and, more recently, Enron.

Equity Funding

The Equity Funding scandal went on for many years and resulted in the collapse of a company highly regarded by Wall Street analysts, with enormous consequences for shareholders, policyholders, and employees. The Equity Funding Corporation of America (EFCA) sold a unique combination package of mutual fund units and life insurance. Customers would buy mutual fund units, which could be used as collateral for a loan as high as 45 percent of their value to pay the premiums. At the end of 10 years, when the life insurance would be fully paid up, unit holders would sell some of their units to pay off the loan and still have a nice nest egg with the remainder. The life insurance offered a hedge against poor market performance by the mutual funds, and the funds offered the opportunity for capital gains while acquiring life insurance. That was the theory anyway.

EFCA went public in 1964 at $6 per share and peaked at 80¾ in 1969. Investigators later concluded that almost immediately fraudulent financial statements were being created that listed as assets nonexistent loans sup-posedly provided to customers to pay the insurance premiums. The most damaging part of the fraud began when the company decided to issue its own policies and get out of the agency business. Unfortunately, it was un-able to write enough new business to meet its contractual obligations with the old insurer. To maintain the appearance of a business with growing as-sets, management began to create and coinsure bogus policies to make up the difference. The growing annual shortfall forced the company to use the money paid by the coinsurers to pay the premiums on the fake policies. In other words, a Ponzi scheme[33] developed. In the end, of the 97,000 policies valued at $3.5 billion that were supposed to be in force, 56,000 or $2 bil-lion did not actually exist.

The Fall

The collapse came on April 2, 1973, when the SEC charged EFCA with stock manipulation by reporting nonexistent earnings. Many other charges were included in a 105-point indictment against 22 men for securities fraud, mail fraud, bank fraud, filing false documents with the SEC, inter-state transportation of counterfeit securities and other securities obtained by fraud, as well as electronic eavesdropping. Other indictments included charges of creating false computer printouts and other records, forging death claims, counterfeiting bank documents, securities purchase confir-mations, and bonds, plus falsifying financial data.

The Aftermath

The first to feel the effects were the nearly 10,000 EFCA shareholders. Be-cause of its remarkable growth record which continued despite downturns in the economy, EFCA had become a Wall Street favorite. At the time of the collapse, its book value of about $300 million in equity and $200 million in bonds was outstanding. Banks, mutual funds, pension funds, and other institutional investors held large positions, but individuals owned at least half the equity.[34] One institution lost $10 million, but none collapsed as a result of the fraud. The thousands of small investors who had also invested part of their life savings on the basis of the same record saw the value of their holdings extinguished within a week of the announcement of the first SEC charge. This was particularly hard on small investors who had bought on margin or were using the shares as collateral for lines of credit. No one knows for sure, but many must have faced foreclosure on their homes or personal bankruptcy as a result of their losses. Expenditures on important items like medical care were canceled and retirement plans destroyed. The largest banks in the country had lent millions to EFCA on the basis of ratios calculated with the fraudulent financial statements. These loans were now irrecoverable. The reinsurers lost at least $10 million when EFCA could no longer create new policies to be sold to new reinsurers in order to pay the old in the Ponzi scheme. Ironically, the policyholders themselves were not affected by the collapse; the trustee informed them that their policies were still in force following a well-managed Chapter 11 reorganization, and so 70 percent stayed with the new company.

Savings and Loan

When President Ronald Reagan signed the Garn-St. Germain Depository Insurance Act into law on October 15, 1982, no one could have foreseen that it would lead to the collapse of the very industry it was designed to transform after 50 years of close government regulation. Instead of permitting savings and loan companies to compete more freely with other financial institutions, the act proved to be an invitation to fraud on an unprecedented scale. In the words of three historians of the tragedy:

> A financial mafia of swindlers, mobsters, greedy S&L executives, and con men capitalized on regulatory weaknesses created by deregulation and thoroughly fleeced the thrift industry. While it is certainly true that economic factors . . . contributed to the crisis, savings and loans would not be in the mess they are today (1989) but for rampant fraud.[35]

Within five years, 500 of the country's 3200 S&Ls were insolvent, and another 500 were on the brink. When President George H. W. Bush brought in his bailout plan in February 1989, estimates of the losses had already reached as high as $360 billion to be paid down over the next three decades.[36] Thrifts in trouble but not yet closed were costing the Federal Savings and Loan Insurance Corporation (FSLIC) $35–40 million a day, or $12.7 billion a year. To give these figures some perspective, the total was twice the then federal deficit and equal to the entire National Aeronautical and Space Administration (NASA) budget for the next 20 to 30 years! Every American taxpayer was going to have to pay an additional $200 annually for 10 years to make up the loss.[37]

The modern thrift was created by President Herbert Hoover with the Federal Home Loan Bank Act of 1932 after the collapse of 1,700 of the country's 12,000 thrifts had wiped out the life savings of thousands of Americans. Congress supplemented this law by establishing the Federal Savings and Loan Insurance Corporation (FSLIC) in 1934 to insure deposits up to $5,000, with funds provided through assessments of the member thrifts.

As housing prices began to rise in the 1960s, Congress tried to protect homebuyers by capping the rate thrifts could pay on deposits to 5.5 percent. With inflation at 13.3 percent in 1979 and the invention of the money market fund and electronic banking making possible the movement of funds to any market on the globe, the S&Ls were simply unable to compete for funds. Congress passed the first interest rate deregulation bill and increased the FSLIC coverage to $100,000 per account from $40,000. Profits were now squeezed between the rising costs of deposits and income from existing mortgage payments, many of whose rates had been set as much as 30 years before.

The Garn-St. Germain Act of 1982 permitted S&Ls to offer money market funds without interest rate regulation and to invest up to 40 percent in nonresidential real estate. Later in the year, other changes now allowed a single shareholder to own a thrift. Formerly, 400 shareholders were required, and no one investor could own more than 25 percent. A thrift could now be purchased using land or other noncash assets as capital. Down payments on property purchases were no longer required; the thrift could now finance 100 percent of the value. The S&L was no longer restricted to making local loans; it could invest anywhere. Loose accounting regulation permitted good-will to swell on the balance sheets. The number of federal and state examiners was cut.

The Fall

This powerful cocktail was sufficiently intoxicating to entice many new investors to take huge risks with federally insured funds under very limited supervision. People who controlled a thrift and were able to attract deposits could invest them in almost anything they wanted. And they did. With millions flowing into the industry, the inexperienced and often criminal new owners went on a nationwide binge of bad investments, fraud in all its many forms, self-aggrandizement, and occasionally even murder. People with federally insured deposits to use threw elaborate parties, bought expensive cars and private planes, built mansions, and vacationed at the best hotels and spas at home and abroad.

The Aftermath

The outcome was all too predictable. After only a few years, acres of unsold apartments, townhouses, condominiums, suburban housing developments, resorts, golf courses, and office buildings were standing dark and empty, especially in Texas and California where state deregulation had supplemented the loosening of controls by the federal government. In the end, the seemingly limitless funds, the bribes, the special deals, the coziness with politicians at all levels and of all stripes could not prevent the impossible financial fantasies from finally collapsing into an enormous multibillion-dollar ruin.

The self-destruction of the S&L industry had repercussions far beyond the monetary losses that would have to be picked up by the federal taxpayer. Enormous resources were wastefully misdirected to projects that would never have economic value, at least not at the prices paid. This money was lost forever for productive investment. Millions more had to be spent on lawyers and other experts to straighten out a mess that should never have occurred in the first place. S&Ls were closed at the cost of thousands of jobs in rural economies where every job is needed.

Perhaps the saddest part of the whole fiasco was the loss of a part of American culture. The thrift industry had been founded in the very heart of small-town America. The word "thrift" as applied to this type of banking was an apt description of the hard work and saving in the pioneer tradition that made the S&L part of the institutional foundation of the community, together with the church and the school. It represented local self-sufficiency. Neighbor helped neighbor in the knowledge that federal insurance made their savings secure even in the rare case of default. All gone as the price of fraud.

Enron

The Enron story is told elsewhere in this book and is not repeated here. Whether the events at Enron constitute fraud will be determined by the courts in the lawsuits now being prepared. Whatever the outcome, the immediate effect of the collapse was enormous and personal. The hardest hit were the employees who held Enron stock in their 401 (k) plans. The stock had reached a high of $90.60 in August 2000 and was trading below $1 by November 2001. On August 14, 2001, chairman Ken Lay sent an e-mail memo to all employees on the occasion of the resignation of president Jeffrey Skilling saying that Enron's "performance has never been stronger; our business model has never been more robust; our growth has never been more certain."[38] The stock was trading at $42. Only two months later, on October 16, Enron announced a $544 million after-tax charge against earnings and a $1.2-billion write-down of shareholders' equity. The very next day, plan holders were told that because of a change in plan administrator they could not trade in the stock for 30 days, a critical period in the collapse of the stock price. The stock was at $33 when the loss was announced and dropped to $16 over the next two weeks, while the plan holders could only sit and watch. During this same period, the company announced it was restating its accounts for the years 1997 to 2001 inclusive. Meanwhile, according to allegations contained in many of the class-action lawsuits, Lay and other senior Enron personnel had been selling hundreds of millions of dollars worth of stock for the 18 months prior to the August 14 memo.

The Aftermath

Plan holders who had believed Ken Lay's memo and had been locked in saw millions in retirement nest eggs vanish.

By the time Enron filed for Chapter 11 bankruptcy protection on December 2, 2001, the stock was virtually worthless and 4,000 employees were let go. The following April 8, Arthur Andersen, the accounting firm that had played such a significant role in auditing and consulting for Enron, laid off 7,000 employees. Important clients Merck and Newell Rubbermaid and many others that had, in some cases, been with Andersen for decades soon began to decamp. Two months later Andersen was convicted of obstructing justice by shredding documents in the Enron audit. By this time, Andersen had lost nearly two-thirds of its former 28,000-person U.S. workforce and faced multimillion dollar lawsuits from Enron investors. The worldwide workforce of 85,000, including the United States, had been reduced to fewer than 3,000 by October, and the company had been fined the maximum $500,000 for obstructing justice. The fine had little meaning since Andersen had almost ceased to exist.

The bankruptcy of Enron was a tragedy, especially for those employees who lost both their retirement funds and their jobs. It was also tragic for the employees of Andersen, who were let go as one of the great names in the accounting industry disappeared bit by bit like the Cheshire Cat. It was catastrophic for the city of Houston, where Enron had been a respected corporate citizen and employed thousands of local men and women. The questionable use of tax shelters may have deprived the federal government of millions in unpaid taxes. The banks lost millions in loans, and the reputations of numerous Wall Street brokerage houses and their analysts were severely damaged.

NOTES

1. *Southern Development Co. v. Silva,* 125 U.S. 247, 8 S. C. Rep. 881, 31 L. Ed. (1888).
2. *Michigan Criminal Law,* chapter 86, section 1529.
3. *White Collar Crime: A Report to the Public,* U.S. Department of Justice, Federal Bureau of Investigation ((Washington, DC: U.S. Government Printing Office, 1989), p. 3, cited in Cynthia Barnett, *The Measurement of White-Collar Crime Using Uniform Crime Reporting (UCR) Data, www.fbi.gov/ucr/whitecollarforweb.pdf*
4. The prices of tulips and the practice of tulip speculation became so extreme that the States of Holland passed a statute in 1637 curbing this activity!
5. Walter Bagehot, *Lombard Street* (New York: Scribner, Armstrong & Co., 1873), new ed. (London: Smith Elder & Co., 1915), rpt. (New York: Arno Press, 1978).
6. *www.cfenet.com/pdfs/2002RttN.pdf.*
7. *www.ftc.gov/reports/Fraud/execsum.htm.*
8. *www.bizstats.com/numberbizs.htm.*
9. *www.cfenet.com/pdfs/2002RttN.pdf.*
10. The intended victim of this scam typically receives a letter purporting to be from a Nigerian official who needs to use the victim's bank account to move millions of dollars out of Nigeria. The letter requests the victim's address and bank account numbers on the promise of a share usually between 15 and 30 percent of the amount.
11. Edwin H. Sutherland, "White-Collar Criminality," *American Sociological Review,* 5, no. 1 (February 1940): 1–12, rpt. in Neal Shover

and John Paul Wright, eds., *Crimes of Privilege: Readings in White-Collar Crime* (New York: Oxford University Press, 2001), pp. 4–11.

12. Sutherland, in Shover and Wright, eds., *Crimes of Privilege,* p. 4.

13. Ibid., p. 7.

14. Ibid., p. 8.

15. Ibid., p. 11.

16. Edwin H. Sutherland, *White Collar Crime* (New York: Holt, Rinehart & Winston, 1949), p. 9.

17. Hazel Croall, *Understanding White Collar Crime* (Philadelphia: Open University Press, 2001), p. 5.

18. M. Levi, *The Prevention of Fraud,* Crime Prevention Unit, Paper 17 (London: HMSO, n.d.), as cited in Croall, *Understanding White Collar Crime,* p. 49.

19. Marshall B. Romney, W. Steve Albrecht, and David J. Cherrington, "Red-Flagging the White-Collar Criminal," *Management Accounting* (March 1980): 51–57.

20. David Weisburd, Stanton Wheeler, Elin Waring, and Nancy Bode, *Crimes of the Middle Classes: White-Collar Offenders in the Federal Courts* (New Haven, CT: Yale University Press, 1991).

21. Weisburd et al., *Crimes of the Middle Classes,* p. 62.

22. David Weisburd and Elin Waring with Ellen F. Chayet, *White-Collar Crime and Criminal Careers* (Cambridge: Cambridge University Press, 2001), p. 29.

23. Ibid., p. 41.

24. Croall, *Understanding White Collar Crime,* p. 55.

25. Ibid., p. 56.

26. Weisburd and Waring, *White-Collar Crime and Criminal Careers,* p. 58.

27. James William Coleman, *The Criminal Elite* (New York: St. Martin's Press, 1989), p 211 ff.

28. For an interesting attempt to combine microeconomics, psychology, and risk analysis into a motivational theory, see Stanton Wheeler, "The Problem of White-Collar Crime Motivation," in Kip Shlegel and David Weisburd, *White-Collar Crime Reconsidered* (Boston: Northeastern University Press, 1992), pp. 108–123.

29. Coleman, *The Criminal Elite,* passim.

30. Sutherland, *White Collar Crime,* p. 234.

31. Gresham M. Sykes and David Matza, "Techniques of Neutralization: A Theory of Delinquency," *American Sociological Review,* 22

(December 1957): 667–670, cited in Coleman, *The Criminal Elite*, p. 211.

32. Weisburd and Waring, *White-Collar Crime and Criminal Careers*, p. 147.

33. A "Ponzi scheme" (according to the Oxford English Dictionary) is "a form of fraud in which belief in the success of a fictive enterprise is fostered by payment of quick returns to first investors from money invested by others." The scheme's name is derived from Charles Ponzi, who immigrated to America from Italy in 1903 and developed a scheme in 1909 to sell notes promising a 40% profit within 90 days. Ponzi did not invest the funds, but used part of each person's money to pay "dividends" to previous investors and kept a certain amount of money for himself. Word got out that people were getting a lot of money from the "fund" and more people wanted to invest. Ponzi's problem was that as the number of people involved grew, it became increasingly impossible for the scheme to continue. The resultant collapse of the scheme thus led to the term "Ponzi scheme." A "Ponzi scheme" is similar to and somewhat interchangeable with "pyramid" and "chain letter" schemes.

34. Ronald L. Soble and Robert E. Dallos, *The Impossible Dream*, (New York: G.P. Putnam's Son, 1975) pp. 275–276.

35. Stephen Pizzo, Mary Fricker, and Paul Muolo, *Inside Job: The Looting of America's Savings and Loans* (New York: McGraw-Hill, 1989), p. 298.

36. Pizzo et al., *Inside Job*, p. 4.

37. Ibid., p. 308.

38. Peter C. Fusaro and Ross M. Miller, *What Went Wrong at Enron* (Hoboken, NJ: John Wiley & Sons, 2002), p. 201.

SUGGESTED READINGS

www.ftc.gov/reports/Fraud/execsum.htm.

www.bizstats.com/numberbizs.htm.

Bagehot, Walter. *Lombard Street*. New York: Scribner, Armstrong & Co., 1873. New ed. London: Smith Elder & Co., 1915. Rpt New York: Arno Press, 1978.

Brooks, John. *The Go-Go Years*. New York: Weybright & Talley, 1973.

Coalition Against Insurance Fraud
www.insurancefraud.org/news/study021303_set.html.

Coleman, James William. *The Criminal Elite.* New York: St. Martin's Press, 1989.

Croall, Hazel. *Understanding White Collar Crime.* Philadelphia: Open University Press, 2001.

Galbraith, J. K. *The Great Crash of 1929.* Boston: Houghton Mifflin, 1979.

Levi, M. The Prevention of Fraud. Crime Prevention Unit, Paper 17. London: HMSO. In Hazel Croall, *Understanding White Collar Crime.* Philadelphia: Open University Press, 2001.

Pecora, Ferdinand. *Wall Street under Oath.* New York: Simon & Schuster, 1939.

Romney, Marshall B., W. Steve Albrecht, and David J. Cherrington. "Red-Flagging the White-Collar Criminal." *Management Accounting* (March 1980): 51–57.

Rosenmerkel, Sean P. "Wrongfulness and Harmfulness as Components of Seriousness of White-Collar Offenses." *Journal of Contemporary Criminal Justice,* 17, no. 4 (November 2001): 308–327.

Shlegel, Kip, and David Weisburd. *White-Collar Crime Reconsidered.* Boston: Northeastern University Press, 1992.

Shover, Neal, and John Paul Wright, eds. *Crimes of Privilege: Readings in White-Collar Crime.* New York: Oxford University Press, 2001.

Sutherland, Edwin H. *White Collar Crime.* New York: Holt, Rinehart & Winston, 1949.

Sutherland, Edwin H. "White-Collar Criminality." *American Sociological Review,* 4, no. 1 (February 1949): 1–12. Rpt. in Neal Shover and John Paul Wright, eds., *Crimes of Privilege: Readings in White-Collar Crime.* New York: Oxford University Press, 2001, pp. 4–11.

Sykes, Gresham M., and David Matza. "Techniques of Neutralization: A Theory of Delinquency." *American Sociological Review,* 22 (December 1957): 667–670.

2002 Report to the Nation: Occupational Fraud and Abuse
www.cfenet.com/pdfs/2002RttN.pdf.

Weisburd, David, and Elin Waring with Ellen F. Chayet. *White-Collar Crime and Criminal Careers.* Cambridge: Cambridge University Press, 2001.

Weisburd, David, Stanton Wheeler, Elin Waring, and Nancy Bode. *Crimes of the Middle Classes: White-Collar Offenders in the Federal Courts.* New Haven, CT: Yale University Press, 1991.

Wheeler, Stanton. "The Problem of White-Collar Crime Motivation." In Kip Shlegel and David Weisburd, *White-Collar Crime Reconsidered.* Boston: Northeastern University Press, 1992, pp. 108–123.

White Collar Crime: A Report to the Public. U.S. Department of Justice, Federal Bureau of Investigation. Washington, DC: U.S. Government Printing Office, 1989, p. 3. Cited in Cynthia Barnett, *The Measurement of White-Collar Crime Using Uniform Crime Reporting (UCR) Data.* *www.fbi.gov/ucr/whitecollarforweb.pdf.*

2

UNDERSTANDING THE BASICS OF FINANCIAL ACCOUNTING

INTRODUCTION

No forensic investigation can be undertaken without some knowledge of accounting principles. Even if you are not examining a company's books and records yourself, you may well be talking to the people who are and need to know how an accounting system works in order to understand their language. The purpose of this chapter is to introduce you to some fundamental concepts that will show you how money moves through a corporation and how business transactions should be recorded. But first, a little historical background.

THE FATHER OF ACCOUNTING

Born in the Tuscany region of Italy in the mid-1400s, Luca Pacioli is best known for his 1494 book *Summa de arithmetica, geometria, proportioni et proportionalita (The Collected Knowledge of Arithmetic, Geometry, Proportion and Proportionality)*. Within this book was a chapter entitled *"Particularis de Computis et Scripturis,"* a treatise on accounting. It was this chapter that dealt with the principle of double-entry bookkeeping. While most people agree that Pacioli did not invent this system of accounting, he wrote of the method used by Venetians during the Italian Renaissance period. Pacioli's accounting system included most of the accounting cycles that we are familiar with today. He wrote of journals and ledgers, and he believed that a person should not go to sleep at night until the debits equaled the credits! The ledger he described included assets (such as receivables and inventories), liabilities, capital, income, and expense accounts. Pacioli talked of year-end closing entries and suggested a trial balance be used to prove a balanced ledger. His work also refers to a wide range of topics from accounting ethics to cost accounting.

One of the most quoted lines from Pacioli's book, which bears so much relevance to our book, is as follows: "He who does business without knowing all about it, sees his money go like flies." Just like the accounting system Pacioli described over 500 years ago, this statement is ageless and as relevant today as it was half a millennium ago. In view of recent events concerning accounting entries and financial statements, one can only wonder what the "Father of Accounting" would have made of today's double-entry chaos.

Over the past 500 years, the primary concept of accounting has not changed. Accounting is a method of tracking business activities in a particular time period (whether it be a week, a month, or a year). Such tracking is needed internally for owners and decision makers to have timely information on the performance of their business. Although most savvy business owners may have day-to-day control over their business, as companies grow larger and their business becomes more complex, the need for more detailed information increases. However, as recent events have shown, people on the outside of a business also need financial information. Their need for information results from the relationship they have with the particular company. An investor will want to know about results and the company's financial stability. Similarly, a creditor will want to know if his debt is likely to be paid, and a potential investor or vendor will need information on the company before moving forward in a financial relationship.

As we will see throughout this book, many corporate frauds are described as crimes committed within the accounting system of various companies. The accounting system comprises the methods by which companies record transactions and financial activities. It tracks the business activity of an entity and is usually categorized as recording data (i.e.; the initial entry into the company's records), classifying information into related items, and then summarizing the data for the end user to readily understand.

Although internal fraud has historically centered on manipulation of accounting entries, recent events have been focused more directly on financial statements and the manipulation of the underlying data. From an early age, accountants are taught that the financial statements are a "snapshot," one point in time to capture the profitability (or nonprofitability) and financial position of an entity. The balance sheet should convey the financial position of the business at one point in time (e.g.; at the company's year-end), listing the company's assets and liabilities, together with the company's equity.

The concept of the balance sheet comprises what is known as the accounting equation—the fact that assets always equal liabilities plus equity. This brings us back to Luca Pacioli, who, we noted earlier, believed that one should not sleep until the debits equaled the credits. Clearly, we are still losing sleep, but not so much over the equation itself: we are now losing sleep over the propriety of what is underlying those debits and credits!

THE FIVE ACCOUNTING CYCLES

To understand how fraud occurs within businesses is to understand how the cycles work within an accounting system. Specifically, the cycles are defined as:

- Sales and Accounts Receivable
- Payments/Expenses and Accounts Payable
- Human Resources and Payroll
- Inventory and Storage/Warehousing
- Capital Expenditures

Sales and Accounts Receivable

The fundamental concept of any business involves getting business from customers, billing for those goods or services, and then making sure the accounts receivable are collected. In terms of the accounting equation and accounting cycle, the revenues from sales appear on a company's income statement, and the respective accounts receivable appear on the balance sheet. Cash sales would directly affect the cash balance, which is also a balance sheet item.

Within this part of the cycle are steps that a business must undertake to minimize its financial risk. These steps include approval potential for credit before entering into a business relationship; having a system for receiving orders from the customers and then invoicing them; and then collecting the amounts owed from the customers, along with the appropriate system for making adjustments to the account for returns, write-offs, and so on.

Fundamental within this accounting cycle are the safeguards put in place by a company—the internal controls to minimize the opportunity for theft or misappropriation. While no different than other aspects of the accounting cycle, it is relevant to note them here. At the same time, the concept behind these controls is similar for all cycles. Specifically:

- **Separation of duties**—This is a fundamental concept of accounting and one through which companies can prevent a lot of frauds by properly segregating the functions of custody, authorization, and recordkeeping. For the sales and accounts receivable cycle, this would apply to separating the credit function and sales function (thereby minimizing the chances of granting credit to an unsuitable potential customer in order to force a sale). Similarly, sales recording and receipt of cash should also be separated.

- **Physical safeguards of assets**—On the most basic level, this should involve restriction of access to computers by specific password, physical locks, and the use of, for example, lock boxes for customers to mail checks, instead of check and cash handling by company employees.

- **Audit trail** (i.e., adequate and proper documentation of transactions)—As with other cycles, the need for adequate documentation in an accounting system is fundamental. At a minimum, this should include prenumbered documents for sales orders, shipping documents, sales invoices, credit memos, and remittance advices (or a computer system that assigns numbers as printed, but with sufficient controls over access limited by specific passwords for users).

- **Approval process**—This process extends to credit approval, write-off approval, and the shipment of products.

- **Independent checks on the system** (whether by an internal audit function or an outside source)—Although many companies have an internal audit function, others do not consider themselves large enough for such a system. In both cases, the organization needs to have adequate awareness that there is some kind of independent monitoring. This should, at a minimum, include independent prepa-

---

CASE STUDY

Accounts Receivable Fraud

The bookkeeper of a small but growing bread company prepared bills to be sent to customers and was responsible for collecting payments. Sales were growing through the acquisition of new customers and increasing sales to existing ones. A surprise internal audit revealed, however, that bank deposits were not as large as would have been expected considering the rate of sales growth. An examination of customer copies of sales invoices revealed that the amounts being billed were higher than the amounts being recorded in the cash receipts journal (see below for a discussion of journals) for the same transaction. Office copies of the invoices had been altered to reflect the falsified journal entry. The bookkeeper had stolen more than $15,000 over a period of a year before the fraud was discovered. The bookkeeper was dismissed and agreed to repay the money in order to avoid having the matter brought to the attention of the police.

---

ration of bank and other account reconciliations, supervision, and perhaps the use of an outside accountant as an additional monitor.

Payments and Accounts Payable

In order to manufacture and/or supply goods and services, a business must obviously procure and pay for the goods and services, which underlie their sales. In terms of the accounting equation and accounting cycle, the expenses appear on a company's income statement, and the respective accounts payable appear on the balance sheet. Similar to cash sales, cash purchases would directly affect the cash balance, which is also a balance sheet item.

As previously discussed for the Sales and Accounts Receivable cycle, the steps and controls for safeguarding a company's assets are of a similar ilk. These steps include approving vendors and ensuring they actually exist and are legitimate businesses; proper processing of purchase orders; proper handling in the receipt and recording of goods and services; recording of liabilities; and processing of cash for payment.

This is one of the accounting cycles that is susceptible to breakdowns in controls, for it involves the flow of funds out from an entity. The safeguarding of a company's assets thus proves just as important, if no more so, in this cycle.

In terms of the accounts that companies typically have in their "chart of accounts" (i.e., their roadmap through their financial statements), this cycle can affect many different balance sheet and income statement accounts. Specifically, the payments and accounts payable cycle can affect balance sheet accounts, including cash, inventory, prepaid expenses, accounts payable (collectively "current assets"), equipment, land and buildings, depreciation ("fixed assets") and other, perhaps longer-term, assets and liabilities.

Similarly, in the income statement, just about every account is affected by this cycle; from cost of good sold (which typically when deducted from sales results in a company's gross profit) to all of the entity's expenses, such as administration, travel, advertising, professional fees, and taxes, among many others.

Within the same guidelines as for the Sales and Accounts Receivable cycle, fundamental controls are essential, especially over the reconciliation of accounts, including the entity's bank accounts. Without a regular (usually monthly) independent reconciliation of the company's bank accounts, the true financial position cannot be known. Similarly, the propriety of transactions and completeness of information cannot be known. At its simplest level, the person who generates checks, the person who signs checks, the person who mails checks, and the person who reconciles the bank account (or accounts) cannot be one and the same. This is a fundamental principle of accounting, which, while it may not exactly date back to Luca Pacioli, still harks back to Pacioli's quote. Once again: "He who does business without knowing all about it, sees his money go like flies."

Along with the reconciliation process, the concepts of budgeting and tendering and vendor knowledge are also key. These processes also include the segregation of duties, proper approvals, and audit trail through proper documentation. Similar to the other accounting cycles, proper documentation includes prenumbered purchase requisitions, purchase orders, receiving reports, and checks. With the advent of sophisticated computer software, many systems now print this information as documents are generated. This therefore puts the onus on a business to safeguard entry to the accounting system and be in a position to identify who enters the system and when. Limiting access at key points therefore makes it more difficult for one person to compromise the system without collusion.

At the entry level of this cycle, acceptance of a vendor, system controls must include background checks on the vendor in order to ensure that the business exists and is legitimate. Adherence to credit limits is another fun-

---

CASE STUDY

Accounts Payable Fraud

The administrator of the school board in a small city had ultimate authority for all items payable from the board's annual budget. As an administrator, he traveled frequently to education conventions and meetings of administrators in the state capitol and across the country. Although he was an excellent CPA and the day-to-day affairs of the board ran smoothly, his prickly personality did not endear him to the board and made his attempts to get approval for his proposals difficult. Frustrated and increasingly embittered, he saw a way to get back at the board by using his signing authority to approve personal expenditures and write checks to himself. He submitted mileage expenses while using a car leased for him by the board, and he used the board credit card to put gas in his own car. Other bills submitted and approved by himself were for meals and entertainment on weekends and repairs to his car. After his secretary blew the whistle on him, forensic investigators found that invoices for many transactions did not exist. The administrator was dismissed from his job, but no charges were ever laid.

---

damental control in the safeguarding of the company's assets. Companies should also have bid and procurement policies to ensure competitive bidding and to minimize the opportunity for purchasing managers to compromise their position.

Human Resources and Payroll

By definition, this aspect of the cycle includes recruitment, disengagement, and remuneration of employees and the related underlying data of time records, expense reports, and other related matters.

From an accounting cycle perspective, there are many accounts affected by this function, specifically, cash and taxes payable on the balance sheet and salaries/payroll, tax, travel and entertainment, and others in the income statement.

The safeguards for this cycle are necessary for the prevention of nonexistent (also known as "ghost" employees), falsified hours and overtime, false expense reports, and false medical claims.

Again, the underlying fundamental concepts are similar to those for all other accounting cycles, with the need for proper documentation (i.e., time cards, time sheets, timely entry into a computerized timekeeping system,

---

CASE STUDY

Payroll Fraud

A suburban construction company employed several hundred laborers at any given time. With a lean operation, the home office included a one-person accounting department, with a long-serving bookkeeper/controller who coordinated the weekly payroll, printed the payroll checks, placed the owner's mechanical signature on the checks, hand-delivered the checks to the job sites, and reconciled the company's bank account.

It came as no surprise, then, that after several years, it was discovered that the bookkeeper had perpetrated a scheme whereby at any point in time, she kept several laborers on the payroll after they had left the company ("ghost employees"). She would endorse the back of their checks and deposit them in her own bank account. At the same time, she paid the withholding taxes, union dues, and other deductions! It was only an alert bank teller who eventually noticed the scheme, after several years and over $600,000 had been taken. The company received $500,000 from its fidelity bond carrier, got back much of the tax and union dues, and reached a settlement with the bank for its lack of oversight.

---

etc.), proper approval (related to hiring, firing, overtime, travel, etc.), and separation of duties. In terms of the last-named, this would include separating the functions of processing and distributing paychecks and approval and payment of expenses, among others.

Inventory and Storage/Warehousing

This part of the cycle encompasses the purchasing function, as it relates to the company's inventory, but it also includes the warehousing of product for both manufacture and then resale. Physical control is therefore as important as the other system controls within the other accounting cycles

The processes for this cycle, from an accounting standpoint, include processing requisitions for purchases; receipt of raw materials and finished goods; storage of raw materials and finished goods; and shipment of goods, among others.

From an accounting cycle perspective, this function affects the inventories on the balance sheet and cost of goods sold in the income statement. Important in this process is the maintenance of an audit trail—specifically, receiving reports, perpetual inventory records, control over requisitions, and shipping documents, among others.

CASE STUDY

Inventory Fraud

Auditors doing their annual review of the books of a gold refiner were unable to reconcile the inventory value of the gold carried on the company's balance sheet with their assessed value. In an attempt to show he was trying to solve the problem, the vice president of finance hired forensic investigators to review the inventory. The discovery of a brass bar of exactly the same weight as a gold bar on the inventory list raised a question in the minds of the investigators. An interview with a smelter worker revealed that brass scrap had been melted down, cast into bars, and added to the inventory. There was no record of brass bars on the inventory lists. Forty-five brass bars had been valued at $8 million on the balance sheet. Another $5 million was classified as gold bars "in transit." The fraud had been going on for about five years when discovered. It had not been perpetrated for the direct personal gain of the VP of finance and his colluding CEO, but as an attempt to hide the operating losses that would have precipitated a fall in the company's stock if made public in the annual report. The VP of finance and CEO were both charged with fraud, convicted, and served terms in prison.

As well as the audit trail, proper segregation of duties is also essential to this accounting cycle—for example, separation of warehouse custody and purchase authorization. In addition, those with custody over the warehouse should not conduct, or be the lead in conducting, the physical count of inventory. It also goes without saying that physical security is critical for this particular cycle.

Capital Expenditures

This part of the accounting cycle is also known as the capital acquisition and repayment cycle or the financing cycle. It includes the borrowing of funds, the debt of a company, and so on. Several transactions surround this part of the cycle, specifically, recording of debt and interest, payment of interest and dividends, and equity financing, among others.

From an accounting cycle perspective, this function affects cash, liabilities (such as mortgages), capital and retained earnings on the balance sheet, and interest paid and received, among other items on the income statement.

An audit trail will once again assist in the safeguarding of the company's assets through, for example, control over bank deposits and authorizations for loans. An entity must ensure proper documentation of loans,

---

CASE STUDY

Capital Expenditures

A government agency responsible for overseeing mortgage brokers was concerned that many brokers were borrowing and lending money as if they were licensed as banks or trust companies. The agency made a random selection of brokers and hired forensic investigators to examine their books.

Under government regulations, the brokers' activities were limited to finding specific mortgages and investors to invest in them. In a typical case, an investor would give the broker $50,000 to be put out in a particular mortgage at the prevailing rate per annum to be paid monthly. The investigators soon discovered that one broker had exceeded his authority by issuing so-called corporate notes secured by the company's guarantee rather than by a mortgage. The money was being used instead to purchase property for the broker, who then reduced his risk by selling partial interests to family members or other relatives. By the time the investigators arrived, more than $5 million had been taken in through the issuance of corporate notes and pooled instead of being directed to specific mortgages.

What should have been securely backed mortgages on the balance sheet turned out to be high-risk investments in other ventures that were not paying the rates of return required to service the corporate notes. The broker was meeting his monthly obligations to his investors through borrowings on a bank line of credit and was rapidly getting overextended. In the end, the government agency revoked the broker's license and closed his operations with the help of several banks that took over the mortgages to protect the investors.

---

journal entries, stock certificates, and the like. In addition, duties should be segregated, such as stock issuance and handling of cash, as well as separating accounting from handling of cash.

Chart of Accounts

So far, we have used the term *audit trail* quite a bit when talking about maintaining the integrity of an entity's transactions. The audit trail, or the ability to go back and trace transactions to their source, is predicated by the company having an effective road map to guide one through its accounting system. Within the accounting system is a document that lists specific accounts, their nature, and reference numbers; this is known as the Chart of Accounts. Exhibit 2.1 contains an example of a Chart of Accounts:

Asset Accounts 1000–1100
1000   Cash
1001   Operating Account
1002   Payroll Account
1003   Petty Cash
1010   Accounts Receivable
1020   Allowance for Doubtful Accounts
1030   Property
1040   Equipment

Exhibit 2.1 Sample Chart of Accounts

It is important that the reader of a set of accounts, or someone who follows an audit trail or is looking to understand the transactions underlying a set of financial statements, be able to follow the chart of accounts. Equally important is an understanding of how each account within the chart, or group of accounts, affects the accounting cycle.

In addition, it is important to understand how each of these accounts affects the accounting equation—the fact that an expense can give to rise to, for example, a charge against income on the income statement (i.e., expenses reduce profit) and a liability on the balance sheet (i.e., in accounts payable as part of current liabilities).

JOURNALS

As we have previously discussed, the activities, and hence transactions of a business, that underlie the entity's financial statements are known as the accounting cycle. Many of us are familiar with the term *month end closing*, which signifies a company closing its books on a particular month of transactions and reconciling its various accounts, to ensure everything is in balance, as well as the propriety of the underlying data. This is therefore known as a monthly cycle. This cycle can be weekly, monthly, quarterly, yearly, or otherwise, but is always known as a particular cycle.

General Journal

So what is a journal? Typically, a journal is described as a chronological listing of transactions or business activities. It has also been defined as an accounting book of original entry where transactions are initially recorded[1]. The journal essentially shows each transaction and the corresponding debit and credit entries and identifies which accounts they affect within the chart of accounts.

These debit and credit entries form the basis from which amounts are transferred to their respective accounts in the ledger. Hence, the controls and audit trail, which we discussed within the various aspects of the accounting cycles, are critical to the ability to trace individual transactions and the documents that support them.

This procedure requires the recording of individual transactions through entries in the general journal, followed by a posting from the general journal to the appropriate ledger account. However, in the practicality of business today, the volume of transactions necessitates the grouping of like transactions and the use of a special journal.

Special Journal

Most transactions fall into one of four categories: sales journal, purchases journal, cash receipts journal, and cash payments journal.

Sales Journal

Exhibit 2.2 contains an example of a sales journal.

Exhibit 2.2 presents an extract from a company's sales journal showing entries made on a particular day to certain customers. The check in the "posted" column indicates the entry was made in the subsidiary ledger, or the ledger, which lists the specific accounts receivable. Thus, the total of $5,200 is posted and shown as the sales for that day, and the individual amounts ultimately are shown in the individual customer accounts. A subsidiary ledger supports the general ledger but is also controlled by the general ledger.

Date	Account	Invoice Number	Posted	Amount
1/2/2003	Arsenal Lumber	1001	√	$1,200.00
1/2/2003	Liverpool Depot	1002	√	$2,425.00
1/2/2003	Manchester Scrap	1003	√	$1,575.00
				$5,200.00

Exhibit 2.2 Sample Sales Journal

Purchases Journal

Similar to the sales journal, the purchases journal handles purchase transactions in the same way as the sales journal handles sales transactions. In a similar vein, the individual invoices from the customer would be posted to a subsidiary ledger, which reflects the company's accounts payable.

Cash Receipts Journal

It may go without saying, but it is nonetheless true, that all cash transactions involving receipts are recorded in the cash receipts journal. Where cash is received from customers, the amounts are posted to the respective customer's account in the accounts receivable subsidiary ledger. The total cash received is posted to the cash account in the general ledger.

Cash Payments Journal

Similar to cash receipts, all cash payments must go through the cash payments journal. Items include payment of accounts payable to creditors, payment of expenses, and other cash payments. Similar to cash receipts, entries are typically posted daily; and then on a monthly basis a business will post cash, accounts payable, purchases, and any other accounts to the respective accounts in the general ledger.

TYING THE THREAD

At the beginning of this section, we spoke of how Luca Pacioli believed that a person should not go to sleep at night until the debits equaled the credits. At the end of a designated accounting period (for example, monthly), an entity will prepare a trial balance—a listing of all account balances in the general ledger. Each subsidiary ledger must also agree to its control account. For example, a listing is prepared of all accounts receivable balances from the subsidiary ledger, which should then be reconciled to the accounts receivable balance in the general ledger.

The simplified explanation of the accounting cycles and the journal system illustrates how relatively simple Pacioli's double-entry system of bookkeeping vision was. However, the complexity of the human mind and the deviation from accepted behavior require business to drill down beneath the surface of simple bookkeeping and maintain control over every transaction and the manner in which transactions are recorded.

Without the controls and checks and balances, the system will be undermined, and the integrity of data will also be compromised.

NOTE

1. *http://investorwords.com.*

SUGGESTED READINGS

Avey, Todd, Ted Baskerville, and Alan Brill. *The CPA's Handbook of Fraud and Commercial Crime Prevention.* American Institute of Certified Public Accountants, 2000.

Luca Pacioli: Unsung Hero of the Renaissance. Paul Jackson (director), with David Tinius, Ph.D., and William Weis, Ph.D. Cincinnati: OH: South-Western Publishing, 1990.

Macve, Richard H. "Pacioli's Legacy." In *New Works in Accounting History,* edited by T.A. Lee, A. Bishop, and R. H. Parker. New York and London: Garland Publishing, 1996.

Pacioli, Luca. *Summa de Arithmetica.* Toscalano: Paganino de Paganini, 1523.

Taylor, R. *No Royal Road: Luca Pacioli and His Times.* Chapel Hill: University of North Carolina Press, 1942.

3

THE ENTITIES

INTRODUCTION

Business entities can be categorized into three major types:

Proprietorships
Partnerships
Corporations

PROPRIETORSHIPS

The Concept

A proprietorship is typically an entity owned by one person and represents the simplest form of business entity. In a proprietorship, the owner and the business are one and the same. In contrast to partnerships and corporations, the initial setup of a proprietorship is relatively cheap and not a complex undertaking. However, what may be considered a trade-off is the fact that from a legal perspective, an owner has unlimited personal liability.

The Operation

For income tax purposes, a proprietorship and its owner are considered a single entity, and business income/losses are reported on the owner's tax return. Hence, all indicators point to the proprietor essentially being accountable to himself and, it must be said, the various authorities to whom he pays taxes! We will later use the analogy of sport as it relates to the various entities, but suffice to say here, the proprietor is not in the game of team sport. While he or she may have staff assisting along the way, the results of the entity and the manner in which the accounting and the integrity of such is maintained fall squarely on the shoulders of the proprietor.

From another accounting standpoint, the owner's entire equity is shown as one amount, without distinction as to initial investment and changes in equity. There are no accounts for capital or retained earnings, just a capital account and a drawing account. The capital account maintains the original investment and additional investments that may be made. The drawing account shows the withdrawal of cash, which is typically offset against the capital account. The drawing account includes items such as withdrawal of cash and payments of personal expenses out of the business bank account.

PARTNERSHIPS

The Concept

Whereas one person owns a proprietorship, a partnership is an entity owned by two or more individuals. As defined by the Uniform Partnership Act, "A partnership means an association of 2 or more persons, including an association of a husband and wife, to carry on as co-owners a business for profit."[1] Most people associate partnerships with professional organizations, such as accountants, lawyers, and doctors.

Typically, a partnership will begin with executed articles of partnership, including the amounts of the partners' investments, the distribution methods, salaries, and the procedures for admission and withdrawal of partners. A partnership can take several different forms, including a General Partnership, in which business is conducted for the benefit of all parties involved and all partners share in the profits and losses of the business, as well as the management of the operations. A Limited Partnership is where one or more partners conduct business but are not liable for the debts of the partnership beyond their contributed funds. Essentially with a limited life, a partnership may end with the death or withdrawal of a partner, or other factors such as bankruptcy. New partners will ostensibly end the old partnership, with a new firm being formed.

A partnership affords the ability to bring together combined capital to conduct the operations of a business. However, it is not without its disadvantages, including the concept of limited life, unlimited liability, and possible limiting factors to raise additional capital, which a corporation may better engender.

From an accounting standpoint, the actual accounting in a partnership is not much more complex than that in a proprietorship, with the exception that the partners must maintain capital accounts and any profits or losses are assessed on the partners according to their agreement. In addition, drawing accounts are used to record the partners' salaries and other interests.

The Operation

The basic accounts and accounting for a partnership are not drastically different from those for a sole proprietorship, or indeed a corporation. As we must keep in mind, the concepts of double-entry bookkeeping and integrity of data apply across the board, regardless of what type of entity one is considering. In moving from a proprietorship to a partnership, the major change in concept is that other people are involved in the accounting equation. The distribution of net income or loss is conducted as noted earlier in this chapter. In a partnership, we have now moved away from the concept of the individual who looks to him or herself when he or she looks back at a particular point in time to two or more people who have entrusted a business to their collective hands.

We have, therefore, placed a greater burden on the partners to be accountable to each other—a burden that brings with it the need for continued integrity and the ability to account for the operations of the business. Once again, although the concepts of accounting have not changed, the playing field in which they are applied has. Using a sports analogy, we have now moved from the golfer who only has himself to blame when he plays a bad shot (with perhaps the exception of wind, rain, and other elements, which can be likened to economic conditions for a sole proprietor) to perhaps a doubles-pairing in tennis or even a hockey or soccer team, where the defense is equally as important and accountable as the offense.

Experience has shown that the greatest accountability for a partnership occurs at the time of admission of a new partner, the withdrawal or death of a partner, or the dissolution or liquidation of the partnership. An understanding of the concepts of how accounts can be undermined and the need for continued stewardship should prevent the discovery of problems for a partnership at just these points in time; rather, stewardship should be an ongoing process, just as it is for a corporation.

CORPORATIONS

The Concept

Unlike proprietorships and partnerships, which are not separate legal entities distinct from their owners, corporations, once they have been approved by the state in which they operate, are considered legal entities separate from their owners. The owners of a corporation (shareholders or stockholders) can transfer stock and hence ownership. Unlike a partnership, the departure of a stockholder, or the replacement of one stockholder by another does not constitute dissolution as in partnership terms. Another important characteristic of a corporation is the owners' limited liability. In the event of bankruptcy, the corporation's creditors have a claim against the company's assets, not the shareholders' personal assets.

Although sole proprietors and partners are typically involved in the day-to-day operations of their business, the shareholders of a company are typically not involved in such operations. Shareholders of a corporation have indirect control by selecting the board of directors to run operations, and many senior members of the corporation may hold stock. Yet, the managers of the business should be held accountable to all the shareholders for the operations of the entity.

In the matter of *Dartmouth College v. Woodward (1819)*, Justice John Marshall opined:

> A corporation is an artificial being, invisible, intangible, and existing only in contemplation of law. Being the mere creature of law, it possesses only those properties, which the charter of its creation confers upon it, either expressly or as incidental to its very existence. These are such as are supposed best calculated to effect the object for which it was created. Among the most important are immortality, and, if the expression may be allowed, individuality; properties by which a perpetual succession of many persons are considered as the same, and may act as a single individual. They enable a corporation to manage its own affairs and to hold property without the perplexing intricacies, the hazardous and endless necessity of perpetual conveyances for the purpose of transmitting it from hand to hand. It is chiefly for the purpose of clothing bodies of men,

60

in succession, with these qualities and capacities that corporations were invented and are in use.[2]

In this quotation, Justice Marshall refers to the "charter of its creations," which we know better as the "articles of incorporation," which are filed with the appropriate state in which the company operates. Justice Marshall recognized that a corporation is a collective of shareholders and has a separate legal personality from these shareholders. As a result, the law perceives that the corporation is a *fictional entity* coordinated and directed by equity investors.

It should therefore come as no surprise that the recent events affecting high-profile corporations, as noted in Chapters 1 and 2 of this book, have caused such a stir within the business community.

The Operation

For those previously unfamiliar with the concepts of proprietorship, partnership, and corporations, it should now be clear that the further one moves away from owners with direct control over an entity, the greater the need for control over the accounting for that entity.

The Board of Directors

The main function of a board of directors is to manage the corporation, while protecting the interests of the shareholders. The directors' duties include policy setting, arranging and authorizing loans; creating and reviewing the system of internal control; liaising with outside accountants; and authorizing other types of contracts and business.

Corporate Officers

The officers of a corporation are typically the president, chief executive officer, chief financial officer, various vice presidents, controller/treasurer, and secretary. It is usually the chief financial officer, together with the controller/treasurer, who is responsible for preparing accounting records and financial statements and maintaining the integrity of the underlying data with adequate internal control.

Although it has been a changing trend over the years, the concept of including individuals who are not corporate officers on the boards of directors of larger companies has been increasingly encouraged. These individuals, it is hoped, will provide an independent view of the company's operations. The entire concept of independence has come under scrutiny in more recent times, both as to corporate officers and the outside accountants (a role that is discussed in greater detail in Chapter 5.

NOTES

1. 1914 by the National Conference of Commissioners on Uniform State Laws.
2. *Trustees of Dartmouth College v. Woodward*, 17 U.S. 4 Wheat. 636 (1819).

SUGGESTED READINGS

Uniform Law Commissioners. The National Conference of Commissioners on Uniform State Laws. *www.nccusl.org/.*

4

FUNDAMENTAL PRINCIPLES OF ANALYSIS

GOOD ANALYSIS = DUE DILIGENCE?

Having looked at what fraud is, how it occurs, who commits fraud, together with some of the underlying principles of accounting and entities involved, it is perhaps time to consider how a "non-expert" can undertake financial analysis and explain what it all means.

For someone who has suffered the ignominy of a loss, born out of lack of financial due diligence or at least some level of financial analysis, the pain of a bad bargain will live on long after the excitement of the particular transaction has faded to a mere memory. Even supposedly well-trained and experienced businesspeople still enter into transactions not only not knowing much about the parties, but also not understanding the metrics of the underlying data.

In the face of recent multibillion-dollar financial statement frauds (discussed in earlier chapters), there still are so few people who truly understand what it all means and understand even the most basic of analyses. The concept of financial analysis, due diligence, call it what you like, is an understanding before a commitment. That commitment could be lending a sole proprietor money to take her business to the next level, it could be buying into a partnership, or it could be investing in a major corporation. It could be joining business with a sole proprietor to create a partnership, or it could be a bank entering into an agreement to provide financing for a new facility. It could even be an investigative journalist trying to get a better understanding of a company's results for a particular story.

Any type of financial analysis will obviously involve numbers. However, depending on the needs of the analyst, it may involve more than just looking at the numbers. It may require a deeper investigation that, among other things, looks at the company in its markets, calculates asset values, discovers hidden liabilities, and examines long-term strategy. Sadly, experience shows that even the most rudimentary analysis is conducted after the fact—the famous historic perspective that financial statements offer us. Anyone who has experience as the victim of fraud or investigating fraud will tell you that there are always red flags that are obvious to the trained eye right from the beginning.

WHY DO IT?

Business has changed since the days of Luca Pacioli. It has changed since the advent of computers. And it has certainly changed since the corporate shenanigans of the past few years. But has business really changed? Or has only the underlying way in which results are captured changed? At the root of it all is one thing—money—specifically, the need to make it, keep it, and grow it, and all driven by the human element. Perhaps the ethos is no different today than it was 500 years ago; perhaps just the pressures have changed. To use our sports analogy again: we're on a different playing field.

Certainly the playing field has changed as to the propriety and reliance an outsider can place on financial statements. Although the recent scandals have mostly surrounded publicly traded companies, with the perception that they can inflict the greatest hurt on outsiders, let us not forget the private companies, the partnerships, and indeed the sole proprietorships, in whom someone on the outside may soon be having an inside interest. The breakdown of confidence in financial statements and their underlying data should apply across the board, not just to public companies.

What and Whom Can You Trust?

Analysts often believe that audited financial statements contain all the information needed for their analysis. This misconception is common not just to companies looking at acquisition targets but is also to be found at banks, bonding companies, vendors' customers, and any other type of business wishing to have some type of fiduciary relationship with another company. The exposed misrepresentations on the financial statements of

Enron, WorldCom, and others should sufficiently demonstrate that making an investment decision based solely on financial statement analysis can be dangerous.

Financial statement fraud has always been with us, but the recent scandals show that not even the most important companies in the economy can remain untainted. In 1998, then SEC chairman Arthur Levitt warned in a speech called "The Numbers Game" that aggressive accountants were exploiting the flexibility of generally accepted accounting principles (GAAP) to create misleading earnings reports: "As a result, I fear that we are witnessing an erosion in the quality of earnings, and therefore, the quality of financial reporting. Managing may be giving way to manipulation; integrity may be losing out to illusion."[1]

Other Factors to Consider

In the post-Enron era, mere analysis of audited financial statements may not be enough, and other key performance indicators may have to be considered. Margin and other ratio analyses will, of course, always be important, but a thorough examination may have to extend to customers, underlying costs, product lines, and market shares, among many others factors. Additional time should be spent talking to vendors and customers to more fully analyze the industry in which the company operates.

When assessing competitor and market risk, prospective acquirers frequently access and rely on information obtained from analysts and self-proclaimed industry "experts." Recent revelations have shown the significant risk of bias in these sources. In addition, in the eagerness to complete a transaction, human nature inadvertently causes greater weight to be placed on positive information and less on negative. Early warnings of potential problems are frequently ignored.

The analytical process should "drill down" to find out who authorizes individual transactions and to ask why. Skepticism should guide the examination of all questionable transactions. In the case of a prospective acquisition, more emphasis should be placed on analyzing whether there is a real need to acquire the target and what its long-term impact on the existing strategy could be. Many badly advised boards of directors have authorized the acquisition of companies in businesses unfamiliar to their own management but argued to be capable of providing what used to be called "synergies." The results have almost always been disastrous.

Lenders, suitors, or any other agent surveying a company need to be alert to factors they may not have considered previously. The old emphasis on net income should now shift to cash flow. It does not matter how a company records transactions once the money is spent; it is the cash flow that should be more closely investigated.

One area that should receive increased attention is the company's governance practices. A board dominated by a multi-titled, charismatic, and/or domineering chairman, president, or CEO should raise a red flag. How many independent directors are there? Are they truly independent? Are they financially literate? Do they have experience in the company's business sector? How much time and energy are all directors devoting to fulfilling their duties? How effective is the audit committee? Is senior management's compensation excessive? Finding these answers can be a challenge because they are not often transparent. If effective corporate governance is not in place—and there is no control or oversight of senior management—then "buyer beware."

ANALYSIS FOR THE NON-EXPERT

As the chart in Exhibit 4.1 shows, in gauging performance, certain ratios can be applied to an entity's financial statements. In this section, we discuss some of the more "popular" or well-known ratios.

The Ratios

Current Ratio

The current ratio is the standard measure of an entity's financial health, regardless of size and type. The analyst will know whether a business can meet its current obligations by determining if it has sufficient assets to cover its liabilities. The "standard" current ratio for a healthy business is recognized as around 2, meaning it has twice as many assets as liabilities.

The formula is expressed as: *current assets divided by current liabilities.*

Quick Ratio

Similar to the current ratio, the quick ratio (also known as the "acid test") measures a business's liquidity. However, many analysts prefer it to the current ratio because it excludes inventories when counting assets and

Liquidity Analysis Ratios

Current Ratio

$$\text{Current Ratio} = \frac{\text{Current Assets}}{\text{Current Liabilities}}$$

Quick Ratio

$$\text{Quick Ratio} = \frac{\text{Quick Assets}}{\text{Current Liabilities}}$$

Quick Assets = Current Assets – Inventories

Net Working Capital Ratio

$$\text{Net Working Capital Ratio} = \frac{\text{Net Working Capital}}{\text{Total Assets}}$$

Net Working Capital = Current Assets – Current Liabilities

Profitability Analysis Ratios

Return on Assets (ROA)

$$\text{Return on Assets (ROA)} = \frac{\text{Net Income}}{\text{Average Total Assets}}$$

Average Total Assets = (Beginning Total Assets + Ending Total Assets) / 2

Return on Equity (ROE)

$$\text{Return on Equity (ROE)} = \frac{\text{Net Income}}{\text{Average Stockholders' Equity}}$$

Average Stockholders' Equity = (Beginning Stockholders' Equity + Ending Stockholders' Equity) / 2

Net Profit Margin

$$\text{Net Profit Margin} = \frac{\text{Net Income}}{\text{Sales}}$$

Earnings Per Share (EPS)

$$\text{Earnings Per Share (EPS)} = \frac{\text{Net Income}}{\text{Weighted Average Number of Common Shares Outstanding}}$$

Business Analysis Ratios

Accounts Receivable Turnover Ratio

$$\text{Accounts Receivable Turnover Ratio} = \frac{\text{Sales}}{\text{Average Accounts Receivable}}$$

(*continues*)

Exhibit 4.1 Popular Ratios

Average Accounts Receivable = (Beginning Accounts Receivable + Ending Accounts Receivable) / 2

Inventory Turnover Ratio

$$\text{Inventory Turnover Ratio} = \frac{\text{Cost of Goods Sold}}{\text{Average Inventories}}$$

Capital Ratios

Debt to Equity Ratio

$$\text{Debt to Equity Ratio} = \frac{\text{Total Liabilities}}{\text{Total Stockholders' Equity}}$$

Interest Coverage Ratio

$$\text{Interest Coverage Ratio} = \frac{\text{Income Before Interest and Income Tax Expenses}}{\text{Interest Expense}}$$

Income Before Interest and Income Tax Expenses = Income Before Interest Income Taxes + Interest Expense

Capital Analysis Ratios

Price/Earnings (PE) Ratio

$$\text{Price/Earnings (PE) Ratio} = \frac{\text{Market Price of Common Stock Per Share}}{\text{Earnings Per Share}}$$

Market to Book Ratio

$$\text{Market to Book Ratio} = \frac{\text{Market Price of Common Stock Per Share}}{\text{Book Value of Equity Per Common Share}}$$

Book Value of Equity Per Common Share = Book Value of Equity for Common Stock / Number of Common Shares

Dividend Yield

$$\text{Dividend Yield} = \frac{\text{Annual Dividends Per Common Share}}{\text{Market Price of Common Stock Per Share}}$$

Book Value of Equity Per Common Share = Book Value of Equity for Common Stock / Number of Common Shares

Exhibit 4.1 (*continued*)

therefore applies an entity's "liquid" assets in relation to its liabilities. The higher the ratio, the higher the level of liquidity, and hence it is a better indicator of an entity's financial health. The accepted optimal quick ratio is 1 or higher.

The formula is expressed as: *current assets less inventory divided by current liabilities.*

Inventory Turnover Ratio

This ratio measures how often inventory turns over during the course of the year (or depending on the formula, another time period). In financial analysis, inventory is deemed to be the least liquid form of asset. Typically, a high turnover ratio is positive; however, an unusually high ratio compared to the market for that product could mean loss of sales, with an inability to meet demand.

The formula is expressed as: *cost of goods sold divided by average value of inventory.*

Accounts Receivable Turnover Ratio

This ratio provides an indicator as to how quickly (or otherwise) an entity's customers/clients are paying their bills. The greater the number of times receivables turn over during the year, the less the time between sales and cash collection and hence, ceteris paribus, better cash flow.

The formula is expressed as: *net sales divided by accounts receivable.*

Accounts Payable Turnover Ratio

Converse to the accounts receivable turnover ratio, the accounts payable turnover ratio provides an indicator of how quickly an entity pays its trade debts. The ratio shows how often accounts payable turn over during the year. A high ratio means a relatively short time between purchases and payment, which may not always be the best for a company (the entity would want to make sure it is taking advantage of all discounts, while not at the same time paying for goods before their time). Conversely, a low ratio may be a sign that the company has cash flow problems. However, this ratio, like all others, should be considered in conjunction with the other ratios.

The formula is expressed as: *cost of sales divided by trade accounts payable.*

Debt to Equity Ratio

This ratio provides an indicator as to how much the company is in debt (also known as "leveraged") by comparing debt to assets. A high debt to equity ratio could indicate that the company may be overleveraged and may be seeking ways to reduce debt.

Aside from the other ratios we have noted, the amount of assets/equity and debt are two of the more significant items in financial statements; they are key evaluators of risk.

The formula is expressed as: *total liabilities divided by total assets.*

Gross Margin Ratio

The gross margin (or gross profit) ratio indicates how well or efficiently a proprietor, group of partners, or managers of a company have run that business. Have the managers bought and sold in the most efficient manner? Have they taken advantage of the market? A high gross margin indicates a profit on sales, together with cost containment in making those sales. However, a high margin, but with falling sales, could be indicative of overpricing or a shrinking market.

The formula is expressed as: *gross profit (sales minus cost of sales) divided by total sales.*

Return on Sales Ratio

This ratio considers after-tax profit as a percentage of sales. It is used as a measure to determine if an entity is getting a sufficient return on its revenues or sales.

Although an entity may make what looks to be a satisfactory gross profit, it still may not be enough to cover overhead expenses. This ratio can provide an indicator of this fact and help determine how an entity can adjust prices to make a gross profit sufficient to cover expenses and earn an adequate net profit.

The formula is expressed as: *net profit divided by sales.*

Concluding Comments on Ratio Analysis

Many other ratios are used in the course of financial analysis, but these are deemed to be some of the most commonly used and understood. It must be remembered that ratios need to be considered in their entirety; unlike in the past, even ratio analysis alone is not to be considered the most useful information. So what if a company made a 25 percent gross profit? So what if its current ratio is 2.1? Given the right circumstances and together with other "due diligence," an analyst can obtain a good picture of an entity's performance and situation.

The ratio analysis cannot be considered in a vacuum; rather, it is important to consider the entity, the type of entity, the industry, the market, the competition, the management, and then consider the calculated ratios.

ANALYSIS THROUGH A CASE STUDY

The following example indicates how valuable analysis can be and why ratio analysis is not enough.

Act I

ABC Corporation conducted a "due diligence" investigation several months after it acquired majority ownership of a medium-sized company. ABC had begun to suspect that the inventory listed in the acquired company's assets was substantially overstated. The investigation proved that concern to be only too real. The vice president of finance was discovered to have been stealing inventory, selling it to one of ABC's competitors, and covering up the fraud by falsifying ABC's inventory figures.

Although ABC, which had based the acquisition value on assets and earnings, benefited greatly from having a true picture of its new acquisition's financial worth, this knowledge was not gained without a significant cost in time, energy, and embarrassment. "Next time we consider a major acquisition," vowed ABC's CEO, "we'll call before the barn door closes." True to his word, the CEO put together a due diligence team well in advance of striking a deal with a supplier that his firm was eager to purchase.

Act II

XYZ Company manufactured a specialized component for one of ABC's most profitable products. The CEO wanted to purchase XYZ both to earn a return and to ensure its component would always be available at a reasonable price. ABC had tried to acquire XYZ for many years, but its owner had always declined. To everyone's surprise, XYZ's owner now confided to ABC's CEO that because of sudden health problems, he was now willing to sell. An agreement was worked out that would give ABC complete ownership of XYZ for 25 percent of the purchase price in cash and the remaining 75 percent in ABC shares to be priced at the close of trading on the last business day before the deal would be signed.

The agreed purchase price was to be $25 million based on a five-times multiple of XYZ's $5-million pretax earnings as reported in its audited financial statements for the most recent fiscal year. The deal would be subject to a due diligence investigation by ABC's team.

Preliminary investigations suggested that the team should determine the key financial and accounting risks associated with the proposed purchase. The team would also analyze XYZ's present and future position within its market and any unforeseen factors that could weaken or endanger XYZ's ability to continue doing business profitably.

Act III—Three Findings

The investigation produced three major findings.

1. Eight main customers plus ABC accounted for 80 percent of XYZ's annual sales of $30 million. Detailed background searches of the eight companies revealed that the same international parent owned three of the companies, either directly or indirectly. By analyzing public documents and interviews with sources familiar with the parent, the ABC team discovered that, although the customers were financially healthy, their parent was undergoing a major debt restructuring of its real estate and plant financing. The restructuring was significant enough to put into question the stability of the parent and, consequently, the future of the largest part of XYZ's customer base.

2. XYZ's success was primarily attributable to the part it manufactured for ABC, plus two other products. The costs of the part made for ABC were kept low by manufacturing it from byproducts of the other two items. Thus any change in raw materials prices or demand for the other two products would affect production costs for the part made for ABC. A second problem was the expiration of the patent on one of the other two products in the near future. XYZ's market share might therefore decrease, since the end of patent rights would open the market to greater competition. A loss

of market share would mean lower production, a reduced level of cheap byproduct, and possibly higher raw material costs to produce the part for ABC.

3. XYZ's controller had recently acquired a second mortgage that brought the total financing on his home above 90 percent of its current value. The mortgage was arranged through a mortgage broker at close to double the going interest rates. As a result, his mortgage payments now accounted for approximately 80 percent of his annual salary. A lifestyle review showed a person who spent far in excess of his apparent income on clothing, entertainment, travel, and material possessions.

Investigation of selected inventory purchases revealed that the controller had been rerouting raw materials directly from their source to a company registered in his wife's name at an address in a nearby municipality. He had then changed the bills of lading and other documents to show that XYZ had received the materials.

Although the inventory had been audited twice during the period in question, the controller was able to direct the inexperienced audit staff to test-check inventory that he knew had been accounted for accurately. Their test-checks of book-to-physical inventory would agree, of course, while he then easily falsified the physical count sheets to agree with the inventory recorded in the books.

The ABC team estimated that XYZ had lost approximately $750,000 of inventory. This information was turned over to XYZ and the controller was immediately dismissed.

Act IV—Impact on Final Analysis

ABC management examined these findings for any "deal-breaker" or "pricing" issues. ABC concluded that the offshore parent would survive its restructuring but would need to be watched closely.

ABC also decided that XYZ would remain competitive despite the loss of patent rights, but that profitability would definitely decline. With respect to the controller and the $750,000 in lost inventory, ABC discovered that the controller had virtually no assets and that recovery would therefore be impossible. A successful claim under the terms of the fidelity bond coverage was also problematic.

ABC concluded that XYZ was still worth buying, but the deal had to be re-priced to reflect the new information. As a result of the $750,000 in overstated inventory, the pretax earnings had to be reduced to $4.25 million from $5 million. The loss of patent rights reduced the purchase price from five times to four times the multiple of earnings. Consequently, the purchase offer was lowered to $17 million ($4.25 million × 4) from $25 million ($5 million × 5). XYZ ultimately accepted the price and the purchase was completed.

"If we hadn't been burned on the previous deal," ABC's CEO said afterward, "I'm sure we would never have conducted such an extensive due diligence review—and we might not have saved $8 million." He learned late but he learned. It is unfortunate that it usually takes a bad experience to teach us the lesson we should know from common sense.

The Concluding Act—Complacency Again?

Once the initial shock of recent scandals has worn off and new reforms are behind us, it is hoped those companies that should use due diligence do not fall back into their old, careless ways. In the short term, at least, there will be an increased scrutiny and skepticism and a recognition of the need for due diligence. The question is whether businesspeople will hear the thunderous collapse of great companies as a wake-up call to pay more attention to the importance of due diligence to protect themselves against deception. As financial tools become more sophisticated, so do the means of covering up the truth. Things are still often not what they seem.

TO THE FUTURE

Until recently, there was an accepted profile of companies susceptible to financial statement fraud. The typical fraud company had revenues of less than $50 million, was a technology, healthcare, or financial services company suffering losses or reaching only breakeven profitability, had an overbearing CEO or CFO, a complacent board of directors, and a poorly qualified audit committee meeting as infrequently as only once a year. The discovery of accounting improprieties at a number of large companies shows that even Fortune 500 companies are not immune to poor governance.

The fear that we are moving into an age of untrustworthy and arrogant management bent on looting their companies is probably exaggerated. The aftermath of the great stock market excesses of the 1920s, the "Go-Go" market of the 1960s, and the collapse of 1987 also brought overvaluations and insider trading scandals to light that were shocking in their size and audacity, but none of them proved to be harbingers of greater corruption to follow. The companies most in need of a due diligence investigation will continue to be those with revenues of less than $50 million. However, all companies must be scrutinized with a healthy professional skepticism at all times.

NOTE

1. Arthur Levitt, "The Numbers Game." Speech presented to the New York University Center for Law and Business, September 28, 1998, *www.sec.gov/news/speech/speecharchive/1998/spch220.txt.*

SUGGESTED READINGS

Levitt, Arthur. "The 'Numbers Game.'" Speech presented to the New York University Center of Law and Business, September 28, 1998.
Silverstone, Howard. "International Business: What You Don't Know Can Hurt You." *GPCC News, the Newsletter of the Greater Philadelphia Chamber of Commerce*, October 2002.
Silverstone, Howard, and Peter McFarlane. "Quantitative Due Diligence: The Check Before the Check." *The M&A Lawyer*, vol. 6, no. 6 (November–December 2002). Used with permission of Glasser Legal Works, 150 Clove Road, Little Falls, NJ 07424, 800-308-1700, *www.glasserlegalworks.com.*

5

THE ROLE OF THE ACCOUNTING PROFESSIONAL

THE IMPORTANCE OF ACCOUNTING PROFESSIONALS IN THE INVESTIGATION

The most important qualities the accounting professional can bring to any fraud investigation are an investigative mindset and skepticism. An investigative professional is a forensic accountant looking for evidence of fraud. He or she asks a set of questions different from those of the conventional auditor who is monitoring the financial statements to see whether they are in compliance with GAAP and thereby fairly represent the financial condition of the company.

This kind of investigator must think like both a thief and a detective and must be constantly looking for the weak links in the accounting system and among the people who staff it. In the course of the investigation, the forensic accountant must be prepared to reach far beyond the company's books to industry and government information, proprietary databases, court records, and any source, for that matter, that might throw light on the case.

The investigative accountant usually comes from either the firm's head office or outside the entity under investigation entirely and thus brings independence and objectivity. Since fraud is a breach of standards of honesty, the investigator must be of irreproachable personal integrity and without allegiance to anyone or anything but the truth. Everyone encountered in the course of the investigation must be dealt with impartially and evenhandedly.

Any fraud investigation is part art and part science. The science element comes, of course, from academic training in accounting theory, especially the audit side, and from knowledge of business practices and legal processes acquired through experience. This serves as the foundation for the investigator's task. As for the art element, many may argue that accounting is an art, not a science, but that is not a discussion for this book! What turns a well-trained and experienced accounting professional into a good financial investigator, however, is the knowledge of human behavior and a sixth sense for "red flags" and a good intuitive "feel" for the significance of evidence. The skeptical mindset should raise questions about the reasonableness of all transactions and the evidence that underlies them. Since the magnitude of amounts taken in a long-term fraud, for example, is often invisible except for a small irregularity in the accounts, the financial investigator must be curious and tenacious enough to follow up even the most initially unpromising clues. The judgments made through this skepticism will open up new hypotheses or close down old ones by testing them against the accumulating evidence until only one explanation is left. "When you have eliminated the impossible, whatever remains, however improbable, must be the truth."[1]

Accounting professionals play two important roles in any forensic investigation: as lead financial investigators and, potentially, as expert witnesses in any subsequent civil or criminal trials. In the first instance, they are *the* key people in any fraud investigation because they understand accounting systems and internal controls and know how to trace the flow of funds into, through, and out of the company. They are also in a position to provide an independent, objective critique of the corporate organization. This critique should not only cover the problems in the accounting system that permitted the fraud to occur in the first place but also address the integrity of the people at the heart of the process. As an expert assisting in case strategy and testimony, accounting professionals know the rules of evidence, what documents to request, whom they should interview and, in civil cases, how to do any associated damage quantification arising out of a particular situation.

The good financial investigator must be knowledgeable about fraudulent practices both in general and for a specific industry. A wide experience of how frauds are committed enables the investigator to act quickly in deciding which classes of documents will be most useful and who needs to be interviewed. Because some industries such as insurance, construction, and banking are especially prone to fraud, some investigators may specialize in those fields.

Since so much information is now created and stored electronically, a good knowledge of computers and information technology is an essential part of the investigator's toolkit. Computer forensics techniques are now also commonplace as part of financial investigations. These techniques can assist in recovering "deleted" information such as emails and proprietary information transferred to unauthorized computers. Then, when the evidence has been gathered and the suspects have been identified, good communications skills are needed to write a report that ties the whole story together and makes a well-supported argument in clear language. The ability to translate complex accounting issues into language the layperson understands is especially important when giving expert testimony. A judge or jury not familiar with accounting concepts and terminology must receive the information in clear, understandable form.

When fraud is suspected, the first job of the investigative accountant is to discover and review the evidence to prove or disprove the allegations. Since the reputations of the suspected principal(s) are at stake, the evidence-gathering process must be extremely discrete. Evidence must also be gathered and preserved in such a way that it can meet the standards-of-proof tests of any court; this is the "forensic" standard to which investigative accounting is held. In criminal cases, the evidence must establish guilt beyond a reasonable doubt; in civil cases, liability is established by the less rigorous standard of the balance of probabilities. Nonjudicial regulatory authorities, boards, and tribunals have yet other standards with which the investigator should be familiar.

Evidence will typically come from two primary sources. The first is the accounting records and any underlying documentation that may exist. In many cases, evidence found in these records might suggest additional research in external databases such as public records and court documents, as mentioned above. The investigator's experience should indicate which issues are well supported, which ones need additional evidence, and which are merely circumstantial.

The second source of evidence is gained through the interview process. Interviews may be conducted with key internal personnel, outside sources, and, ultimately, the suspects and any outside parties such as vendors or contractors who have done business with the individuals in question. The nature and timing of the interviews will be driven by the conduct of the case. (Interviews are discussed at greater length later on this book.)

The financial investigator must also be a good psychologist and be able to assess the greater or lesser likelihood that any given suspect is a fraudster. The paper and electronic evidence may show that accounting irregularities exist, but unless the evidence is connected to individuals, no fraud can be established. The investigator must be able to pick up on the motivational and behavioral clues that define a suspect. A winter tan, a better car, an affair, domestic financial worries, and a thousand other clues can all raise suspicions that might develop into a picture of criminal activity. Again, this process is discussed later in this book.

THE AUDIT PROCESS

Every fraud has an institutional context. Fraud is less likely to occur in an ethical corporate culture created by a principled management that respects the law and its employees, pays them adequately, and deals fairly with its customers and suppliers. A permissive corporate culture driven by greedy and even charismatic management that turns a blind eye to cutting corners, overlooks infractions of regulations, and has an inadequate accounting system gives unscrupulous employees the green light to commit fraud.

Some frauds show amazing ingenuity, but most are quite straightforward if the investigator knows where to look. Many very clever people have committed fraud but have been caught because every fraudster leaves a trail and makes mistakes. Since only a small proportion of fraud is actually discovered by investigation, most of the investigator's initial work involves checking out preliminary information.[2] This is especially true of so-called off-book frauds (i.e., bribery and kickbacks), which do not leave an audit trail and are often discovered by tip-offs.

The fraud itself may be entirely internal, directed against outsiders or directed by outsiders against the company. Internal frauds are usually abuses of the accounting system to steal cash. Frauds directed against outsiders frequently take the form of misrepresentations of financial information to creditors, shareholders, or insurance carriers. Outsiders defrauding the company are most often vendors, contractors, and consultants who supply shoddy goods, over-bill, or seek advantages through bribing employees.

Given the statistics and the fact that approximately 12 percent of initial fraud detection is through external audit (and approximately 19 percent is from internal audit), one would hope that we have all learned from the lessons of the past, and have become smarter and better equipped to detect fraud. Certainly, the American Institute of Certified Public Accountants and the accounting bodies have gone a long way to instill the fraud "mindset" in external auditors. Through Statements on Auditing Standards (SAS)

53, 82, and, most recently, 99 ("Consideration of Fraud in a Financial Statement Audit), auditors have been given expanded guidance for detecting material fraud.[3]

As stated by the AICPA, "The standard reminds auditors that they must approach every audit with professional skepticism and not assume management is honest. It puts fraud at the forefront of the auditor's mind."[4]

SAS 99 provides primarily for an increased professional skepticism and the auditor must plan for brainstorming how fraud can occur and put aside prior mindset as to management's honesty and integrity. At the planning stage, the auditor is required to identify the risks inherent in the client organization and to keep in mind the essentials of fraud factors, such as incentive, opportunity, and rationalization. In addition, there must be discussions with management, and inquiry must be made as to the risk of fraud and as to whether management is aware of any fraud. Auditors must also talk to employees and outside management, and give people a chance to bring to light problems that may exist (the concept of "whistle-blowing"). This particular factor emphasizes the psychological deterrent to potential perpetrators of knowing there is a better chance they will be turned in if people who are aware of the problem have a chance to provide information in a controlled, somewhat anonymous forum.

SAS 99 also places emphasis on surprise testing (i.e., testing of locations and accounts), which might otherwise not be tested and which are therefore a surprise to management and employees alike. The standard also includes procedures for auditors to test management's potential override of controls.

From a historical perspective, the debate on the auditor's role as "watchdog" versus "bloodhound" and the auditor's responsibilities is nothing new. Two AICPA committees, the Cohen Commission of 1978 and the Public Oversight Board of 1978, were established to look at the public perception of the auditor and his perceived role versus his actual role. In addition, the AICPA held a conference in 1992 called the Expectation Gap, which identified fraud as a problem in the industry. It was found that the public truly believed that the independent auditor would detect material misstatements owing to fraud.

The Cohen Commission also noted that users of financial statements were confused as to the respective responsibilities of auditors versus those of management. The most troubling aspect of the Cohen Commission's findings was the confusion that appeared to be prevalent among what could be considered educated users such as bankers, analysts, and shareholders.

It was hoped that the Auditing Standard Board's Statement of Auditing Standards No. 58, "Reports on Audited Financial Statements," would clarify the understanding of management and auditor responsibilities. However, as business transactions became more complicated and entities more complex, it became clear that the nature of business left prior perceptions behind. Perhaps because of this business complexity, the standards began to address the role of the auditor, specifically in detecting fraud, and emphasized that the concept of the professional skeptic had to be spelled out not only for the auditor to understand, but for the users of financial statements who needed to comprehend the auditor's role and separate existence from management.

Sadly, the accounting "shenanigans" discussed in earlier chapters once again brought into question the auditor's role and the perceived value of an audit. It is the users and the regulators who want the auditor to probe deeper, and it is out of this need and expectation that SAS 99 was born. We have discussed earlier in this book some of the traditional analytics used in conjunction with a company's financial statements. Auditors must use analytical techniques during the planning of their audit. These results can now be used in conjunction with other evidence gathered for purposes of identifying material misstatements.

So what does all this mean in the context of understanding basic accounting concepts, the concept of fraud, and the use of analytics in conjunction with all other knowledge? What it means is that today's auditors must think like their investigative accounting counterpart. They have to think like a potential fraudster. They have to be experienced in understanding the concept of fraud and must continually be the skeptic. Although this will put pressure on other aspects of the audit—such as staffing and budgeting (a subject near and dear to most clients' hearts!)—it will hopefully narrow the expectation gap that has existed for so long now.

INTERNAL CONTROLS

Internal controls are part of the protective system against fraud. They are designed to prevent irregularities and ensure early detection. Indeed, the Association of Certified Fraud Examiners 2002 Report to the Nation on Occupational Fraud and Abuse noted that: "a strong system of internal controls was viewed as the most effective anti-fraud measure by a wide margin."[5]

Internal controls, or the lack thereof, become a concern to both the auditor and financial investigator when these controls are absent or vulnerable to manipulation by fraudsters. Controls ensure that transactions are carried out only with appropriate authorization and are recorded correctly according to transaction type, amount, and time of execution. With good internal controls, restricting access and segregating responsibilities should safeguard assets. Access to data processing centers and to the computers themselves should be strictly controlled. Assets are further controlled through comparing physical inventory counts with the financial records.

In light of recent events in the business and accounting world, one of the more important controls over the accounting system is the ethical conduct of management. As already mentioned several times in this book, the ethical tone of the company is established at the top and works its way down. Good management should ensure that employees are properly trained, that they read and abide by a written code of conduct, and that they know that a policy of integrity will be enforced. The owners must also ensure that the board of directors is composed of financially experienced and honest people. It is especially important that the audit committee include financially educated and sophisticated members who meet regularly and carry out their responsibilities conscientiously.

Hiring at all levels should be done carefully through screening processes in which HR people or background-check specialists actually make the phone calls to verify education and experience claimed on the application form. All employees must take their vacations. This is one of the most basic tenets of business, but also one that is not readily enforced and has been shown to be the roadmap to fraud on so many occasions.

Although the cost of good controls can be significant, they should not be more than their anticipated benefit. Smaller companies are sometimes forced to combine duties that would be separated in larger firms. The audit committee as well as the internal and external auditors should be aware of this fact. People with multiple responsibilities must be supervised closely. Many companies have introduced the concept of self-audit, whereby different groups or locations within a company audit each other on a monthly basis, checking certain aspects of the other's business. This process demonstrates not only that controls are actually in place, but also that any fraud likely to be perpetrated would then have to comprise more people in its collusive manner, hence increasing the difficulty of its execution.

Another simple concept, but one that is easily missed, is that of preparing an organizational chart that defines responsibilities. This eliminates

"I didn't know that was my job" from the excuse and/or rationalization stage. In addition, forms used within the company should be designed for accurate recording of data. The data itself as recorded should be complete enough to be accepted as evidence in court. Accounting personnel should be rotated to different duties on a regular basis. Recordkeeping should not be handled by operating personnel, and there should be a clear records management policy with a schedule for retention, archiving, and destruction that meets statutory, legal, and regulatory requirements.

Special attention should be paid to the control of cash and inventory, two of the most common targets of fraud. Only a reasonable amount of cash should be kept on hand at any time, and the custodian should have no access to the accounting records. Cash receipts should be deposited by way of a lock box arrangement with a bank. Where a lock box is not practical due to company size or nature of business, cash should be deposited daily by bonded custodians and bank accounts should be properly authorized. The cashier should have no accounting duties. Cash disbursements should be made only through computer-generated checks, and all signing authorities should be limited. Inventory counts should be made by employees other than those responsible for managing the stockroom or warehouse. Insurance coverage should reflect the real value of the current inventory at all times. Periodic counts should be compared to the perpetual record.

So many times we hear about the "red flags" of fraud, the quotes of management playing Monday morning quarterback, the specialized sense of hindsight, and many of the other "should have known" vernacular. Through qualified professionals, a healthy serving of professional skepticism, suitable guidance from the accounting profession, and adequate assistance from business itself, business has the chance to minimize the chance of fraud occurring. However, as we have seen and will continue to see throughout this book, none of these factors is mutually exclusive, and none of the players is mutually exclusive.

NOTES

1. Sherlock Holmes in Sir Arthur Conan Doyle's *The Sign of Four.*
2. Bologna and Lindquist state that 90 percent of fraud is discovered by accident. See G. Jack Bologna and Robert J. Lindquist, *Fraud Auditing and Forensic Accounting: New Tools and Techniques* (Hoboken,

NJ: John Wiley & Sons, 1995), p. 32. This estimate has changed in recent years, as reported by the Association of Certified Fraud Examiners. Of the 532 cases whose discovery was studied for the *2002 Report to the Nation: Occupational Fraud and Abuse*, only 18.8 percent were found by accident. This figure is especially startling because it is higher than those discovered by internal audit (18.6%), internal controls (15.4%), or external audit (11.5%). Tips from employees were the single largest source of information that fraud was suspected (26.3%). *www.cfenet.com/media/2002RttN.*

3. As defined in *Statement of Financial Accounting Concepts No. 2* (FASB, May 1980), materiality is "*the magnitude of an omission or misstatement of accounting information that, in the light of surrounding circumstances, makes it possible that the judgment of a reasonable person relying on the information would have been changed or influenced by the omission or misstatement.*"
4. Barry Melancon, AICPA president and CEO.
5. *www.cfenet.com/media.*

SUGGESTED READING

G. Jack Bologna and Robert J. Lindquist, *Fraud Auditing And Forensic Accounting: New Tools and Techniques.* (Hoboken, NJ: John Wiley & Sons, 1995).

——— PART TWO ———

FINANCIAL CRIME
INVESTIGATION

6

BUSINESS AS A VICTIM

INTRODUCTION

Business can be a victim of both internal and external fraud. Internal fraud is perpetrated by employees at any level, from the cashier stealing out of the till to the complex collusion to steal inventory by manipulating computer data and shipping the stolen goods to offsite locations. External fraud is deception committed by an outsider against the company. Insurance companies are common victims of this type of fraud through false applications and false claims. Banks are also frequently victimized, as are government agencies.

As indicated in the 2002 report of the Association of Certified Fraud Examiners mentioned in Chapter 1, asset misappropriation accounts for an overwhelming 85.7 percent of all occupational fraud. Corruption schemes are a distant second at 12.8 percent, and fraudulent statements represent only 5.1 percent[1]. These figures were consistent with the findings in the 1996 report and can probably be taken as an accurate picture of the distribution of occupational fraud by type.

EMPLOYEE THEFTS

Cash

Cash is the favorite target of fraudsters and accounts for 77.8 percent of all asset misappropriations. Much is taken by outright cash larceny and skimming, but the majority is stolen through more elaborate disbursement schemes, including some manipulation of the billing and payroll systems or falsification of expense reimbursements and check tampering.

All accounting cycles pass through the cash account at some time. The cash produced in these processes becomes either petty cash or demand deposits, such as checking accounts, interest-bearing accounts, certificates of deposit, or other liquid investments. The mechanism of these thefts is usually quite simple. Petty cash is stolen by forging authorizing signatures or creating false vouchers for reimbursement.

Dishonest employees often manipulate receipts being prepared for deposit. This is common in small companies where the same person is responsible for booking the cash receipts and writing the checks for deposit. It is not uncommon for the long-term "trusted employee" to become an "opportunity taker" type of fraudster in the face of this temptation. Because the money is so available and the in-and-out transactions are so simple, the fraudster frequently rationalizes the theft as "borrowing" with the intent to return the cash later. Of course, since the money is easier to take than to return, the accrued amount stolen soon becomes too great to replace and the fraudster becomes locked into an endless round of theft and cover-up.

CASE EXAMPLE

Cash and Carry

An example of cash theft is the case of the security officer who had custody of the petty cash account at a small manufacturing company. For most of the seven years of his service with the company he had been altering the numbers on legitimate receipts for such loosely watched items as postage and office party expenses. He was caught during a surprise count when the auditors found only a few hundred dollars instead of the $3,000 that should have been in the account.

The consequences of this fraud were felt almost exclusively by the security officer. The company was out an unknown few thousand dollars but suffered no significant harm. The security officer, on the other hand, was out of a job and at risk of having his prospective new employer call the old company for an explanation of his departure. His wife was now forced to support the family on her salary alone, which was not sufficient to maintain their lifestyle. He was unemployed for six months before getting a lower-paying job that allowed the family some comfort but forced them to reduce their standard of living.

PAYROLL FRAUD

Fraud through the payroll department is commonly committed by using ghost employees, inflating hours of work and overtime, as well as overstating expense accounts or medical claims.

CASE EXAMPLE

The Trusted Employee

A divorced woman in her 40s became the bookkeeper and office manager of a husband and wife team operating a highly successful and growing catering business. The bookkeeper was the classic "trusted employee" responsible for all cash transactions from depositing the customers' checks to paying suppliers and managing the line of credit at the bank. The bookkeeper had no signing authority, but the husband or wife put their names to whatever their employee presented.

The bookkeeper's first marriage had not provided her with a high standard of living and her current income, which was excellent for her level of responsibility, was not sufficient to satisfy her growing taste for the finer things. The owners' combined trust and carelessness in not doing regular reconciliations provided their trusted employee with the opportunity to start forging their signatures and deflecting money to the bookkeeper's own account. The business was growing rapidly, and the bookkeeper began stealing larger and larger sums. The amounts stolen soon became greater than the monthly income of the business. She was discovered when the bank called the owners to inquire about the huge NSF charges that seemed strange given the size and regularity of the deposits.

In this case, the woman had not reported for work on the very morning the bank called about the NSF charges. When she did not come in the next day either and could not be reached on the phone, the police were sent to her apartment. They found that she had left town leaving no forwarding address.

CASE EXAMPLE

The Bank Teller

The huge amounts of cash passing across the counter every day at any bank branch frequently provide all the temptation a teller may need to become dishonest. A client complained she could not account for the withdrawal of several thousand dollars recently deposited following the sale of her car. She remembered the name on the tag of the teller who had processed the deposit. The

(continues)

(*continued*)

employee was interviewed and confessed she had obtained the client's identifiers (her mother's maiden name and birth date) and created a duplicate bankbook. This was a particularly sad case because the teller was just in her early 20s. The motive for her theft was her large credit card debt, which left her without enough money to pay her rent. She was dismissed from the bank but was not prosecuted.

CASE EXAMPLE

Simple Payroll Fraud

When an employee at a large advertising agency tried to pick up his paycheck, he was told it had gotten lost and he would have to wait for the new paperwork to be done before another could be issued. After finally getting the new check, he noticed his year-to-date earnings included an amount for the missing check. An inquiry discovered that a payroll clerk had generated the "missing" check by entering false information into the computer and had cashed it by forging the employee's name.

The payroll clerk was a young married woman with a small family. She and her truck driver husband were not making ends meet, and she had turned to fraud to generate the difference. With only a high school education, she found it difficult to get another job. She collected unemployment insurance for a while before turning to a government program to upgrade her computer skills. In the meantime, she and her husband had to reduce an already inadequate standard of living in order to feed and clothe their two small children. In the end, she was able to get a job as a data processor.

CASE EXAMPLE

Expense Report Fraud

Expense reports are quickly turned into cash in the payroll department and offer a rich opportunity for padding. The sales director of a large region in the central United States knew that his managers incurred a lot of expenses generating sales but showed little concern as long as the sales numbers were meeting projections. During a downturn in the economy, the sales director began looking more closely at the managers' expenses and noticed that one man's seemed excessive in relation to the sales generated. He had heard rumors the man was having an affair and now began to suspect it was being financed through the expense account. A review of restaurant and hotel receipts attached to the expense reports obtained from the payroll department showed that all the expenses could be supported with documentation. Nevertheless, the director remained suspicious. Since he knew the territory well and had done business with most of the persons named as dining companions in the manager's expense reports, the director decided to make a few discrete phone calls. It was soon clear that many of the dinners had not been with clients. When confronted with the evidence, the manager confessed to having an affair with one of the saleswomen of a ___ ___ their sales trips to put them in ___ ___ xpense accounts to both co

The sales direc___ ___ er was forced to explain the ___ im out of the house and sta___ ___ ob but only as a full-commi___ ___ famil- iar in a new territor___ ___ oe for many years since his ___ s wife was forced to return t___ ___ e was sold, and they lost the

FRA

These frauds are usually ___ pliers, and contractors of vario ___ ission of false invoices for go ___ ___ces for goods or services of inf ___ ___ty. These frauds often involve collusion between outsiders and internal employees and can become quite complex. Collusion allows controls to be circumvented.

CASE EXAMPLE

Construction Fraud

Because the competitive bidding process for construction contracts often makes profit margins razor thin, contractors may be tempted to increase their profits through fraud. A developer negotiated a $550 million guaranteed max-imum-price contract with a prime contractor and subcontractors to erect a 40-story building. To the developer's surprise, the allowances and contingency holds for unexpected costs and emergencies were exhausted before even the core and shell had been completed. This left the interior work unfunded. Puzzled and suspicious, the developer hired private investigators who discovered the prime contractor had bribed the architect and were now colluding to defraud

(continues)

(*continued*)

the developer. The contractor was purchasing goods and services beyond those required for the developer's building, diverting the excess to other jobs on which he and the architect were working and submitting the invoices to the developer. The excess expenses were approved and explained away by the architect. The contractor and the architect had convinced themselves that the developer's cost controls were shortsighted and would make the job unprofitable for them. When the architect and contractor were confronted with the evidence of the private investigation, they agreed to pay for the remaining construction from their own funds rather than be prosecuted.

The developer did not press charges against either the architect or the contractor, but he did report the architect to the licensing board. At the hearing, the investigators produced the evidence they had discovered for the developer and the architect received a written reprimand. This effectively put the architect on an industry blacklist, which made it difficult for him to find well-paying jobs. As with other fraudsters, the consequences of the dishonest architect's fraud affected his family. He was no longer able to keep his children in private school, and he had to drop a club membership he had enjoyed with his wife. Life went on, but not at the carefree level the family had enjoyed before.

CASE EXAMPLE

Insurance Fraud

A medium-sized clothing manufacturer had a warehouse fire in which it lost its summer inventory and financial records. The insurer became suspicious and started an investigation when a multimillion-dollar claim was filed less than two weeks after the fire. The investigators found the inventory was three times as large as that of the previous year, despite the fact that the industry was suffering a downturn and everybody was cutting back. The only records lost in the fire were those related to the inventory; everything else had been moved to another building a few weeks earlier. On the last renewal date before the fire, the insured had tripled the coverage. The documents submitted in support of the inventory valuation proved to have been created by the owner's brother allegedly for the owner's wife in an angry divorce action. The owner had, in fact, paid his brother $100,000 for the valuation. When the fire marshall's investigation proved arson, the insurer refused to pay the claim. The owner was convicted of arson and sentenced to prison.

With the building destroyed and the insurer refusing to pay the claim, the clothing manufacturing business was worthless. The only value lay in the land on which it had stood. The owners had taken a huge risk and lost everything. They now had to lay off warehouse staff and bookkeepers as well as cutters and other skilled employees. Suppliers lost a customer and were forced to lay off part of their workforce.

FRAUD COMMITTED BY OUTSIDERS

Credit card and insurance fraud are perpetrated against companies by outsiders. Credit card fraud is estimated to have caused $650 million in losses to American business in 2001.[2] The impact of this type of fraud can be especially devastating to small retailers. According to the Coalition Against Insurance Fraud, fraudulent claims now cost the U.S. insurance industry an estimated $80 billion annually.[3] Bogus property and casualty claims alone account for $24 billion, or 10 percent of all property and casualty claims paid.[4] The insurance industry is at risk not just from paying on fraudulent claims but also from providing coverage where the real risk of loss is actually greater than can be actuarially determined on the basis of the false data in the original application.

MANAGEMENT THEFTS

Fraud by management can be extremely serious since senior personnel can override the controls that have been put in place to prevent the very fraud they are committing. The effects of management misconduct can also have severe consequences for the company's overall morale and set a negative model for employees farther down the company ladder.

CASE EXAMPLE

A Misused Credit Card

A disgruntled employee in the accounting department informed the new president of the publishing company that the secretary-treasurer was defrauding the company through misuse of her credit card. The secretary-treasurer was then covering her tracks by manipulating the accounting records. The new president realized immediately this was a political hot potato that could not be left uninvestigated but could also destroy his effectiveness if it proved to be untrue. He was unknown, and the secretary-treasurer had been with the company for seven years. Forensic accountants were brought in to examine her accounts. They discovered that she had charged personal items to a general corporate expense account and to the advance accounts of several employees. (The company permitted employees to charge personal expenses to their advance accounts from which they would be deducted later.) The false journal entries were in the

(*continues*)

(*continued*)

secretary-treasurer's own handwriting. On the basis of the investigators' evidence, the president was successful in persuading the board of directors to dismiss her.

The departure of the secretary-treasurer created problems for everyone. When confronted by the board, she admitted taking the money and signed a promissory note for the full amount. She originally threatened a suit for wrongful dismissal but dropped it when confronted with the evidence uncovered by the forensic investigators. She now faced disgrace and loss of employment and was forced to live on her savings for 18 months before she found another job in an inferior position at a lower salary with a less prestigious company.

Those at the publishing house lost a friend and colleague. The company was now faced with the expense of an executive search and the prospect of hiring an unknown for a sensitive position. Everyone was shocked that such a trusted person should have committed fraud. The company incurred the additional expense of developing an educational program for employees in fraud prevention and detection and reviewing its accounting controls.

CASE EXAMPLE

Meaty Matters

A medium-sized meatpacking company in a small Texas town began to experience financial difficulties following a fire that did extensive damage to the plant. The insurance company promptly settled the property damage claim but a lengthy delay in coming to an agreement on a $1 million business interruption claim caused significant hardship as customers were forced to look elsewhere for their meat. The owners were concerned that a decline from their $40 million in annual sales and its effect on accounts receivable would jeopardize their line of credit with the banks. To keep their working capital ratio healthy, they began pre-billing and inflating inventory records.

When the company was eventually forced into bankruptcy, the receiver discovered only $2 million in inventory instead of the stated $10 million and $6 million in accounts receivable from clients who denied owing anything. No money, however, had been diverted to the personal use of the owners; they had acted solely to save the business.

The two owners pleaded guilty to fraud and received prison terms. The lives of two otherwise productive citizens had received blows from which no one ever really recovers. Their families were not only deprived of the presence of two husbands and fathers, but the lives of their wives and children were completely changed. The fraudsters' families were ostracized as they suffered the reflected disgrace of the two men. The wives who had not worked in 20 years now had to find jobs to support their families. The children became the target of other children's taunts. In the end, the situation became unendurable, and both families moved away to start new lives elsewhere. When the men came out of prison they had no money and were forced to begin again at a much lower standard of living. One of the couples divorced.

The effect of closing the meatpacking plant reached far beyond the immediate families of the convicted fraudsters. The company had been a major employer and had a significant impact on the local economy through its own spending and that of its employees. Of the 50 or so employees at the plant, only about 10 were able to get jobs in the town. Others found it difficult keeping up their mortgage payments and were forced to take odd jobs or look for employment in the next major center, which was about an hour's drive away. The local retailers suffered a noteworthy loss of business.

CASE EXAMPLE

The Whole Shebang

A manufacturing company was headquartered on the East Coast of the United States but had its main facility in the Midwest. Consequently, there was little day-to-day communication between the board of directors and senior management with management of the main operation in the Midwest. The chief financial officer, based in the Midwest, had been with the company for many years and had worked his way up from bookkeeper to assistant controller to controller and ultimately to CFO.

What was most interesting about the CFO's role is that with all the promotions leading finally to CFO, he retained custody over the bank reconciliations. For all the "best practices" discussed earlier in this book, the company, perhaps unwittingly allowed its CFO to authorize contracts with vendors, approve payments, actually print and sign checks, receive bank statements, and perform the bank reconciliation.

It was no surprise, then, that over seven years, the CFO was able to embezzle over $600,000 through almost a dozen different schemes. The schemes ranged from a falsified employee workers compensation claim (under which the CFO paid for his children's braces) to an expense account fraud whereby the company paid the CFO's credit card bill through a corporate check, while at the same time he submitted the charges on his expense account and was

(continues)

(*continued*)

therefore reimbursed twice. He also paid for lavish family travel and entertaining at the company's expense and was part of a scheme with vendors whereby he received kickbacks in return for giving them various contracts.

When questioned how these schemes could go unnoticed for so long, it became apparent from his former staff that he had created a barrier between himself and anyone who worked for him. In addition, his physical size and manner reportedly intimidated anyone who wished to confront him. The schemes were ultimately discovered when a disgruntled secretary approached Human Resources and informed them that she thought something was peculiar about the handling of the CFO's expenses. She also questioned why he was still handling the bank reconciliation. An internal investigation ensued, and the schemes were discovered.

The company ultimately recovered $500,000 of its losses under a fidelity bond; an agreement was made between the company, the bonding company, and the U.S. attorney to keep the principal out of jail and working at another company in a nonfiduciary position, where he was able to start making restitution.

CORPORATE THEFTS

Corporate fraud is committed by senior management to benefit the corporation as a whole. This type of fraud includes financial statement fraud, antitrust violations, securities fraud, tax evasion, false advertising, environmental crimes, and the production of unsafe products.

Financial statement fraud is usually committed in order to improve the earnings and hence the stock price of publicly traded companies or the ratios supporting loan covenants at private companies. Generally accepted accounting principles (GAAP) provide accountants with a certain amount of interpretive leeway in creating their accounts. What can be justified as a liberal but understandable interpretation of GAAP can easily become a policy of deliberate earnings management and ultimately slip across the line into fraudulent manipulation. Managements of publicly traded companies are often under pressure from Wall Street analysts to meet earnings expectations by showing steady growth despite any downturns in the economy. The Equity Funding and Enron cases discussed earlier in this book are examples of what can happen when real life cannot perform up to expectations.

CASE EXAMPLE

Price Fixing

Although price fixing has been discovered in many industries, one of the most outstanding recent cases was that of Archer Daniels Midland. In October 1996, the company paid a $100 million fine after pleading guilty to felony charges alleging a conspiracy with other producers of citric acid, lysine, and other commodities. It was estimated that makers of soft drinks, processed foods, detergents, and other products paid $400 million extra to buy citric acid from ADM and its co-conspirators between 1992 and 1995. Poultry, swine, and other livestock producers paid an extra $100 million in the same period for lysine, a growth additive used in feed.[5]

During the late 1940s through the 1950s, electric equipment manufacturers, including General Electric, Westinghouse, Allis-Chalmers, and Federal Pacific, conspired to fix prices in a market worth $1.75 billion annually.[6] Utilities, all levels of government, the military, and industry were victimized by prices that rose by double and sometimes even triple digits, despite slow growth in the wholesale price index. By the early 1960s, four grand juries handed down 20 indictments against 45 individuals and 29 companies. The power of rationalization and "neutralization" referred to in Chapter 1 is well exemplified in the remarks of some of the industry executives. One company president defended his actions this way: "It is the only way a business can be run. It is free enterprise." Another, in a statement worthy of Yogi Berra, said: "Sure, collusion was illegal, but it wasn't unethical."[7]

Antitrust laws, starting with the Sherman Antitrust Act of 1890, are designed to encourage competition by preventing monopolies or conspiracies to monopolize. The willingness to enforce these laws has varied from administration to administration. The principal instrument of monopoly power is price fixing.

NOTES

1. The sum of the percentages exceeds 100% as some cases involved more than one type of fraud.
2. "The Growing Toll of Identity Theft," *Credit Card Management*, 1, no. 6 (September 2002), p. 13, *www.aba.com/industry+issues/ealertii20. htm.*

3. *www.insurancefraud.org/site_index_set.html.*
4. *www.insurancefraud.org/news/study021303_set.html.*
5. David R. Simon, *Elite Deviance*, 6th ed. (Boston: Allyn & Bacon, 1999), p. 107.
6. Ibid., p. 108.
7. Quoted in ibid., p. 110.

SUGGESTED READINGS

http://insurancefraud.org/site_index_set.html.
www.insurancefraud.org/news/study021303_set.html.
"The Growing Toll of Identity Theft." *Credit Card Management,* vol. 15, no. 6 (September 2002): 13. *www.aba.com/industry+issues/ealertii20.htm.*
Simon, David R. *Elite Deviance*, 6th edition. Boston: Allyn & Bacon, 1999.

7

BUSINESS AS A VEHICLE

INTRODUCTION

In any discussion of financial crime in the context of business, it is imperative to remember that, in addition to the supporting role of the victim, a company or business enterprise may take center stage as the star of the show, becoming the vehicle to commit the crime.

Business's role as the vehicle for criminal conduct, though not new, is more readily apparent in the wake of such recent debacles as Enron, Worldcom, and Tyco. These tailor-made-for-TV dramas only serve to illustrate what experienced financial investigators and forensic accountants have known for years: Businesses are used to further criminal enterprises. Criminal enterprises have used businesses both to directly engage in criminal activity and to facilitate its commission through concealment or escape from prosecution. Therefore, no text on financial crime would be complete without examining how a business's less-palatable role as the vehicle for crime commission can influence your decisions as an investigator. After all, business is where the money is, and as you will soon see, following the money inevitably leads to identification of the suspect.

ORGANIZED CRIME AND BUSINESS

Historical Trends in Organized Crime

Organized crime—the very mention of those two words conjures up images of ruthless ethnic criminals with colorful nicknames like "Fat Tony" and "Sammy the Bull." Historically in America, though hardly not the only group of organized criminals, the Italian-dominated crime families have received more renown and publicity than perhaps any other. One need look no further than Martin Scorsese's *Goodfellas* or Mario Puzo's *Godfather* trilogy to immerse oneself in the seedy, often overglamorized world of the Italian Mafia. Commercialization of the exploits of "La Cosa Nostra" (LCN)—Italian for, "this thing of ours"—catapulted the secret, highly structured society of soldiers and bosses, *consigliere* and lieutenants, into the front of the collective conscience of Americans.[1] It is for that reason that most readers' thoughts turn to men like John Gotti, Carlo Gambino, and Lucky Luciano when the term *organized crime* is first encountered.[2]

In reality, however, the operations of the traditional Mafiosi comprise only a small, some would argue insignificant, portion of the organized criminal enterprises that those charged with the investigation of financial crimes are likely to encounter.[3] Today, financial crime investigators are likely to discover organized groups from all ethnic origins. Chinese (Tongs and Triads), Japanese (Yakuza), Colombian (drug cartels), Jewish, Jamaican (Jamaican Posse), Mexican (Nuestra Cosa), Nigerian, Vietnamese (Triad), and, most recently, Russian ethnic groups present a significant presence in the world of organized crime.[4] In addition, the face of today's organized criminal enterprise is no longer defined by nationality or ethnicity. In fact, today's definition of organized crime may apply equally to traditional ethnic-based organizations and to nontraditional groups who are associated solely through a shared desire to capitalize on illegal conduct monetarily. This definition includes the likes of corporate directors, managers, and officers.

Therefore, when discussing organized crime, it is essential that the reader expand the definition of organized criminal enterprise (OCE) to include nontraditional groups. That is why we have adopted the following definition.[5] An OCE is any association of two or more entities (note that this definition expands to include associations of corporations) whose acknowledged purpose is to profit from illegal activity. It is important to note that this definition makes no distinction regarding the stage at which criminal activity enters the equation. Therefore, no distinction is drawn between the cocaine cartels of Colombia and the top-level executives who conspire to conceal liabilities or to misstate expenses, thereby defrauding stockholders.

THE LIFE-CYCLE MODEL OF TRADITIONAL ORGANIZED CRIME

Historically speaking, traditional OCEs, regardless of ethnic origin, traverse a classic pattern—a life cycle. In the beginning, the organization involves itself in low-level street crime and violence.[6] This has been seen quite clearly in the origin of the Italian Mafia. Originally syndicated to protect fellow immigrants, the mob evolved into the business of providing protection as a product. During Prohibition, the product focus shifted to illegal alcohol. The violence that was so inherent in the organization from the beginning became a way to reinforce the power of the organization. The product became the means to the end—maximization of profit.

During this stage of the life cycle, the OCE expands its product line into other areas such as prostitution, gambling, and other goods—either illegal per se or obtained through illegal means. The violence remains a staple of the group's method of operation. It is at this stage that organized crime begins to resemble legitimate business.[7]

As the organization continues to evolve, a gradual movement into legitimacy can be observed. In the Italian Mafia, this shift was evident in its transition into the entertainment industry. During the 1950s, the mob became active stockholders (though not stockholders of record due to gaming regulations) in several major legitimate hotel chains and Las Vegas casinos. At this stage, organized crime not only looks and operates like a legitimate business, but the product of their labor—the profits—are, for all outward appearance, legitimate revenues. That isn't to say that groups within this stage of the evolutionary life cycle have extricated themselves from illegitimate business activity such as narcotics sales, gambling, and extortion. But the outward appearance of the organization remains that of a legitimate business. In fact, many organizations adopt formal structures for management of both their legitimate and illegitimate operations, making the distinctions between each operation less clear than ever. As is true for all organizations, the life cycle of each OCE may be more or less distinct than the next. One OCE's period of expansion of the product line may occur quite early on—even imperceptibly so—while another OCE may dwell in the later phase of its illegal enterprise stage for an extended period of time before transitioning into the appearance of legitimacy, if at all. The Life-cycle Model is not intended to illustrate that all OCEs follow an identical blueprint. Instead, much like legitimate businesses, OCEs undergo an evolution that draws them more and more directly into the business world. Therefore, there is a greater likelihood of impact on financial investigators such as auditors, criminal investigators, and financial managers.

Because both legitimate business and organized crime share this common thread, the profit motive, money is the one unifying element among these groups and across all phases of the life cycle. The goal, and therefore the driving force, for all organized criminal enterprises, without exception, is the amassing of as much money as possible while incurring the least amount of cost. In that regard, organized crime is no different than big business. The result is money, usually in the form of cash, and lots of it.

THE SHARED PROFIT MOTIVE

The challenge that the profit motive presents to organized crime is how to conceal large sums of cash. This becomes a problem for organizations in both the legitimate and the illegitimate phases of the life cycle. This is so because, as noted earlier, the goal of the enterprise is to produce the most income at the least cost. If an enterprise, even one operating under the guise of legitimacy, reports accurately all of its revenue, intrusive questions inevitably arise—questions that the criminal enterprise cannot legitimately explain away. The challenge of concealing large sums of cash leads naturally to migration into the world of money laundering.

Through money laundering, illegitimate businesses and legitimate businesses operating as a cover for illegal operations can hide, distribute, and repatriate large sums of money through legitimate sources. For organized criminal enterprises, this is often exactly what the doctor ordered.

MONEY LAUNDERING

Because money laundering by its nature is a crime of concealment, the scope of money-laundering activity is not precisely known. It is safe, however, to assume that huge sums of illegal funds course through the international economy on a daily basis. The International Monetary Fund (IMF) has estimated that, annually, laundered funds are equivalent to roughly 3 to 5 percent of the entire world monetary output. Other estimates place the figure at $300–500 million worldwide.[8] In the United States alone, it has been estimated that more than $2 million in laundered funds flow through the U.S. economy daily.[9] These figures, though imprecise, are a sobering illustration of the degree to which law enforcement in this area is seemingly a needle-in-a-haystack effort.

Money laundering, though a distinct crime in its own right, is also a collateral crime associated with many forms of organized crime. As we discussed earlier, the large sums of cash that criminal activity tends to generate pose logistical problems for OCEs. In order to ensure the contin-

104

ued existence of the enterprise, its managers must quickly and surreptitiously convert this mountain of dirty money into legitimate-appearing income. Money laundering is the process by which OCEs accomplish this task—more or less successfully depending on the efficacy of the laundering scheme employed. Generally speaking, the more successful a money-laundering operation is at imitating the patterns and behaviors of legitimate transactions, the less likely the operation will be exposed. For an investigator, this rule-of-thumb is the key to success.

No matter how hard the OCE tries to emulate the patterns of legitimate business activity, however, appearances will eventually break down. Many times, the cracks in the armor will be imperceptible unless you as the investigator are knowledgeable about the legitimate patterns of activity and behaviors of an actual going concern. Armed with this knowledge, you are poised to spot the impostors through financial analysis paired with conventional investigative techniques.

It is widely accepted, and rightly so, that the investigation of money-laundering activity is an effective means to dismantle any OCE. It wasn't until "Deep Throat," the key informant in the Watergate scandal, urged Bob Woodward of the *Washington Post* to "follow the money" that the phrase "money laundering" even appeared in print.[10] However, this approach to investigating had been employed successfully in all types of criminal enterprises ranging from traditional LCN networks to modern terrorist cells. As early as 1932, law enforcement had applied this collateral attack technique to solve the predecessor crimes. For example, Bruno Richard Hauptmann was eventually arrested for the Lindbergh kidnapping because his efforts to launder the ransom money were unsuccessful.[11]

This collateral attack is in essence a "reverse engineering" method that is predicated upon the idea that once the origin of laundered funds is uncovered, both the source of the money and the persons responsible for generating the illegal income will be revealed. Much like the laundering process itself, the success of the investigative process depends largely on the efficacy of the scheme employed and on the skill of the financial bloodhound tracking the source of funds.

From the perspective of a financial investigator, money laundering may be broken down into a series of three stages—placement, layering, and integration.[12] Within these three stages, which may overlap, various methods and techniques are employed to accomplish the individual goal of that stage. These methods vary widely in complexity and detail, but when combined, they can produce a total break in the link between illegal activity and assets.

Step One: Placement

Placement is the introduction of the dirty money into the global financial system. It is the starting point of all money-laundering activities, and because of the volume of funds involved, it is often the most difficult stage. It is at this stage that the form of the funds must be converted to hide their illegal origin. Since most illegal activities generate large sums of cash in small denominations, OCEs must break these large amounts of dirty money into smaller, less conspicuous sums. This is accomplished in a variety of ways.[13]

In theory, the OCE's creativity is the only limit to the ways in which placement can be accomplished. In practice, launderers try to make their choices reflect, as closely as possible, the profile of legitimate businesses in the areas in which they operate. In addition, the OCE's choices as to placement methods will often depend on the magnitude of the criminal activity. The methods of placement used to integrate small sums periodically will vary greatly from the methods used to place large sums regularly.

If the sums are small, or the nature of the revenues is generally infrequent, there are a number of techniques that efficiently combine all three stages into the placement stage. For example, small sums can be placed, layered, and integrated using the racetrack method.

In this scheme, the OCE purchases winning betting slips from patrons at local racetracks for a percentage over the actual payout: The OCE in turn redeems the slips for face value, instantly legitimizing the funds as gambling earnings. For obvious reasons this method is limited in the amount of cash that can be legitimized efficiently.

One of the most common methods of placement is a technique used for larger, more regularly occurring flows of cash known as *smurfing*. Smurfing is accomplished by dividing large sums of cash into smaller amounts— less than the currency transaction reporting (CTR) requirement.[14] These bundles are distributed to a large network of "mules," who take the allotted cash and deposit it into special accounts set up for that purpose. By keeping the deposits below the CTR threshold (currently $10,000 in a single transaction or multiple structured transactions to that limit), and distributing the sums across a wide geographic area, the OCE can fly under the radar of most watchdog agencies. Once the cash is successfully placed into the financial system, the first link between illegality and the money is broken.[15]

By concealing the illegal nature of the money by associating it with legitimate sources of income such as cash businesses or charities, the red flags associated with large-value cash deposits are avoided. Therefore, the links tying the money to its source—OCE-sponsored illegal activity—are no longer visible.

Popularized by the drug cartels of the 1980s, this technique has its limitations. As the operation grows, more mules are required, and the probability of detection increases—both through betrayal and by suspicious bank personnel. Although still in use, smurfing is becoming less popular. Instead, financial investigators, fraud auditors, and criminal investigators are more likely to encounter the next technique—placement through legitimate businesses.[16]

This technique employs cash-intensive legitimate businesses as fronts for the placement operation. The complexity of this operation may run from the occasional mingling of dirty cash with legitimate receipts to complete support of the business with illegal proceeds. In keeping with the OCE's desire to mirror the profile of legitimate businesses, bars, restaurants, casinos, and other cash-only businesses are prime targets for laundering activity. Large cash deposits of small-denomination bills are expected by the local bank, and, absent inside information, local officials rarely notice anything out of the ordinary.

Although not exhaustive, the following methods are commonly employed, either individually or in tandem, to accomplish the successful placement of dirty money:

- Exchange of cash for money orders and other negotiable instruments.
- Smuggling hordes of currency across the border to a haven nation for deposit.
- Conversion of cash into high-value/low-bulk items such as diamonds and precious gems.
- Collusion with banking officials to avoid reporting of large-value deposits.
- Use of parallel banking systems.
- Conversion of cash into insurance products and long-term capitalization bonds.
- Concealment of cash in trading losses of derivatives and securities brokers.

Regardless of the method employed, the goal remains the same: insert large amounts of cash into the global financial system. By keeping this goal in mind, the financial investigator is much more likely to recognize the potential for money-laundering activity at this stage.[17]

Step Two: Layering

Once the funds are introduced into the system, the OCE must further conceal their origin and ownership in an attempt to destroy the audit trail. This is accomplished through layering. Layering consists of moving the funds through a series of transactions within the financial system—often more than a dozen.[18] These transactions appear to be normal business transactions and routinely pass unnoticed by even the most watchful eye.

Similar to the placement stage, the OCE's options are often limited only by the creativity and imagination of the money movers. Recently, with the advent of smart cards and e-cash, a whole new area of financial transaction has become ripe for exploitation by sophisticated OCEs.

In the conventional scenario, an OCE will shift funds between various banks using electronic funds transfers (EFT). Electronic funds transfers are instantaneous and, given the sheer volume of daily EFT activity, practically invisible. In 1998, it is estimated that there were approximately 70,000 wire transfers per day, moving nearly $2 trillion in funds. With that volume of activity, it is no wonder OCEs feel secure in their anonymity.[19]

It is at this stage that shell corporations, offshore financial centers (OFCs), and Non-Cooperative Countries and Territories (NCCTs) play a significant role. In addition, the advent of on-line banking services, electronic cash payment systems, and smart cards has combined to greatly complicate the financial investigator's job. We will briefly discuss several of the most popular techniques.[20]

The Use of Shell Corporations

The corporate structure, particularly the existence of the corporation as a legal entity, lends itself well to the task of structuring financial transactions to increase anonymity. Nowhere is this more evident than through the use of offshore entities whose ownership is held through bearer securities.

Bearer securities consist of bearer bonds and bearer stock certificates. Although the use of bearer bonds to launder money has not been officially documented, the use of bearer stock certificates is commonplace. In a conventionally created corporation, ownership of the entity is signified by the issuance of registered shares. Registered shares are exactly that: shares whose ownership is registered on the books of the entity. Determination of actual ownership and control of the entity at any given point in time is a simple matter of referring to the books.

Bearer shares, in contrast, are unregistered. They are owned solely based on possession or physical control of the actual share certificate. There is no registered owner, and determination of actual ownership and control of the corporate entity is difficult where possible at all. Although some countries now prohibit the issuance of bearer shares, in a number of countries, such forms of corporate ownership are still commonplace.[21] An investigator will often encounter such a structure in Less Developed Countries (LDCs) and OFCs. By creating a legally viable entity with bearer shares, an OCE can almost completely defeat attempts to learn the true identity of the shareholders of the corporation.[22]

Haven Countries and Offshore Financial Centers

Offshore finance is the provision of financial services by banks and other agents to nonresidents. Such services are legal and do serve a legitimate purpose. However, because these financial centers are often in LDCs with weak or ineffective anti-money-laundering programs, the use of their facilities for money laundering is common. A common denominator among many of the Less Developed Countries' OFCs is the existence of strict bank secrecy legislation.

Unlike the United States, many LDCs have enacted strict laws making the release of account holder and transactional information difficult or illegal. A number of NCCTs have even enacted laws that prohibit bank officials from releasing any information about customers, accounts, or transactions under penalty of imprisonment. By opening an account within one of these NCCTs, an OCE is assured of total secrecy regarding the flow of funds into and out of the account.[23]

Correspondent Banking

Correspondent bank accounts are accounts that banks maintain with each other in their own name. In the course of international banking, correspondent banking has a significant legitimate purpose. For example, by establishing multiple correspondent relationships globally, one bank can undertake various financial transactions internationally without the need for a physical presence in a host country. These services include such legitimate transactions as international wire transfers, check-clearing services, and foreign exchange services.[24] However, such relationships are well suited for misappropriation by OCEs to perpetuate their money-laundering schemes.

The indirect nature of the correspondent relationship means that the correspondent bank (the international bank supplying the transfer services to the OCE's bank) is essentially supplying services for individuals or entities for which it has no verifiable information. In correspondent banking, the correspondent bank must rely on the respondent bank (the bank in which the OCE has funds on deposit) to verify the nature of the transactions and perform the necessary due diligence and monitoring of the customer's account. In some cases, the respondent bank may be providing correspondent services to another institution. Transactions thus structured are twice removed from the scrutiny necessary to detect suspicious financial activity.[25]

Adding to this difficulty is the fact that most correspondent banks that provide fee-based services (as opposed to granting of credit) such as wire transfers and check clearing rarely perform any due diligence examination of the respondent bank or the customer on whose behalf the transaction is undertaken.

Shell Banks

Much like shell companies, shell banks are institutions with no physical presence in the jurisdiction in which they are incorporated. Instead, they are often called brass plate institutions because they have no affiliation with a regulated financial group and are frequently nothing more than a brass nameplate on the door.[26]

For obvious reasons, these institutions, while performing marginally legitimate functions, are tailor-made for employment in layering transactions. By using a shell bank, which is often owned and operated in an OFC itself, a correspondent relationship may be established between the shell bank and a registered financial group within the OFC. Once the correspondent relationship is established, the shell bank, acting as a respondent, can essentially transfer limitless amounts of money between banking institutions. This unlimited access to untraceable wire transfers eliminates any audit trail that may have existed.[27]

By combining several of these techniques, the OCE creates a complex web of anonymous, or nearly anonymous, transactions. For example, an OCE will establish a web of shell corporations in various OFCs incorporated using bearer shares. This form of corporate structure effectively eliminates the ability to trace the ownership of the company, separating the OCE from the shell company, The OCE has already placed the funds, through whatever placement method the OCE chooses, into a domestic bank account. The OCE then moves the funds by wire transfer through the various bank accounts held by the shell corporations in strict bank secrecy nations. Once the OCE is satisfied that the web of transactions is sufficiently complex, the distributed funds can be collected into an account at the shell bank in an OFC. From there, utilizing the correspondent relationship, the OCE wire transfers the balance in the account to a legitimate account in an overseas branch of a domestic bank. Once the funds reach the domestic bank, there is effectively no possibility of tracing the funds to any criminal activity. The typology of the layering scheme aside, the end result is the total destruction of the link between illegal activity and the money. It is here that the investigator's attempt to follow the money is often thwarted.

Step Three: Integration

After completion of the first two phases, all connection with illegal activity is broken. The OCE must now reintroduce the money into the economy. After all, the end motive for the criminal enterprise is profit. Without access to the money, the existence of the OCE would be pointless.

The techniques for integration, like the first two stages, can range in complexity from simple repatriation schemes to a series of complex financial transactions. The methods used vary, but the goal is the same. The laundered money must be reunited with the members of the OCE in a manner that emulates legitimate business activity.[28]

To this end, OCEs often establish additional shell corporations. These businesses are frequently incorporated using legitimate registered shares in the jurisdiction of the OCE. It is at this point that the OCE wishes to establish a legitimate connection between the clean funds and themselves. They must convince the authorities that they have a legitimate source of revenue to justify their lifestyle. Establishing a cash-intensive business is a start toward accomplishing this objective.[29]

Using cash-heavy businesses, such as bars, nightclubs, vending machine businesses, and casinos, the OCE mixes the laundered funds with legitimate income and reports the entire amount as legitimate earnings. In addition to the use of front businesses, other popular techniques include loan-back schemes, import/export operations, and real estate or luxury item transactions.

In the loan-back scenario, the OCE arranges for the shell bank to extend a business "loan" to the domestic business controlled by the OCE.

The loan proceeds, in reality the laundered cash, are transferred to the OCE's business as a nontaxable business loan. Once the loan is executed, the OCE begins repayment with funds consisting of dirty money (often commingled with legitimate business receipts). In effect, the OCE is repaying the loan, including the tax-deductible interest, to itself. In this way, the loan-back scheme may also become a component of the placement process.[30]

In the import/export scenario, the OCE establishes a domestic corporation engaged in the business of exporting. The domestic exporter in turn engages an offshore importer (occasionally also owned by the OCE) and exports goods at overvalued prices. Occasionally, no goods will be exchanged; however; it is much safer if the goods actually exist but are highly overvalued. A slight variation of this scheme involves the financial takeover of a legitimate, reputable foreign importer. This method allows the OCE to assume the sound business reputation of the going concern, gaining immediate business legitimacy as well as a viable source of legitimate income with which to commingle dirty money for placement.[31]

Once all three stages have been completed, what began as traceable—and forfeitable—fruits of a criminal activity have evolved into untraceable, legitimate-appearing income—the holy grail of all organized criminal activity.

The concept of money laundering has changed under the influence of the Internet and the globalization that has accompanied it. Although the basic framework, the motivations, and the end goal have not changed, the methods used have been heavily influenced by the advent of electronic commerce and Internet banking.

CYBER-LAUNDERING

In our discussion of the influence of Internet banking on money laundering, it is important to first draw a distinction between a mere presence and a "transactional" presence. In terms of exploitable vulnerabilities, mere Internet presence does not generally provide an OCE with any greater opportunity for money laundering than conventional, legacy topologies.

Conversely, the existence of "transactional services"—in other words, the ability to conduct financial transactions such as direct payments, electronic funds transfers, and other exchange operations—does add an enhanced level of protection against detection to the OCE.

Of major concern to investigators is the obvious reduction of face-to-face contact between the financial institution and banking customers. Since customer access over the Internet is indirect, the institution's personnel have no opportunity to verify the identity or location of the customer. Thus, the Internet can give the customer what amounts to nearly unrestricted anonymous control of bank accounts from any location.

In the non-Internet environment, the "know your customer" policy is an invaluable tool in identifying suspicious banking activity. At a minimum, banking institutions verify identifying information at the onset of the relationship. As more and more institutions shift to an Internet transactional presence, it will become increasingly difficult to identify what constitutes normal business practices. In fact, information that is routinely available to investigators today, such as who accessed the account and from what location, will become obscured under the veil of Internet anonymity. In the Internet banking environment, a single individual may have ultimate control over a number of accounts simultaneously without raising the suspicions of banking officials who, in a face-to-face world, would become suspicious of such activity.

On a more pragmatic note, the evolution of the Internet has literally dissolved international borders—borders that were once a substantial hurdle to money launderers. The ability to instantaneously move unrestricted amounts of cash between banking institutions in the United States and abroad through Internet transactions has eliminated the cumbersome need to "mule" large caches of currency out of the country. As with most advances in technology, the manual laborers are the first casualties of the new age. In this case, the transporter carrying the briefcase full of currency to offshore financial centers has become obsolete. With this obsolescence has come a concomitant reduction in an investigator's ability to identify suspicious behavior.

The Internet environment is not the only new frontier for exploitation by the techno-savvy financial criminal. The growth of electronic mail communication has given new life to a time-honored financial practice known as the alternative remittance system (ARS). Although predominantly a cultural phenomenon with idiosyncratic nuances, all ARSs share one consistent element that makes them ideal for the global movement of cash.[32] In broad strokes, all ARSs, sometimes referred to as parallel banking systems, rely on some form of "book transfer" procedures—commonly referred to as netting—to transmit value. Although nearly every nation in the world has reported some ARS activity within their jurisdiction, three systems comprise the majority of ARS activity: the Black Market Peso Exchange (BMPE); the Hawala/Hundi system; and the Chinese or East Asian system.[33] Because these systems started in immigrant communities where they were originally used to circumvent restrictive currency exchange policies in order to transfer money from overseas, they have developed a distinct cultural mystique. In addition, as a result of their clandestine nature, they offer a certain amount of anonymity, making them ideal for exploitation by OCEs.

As stated earlier, each ARS has its own unique characteristics, but all operate through roughly the same process based largely on trust. In an ARS, a customer who wishes to move currency from an origination country to a destination country contacts an underground broker in the originating country. The customer provides the amount of currency to be transferred—generally in the currency of the originating country. That broker contacts a broker in the destination country and directs that an equivalent amount, less a broker's fee, be paid to the recipient in the destination country. No money is actually transferred. Instead, the accounts are settled over time as remitters in the destination country deposit funds to be transferred back to the originating country. As funds move back and forth, a balance of payments eventually occurs.[34]

Although these systems are low-tech, they are commonly found in areas of high-immigrant population. In addition, recent developments in the area of international terrorism have led to close scrutiny of ARSs as a means of concealing the transfer of funding to terrorist cells abroad. Because members of immigrant communities often use ARS as a legitimate means of sending money back home, terrorist organizations can conceal their activities by blending in with the local immigrant population.

The impact of the Internet and electronic communications on this ancient clandestine network may not be readily apparent. However, by examining the East Asian system, it is possible to see how technology may be exploited to add a layer of sophistication tailored to the needs of OCEs.

In the East Asian system, often referred to as the "Chit system," a customer desiring to remit funds to a distant location will go to a remitting agent and deposit the funds. The remitting agent will provide a chit to the customer, who sends the chit to the recipient at the distant location. The recipient will then go to another remitter at the distant location and present the chit to redeem the funds.

If, instead, an ARS remitter encrypts a unique electronic token with specific payee and amount information and provides it to a customer, the electronic token becomes the chit. This electronic chit can then be e-mailed instantaneously with all the security and confidence that digital technology affords. The recipient, having received the unique electronic chit, presents it to a remitter at the destination location in exchange for the money. No money is actually transported, but cash is effectively moved from point "A" to point "B"—completely outside regulatory oversight.

On a global scale ARS plays a key role in a significant portion of international money movement for certain segments of the population. Because these systems were designed to move large volumes of money clandestinely, with little or no actual recordkeeping, they are a key vector for laundering proceeds of criminal activity. It is imperative that the financial investigator take the cultural makeup of the local community into consideration when the potential need for large-volume currency movement is suspected. These parallel banking systems exist, to a greater or lesser degree, in all major communities and cannot be overlooked as potential money-laundering vectors.

SUMMARY

In the course of any investigation into financial manipulation, whether based on criminal misconduct or civil wrongdoing, money is pivotal. Your skills as a forensic accountant and financial investigator become pointless unless you can track down the proverbial pot-of-gold. To do that, you must understand the basic concepts that underpin even the most elaborate asset-hiding scheme—placement, layering, and integration.

Without these stages, no asset concealment attempt can hope to succeed. The converse is also true. All successful concealment and repatriation schemes employ all three steps. As a financial investigator, your task is not only to find the assets, but also to establish a nexus between the criminal (or tortuous) conduct. By linking the money to the conduct through a detailed, well-articulated paper trail, you will provide the basis for damage awards or forfeiture proceedings. By coupling the foundational knowledge of where the money goes, and more importantly why, with the ability to build a tangible trail of documentary evidence, you can ensure both a successful prosecution and a successful recovery.

As you proceed through the remaining chapters of the text, pay careful attention to the techniques you will learn and consider the ways you might apply them to pursue an investigation of organized money-laundering operations.

NOTES

1. J.D. Torr, *Organized Crime: Contemporary Issues Companion* (San Diego, CA: Greenhaven Press, 1999), pp. 15–17.
2. Ibid., pp. 38–40.
3. Ibid., p. 64.
4. Ibid., pp. 67, 69–70, 75–79, 86–93.
5. Ibid., pp. 9–13.
6. J.M. O'Kane, *The Crooked Ladder: Gangsters, Ethnicity and the American Dream* (New Brunswick, NJ: Transaction Publishers, 1992), pp. 64–65.
7. Ibid., pp. 76–78.
8. Financial Action Task Force on Money Laundering (FATF), *2001-2002 Report on Money Laundering Typologies* (Paris, France: FATF Secretariat, OECD, February 2002).
9. Ibid.
10. J.R. Richards, *Transnational Criminal Organizations, Cybercrime and Money Laundering: A Handbook for Law Enforcement Officers, Auditors and Financial Investigators* (Boca Raton, FL: CRC Press, 1999), pp. 28–40.
11. Ibid., pp. 152–157.
12. Ibid., pp. 46–47.
13. Ibid., pp. 47–48.
14. Ibid., pp. 122–123.
15. Ibid. See also R.E. Grosse, *Drugs and Money: Laundering Latin America's Cocaine Dollars* (Westport, CT: Praeger Publishers, 2001), p. 4.
16. Grosse, *Drugs and Money*, pp. 4–7.
17. Ibid.
18. Richards, *Transnational Criminal Organizations, Cybercrime and Money Laundering*, p. 49.
19. Ibid.
20. Ibid., pp. 53–56.
21. J. Madinger, and S.A. Zalopany, *Money Laundering: A Guide for Criminal Investigators* (Boca Raton, FL: CRC Press, 1999), p. 409. See also FATF, *2001-2002 Report on Money Laundering Typologies*, p. 4.
22. Ibid.
23. J.A. Blum, M. Levi, R.T. Naylor, and P. Williams, eds., "Financial Havens, Banking Secrecy and Money Laundering," in *Crime Preven-*

tion and Criminal Justice Newsletter, vol. 8 (New York: United Nations Publications Board, 1998), pp. 19–33.

24. N. Wilkins, *The Correspondent Banking Handbook* (London: Euromoney Books, 1993), pp. 11–17.

25. Ibid., p. 103.

26. Blum et al., "Financial Havens, Banking Secrecy and Money Laundering," p. 65.

27. Ibid.

28. Richards, *Transnational Criminal Organizations, Cybercrime and Money Laundering*, pp. 48–50.

29. Ibid.

30. Ibid., p. 57.

31. Ibid., p. 55.

32. Ibid., pp. 47, 80.

33. Ibid., pp. 60–61.

34. Ibid. p, 35. See also Madinger and Zalopany, *Money Laundering*, pp. 241–242.

SUGGESTED READINGS

Abadinsky, H., ed. *Organized Crime*, 3rd edition. Chicago, IL: Nelson Hall, 1990.

Bauer, P., and R. Ullmann "Understanding the Wash Cycle." *Economic Perspectives*, 6. Retrieved May 5, 2002 from *http://usinfo.state.ov/journalsl/journala.htm*.

Cassard, M. *The Role of Offshore Centers in International Financial Intermediation, IMF Working Paper 94/10*. Washington, DC: International Monetary Fund, 1994.

Financial Action Task Force—OECD. "Policy Brief: Money Laundering." *OECD Observer*. Paris, France: FATF Secretariat, OECD, 1999.

Financial Action Task Force on Money Laundering. *1998–1999 Report on Money Laundering Typologies*. Paris, France: FATF Secretariat, OECD, February 1999.

Financial Action Task Force on Money Laundering. *1999–2000 Report on Money Laundering Typologies*. Paris, France: FATF Secretariat, OECD, February 2000.

Financial Action Task Force on Money Laundering. *2000–2001 Report on Money Laundering Typologies*. Paris, France: FATF Secretariat, OECD, February 2001.

Gustitus, L.E. Bean, and R. Roach. "Correspondent Banking: A Gateway for Money Laundering." *Economic Perspectives*, 6, retrieved May 5, 2002, from *http://usinfo.state.gov/journals/jounala.htm.*

Harvey, J. *Money Laundering and the LDC Offshore Finance Centres: Are They the Weak Links?* Paper presented at the Development of Economics Study Group Annual Conference 202, Nottingham, UK., University of Nottingham, April 18–20, 2002.

International Federation of Accountants. *IFAC Discussion Paper on Anti-Money Laundering*. New York: International Federation of Accountants, 2002.

Joseph, L.M. "Money Laundering Enforcement: Following the Money." *Economic Perspectives*, vol. 6, retrieved May 5, 2002, from *http://usinfo.state.gov/journals/journala.htm.*

Lorenzetti, J. "The Offshore Trust: A Contemporary Asset Protection Scheme." *Journal of Commercial Law Review*, vol. 102, no. 2 (1997).

Mahan, S., and K. O'Neal. *Beyond the Mafia: Organized Crime in the Americas*. Thousand Oaks, CA: Sage Publishing, 1998.

Monkkonen, E.H., ed. *Crime and Justice in American History: Historical Articles on the Origins and Evolution of American Criminal Justice. Vol. 8: Prostitution, Drugs, Gambling and Organized Crime, Part 1.* Munich, Germany: K.G. Saur, 1994.

Pace, D.F., and J.C. Styles. *Organized Crime: Concepts and Control.* Englewood Cliffs, NJ: Prentice Hall, 1975.

The Ten Fundamental Laws of Money Laundering. Retrieved April 8, 2002 from *www.unodc.org/money_laundering_10_laws.html.*

United Nations Office of Drug Control and Crime Prevention. *Attacking the Profits of Crime: Drugs, Money and Laundering*. Vienna, Austria: UNODC, 1998.

United States Department of the Treasury. *A Survey of Electronic Cash, Electronic Banking and Internet Gaming*. Washington, DC: U.S. Government Printing Office, 2000.

United States Department of the Treasury, Financial Crimes Enforcement Network. [Electronic version,] *FinCEN Advisory: Transactions Involving Israel*. Issue 17. Washington, DC: U.S. Government Printing Office, July 2000.

Woodiwis, M. *Crime Crusades and Corruption: Prohibitions in the United States 1900–1987*. Totowa, NJ: Barnes and Noble Books, 1988.

8

CASE GENERATION

INTRODUCTION

Investigations of financial crimes may be divided into two general categories: reactive and proactive. Traditionally, reactive investigations occur as the result of victim/citizen-initiated actions. They are investigations that result from citizen notification that a crime has occurred. Whether initiated by disgruntled employees, lovers or former spouses, or, as occasionally happens, by auditors, stockholders, or corporate management, the investigator reacts only after the crime has been committed and the suspect has fled. The majority of investigative efforts fall into the reactive category.

Conversely, proactive investigations occur as the result of investigator-initiated action. In a proactive posture, surveillance and undercover operations often play a vital role. Proactive efforts often involve the discovery of a defalcation in progress, whereas reactive investigation is concerned with putting the puzzle together once the theft has been consummated. Both require a unique skill set and different approaches with different goal sets.[1]

In the case of fraud investigation, these general categories are not mutually exclusive. Often, an investigator will be faced with a reactive case in which proactive techniques may be beneficial. For example, an auditor from XYZ Company may report that he has discovered a possible discrepancy in the company's accounts receivable. He suspects that an employee has been engaging in lapping.[2] Although this case may be approached from a strictly reactive posture by stitching together a paper trail of documents, a proactive approach, such as covert surveillance of the employees, might prove valuable as well.

Traditional proactive techniques such as surveillance and "undercover" operations are not usually thought of as the bread-and-butter of financial-crime investigators. Yet they may yield invaluable evidence that can prove to be the smoking gun in an embezzlement that would otherwise be difficult to prove. In fact, it might be the essential element necessary to tie a specific employee to specific acts.

In today's business world where computers often control the entire revenue generation cycle, employee surveillance may become an essential part of nearly every investigation. As more and more transactions are documented digitally, assigning responsibility, and in the case of investigations, culpability for a specific transaction cannot be done by traditional methods. Long gone are the days when forensic document examiners were the most essential components of financial crime investigations.

In today's digital environment, linking an employee to a transaction is often done with no more than a secret code or password. In the day-to-day business world, the audit trail left by most software and computer systems is more than adequate for productivity and "business" purposes. However, from the viewpoint of an investigator, poor information technology security, or ITSEC, can make proof of culpability impossible as a practical matter.

Although it may be desirable for productivity purposes to allow clerks to cross-login under other employees' ID numbers, it destroys all hopes of conventionally following the forensic audit trail and indisputably assigning a specific transaction to a specific employee. When an investigator is faced with such a situation, a combination of reactive and proactive techniques will bridge the gap.

Actual surveillance of the employee, combined with the documentary evidence produced by the computer audit log, can reliably link a suspect employee to each and every suspect transaction. Therefore, as crucial as reactive techniques are to a fraud investigator, it is essential to remember the value that proactive techniques can add to many cases.

THE INVESTIGATIVE PROCESS—THE INVESTIGATION LIFE CYCLE

Once the need for investigation becomes apparent, its flow must proceed as logically and efficiently as possible. Although every investigation is unique, with its own intricacies and obstacles, success depends entirely on a combination of the skill and knowledge of the investigator with the soundness of the investigative process. A skillful and knowledgeable investigator who proceeds in a haphazard manner with slipshod techniques is no more likely to succeed than one who is inexperienced and ignorant and yet proceeds with a carefully designed investigative plan. Armed with an understanding of the unique nature of financial crimes, and an awareness of the logical flow of a successful investigation, it is possible to produce reliable and consistent cases. One key to this understanding is the consciousness that every investigation has a life cycle: There is a beginning, a middle, and an end. Neglect during any stage will compromise the probability of a successful prosecution. For the purposes of analysis, we have broken the investigative process into six discrete stages. Stage I is the beginning, Stages II through V comprise the middle, and Stages VI and VII are the end.

As with most everything in life, every stage overlaps the other, and often progress from stage to stage may be barely perceptible. In fact, especially in financial crime investigation, it is possible to be in two distinct stages simultaneously. Therefore, the entire process from beginning to end must remain a living, breathing entity.

Stage I

Assessment and Goal Setting

The beginning of every investigation, regardless of whether it is generated proactively or reactively, results from a complaint. In the proactive posture, the investigator generates the complaint; in the reactive posture, a reporting party generates the complaint.

In financial crime cases, reactive investigations often result from reports by investors, insiders, or auditors who have discovered an imbalance in the accounts. Often, these reports are sketchy at best and contain a mixture of fact, speculation, and hyperbole. Therefore, this stage requires that the fraud investigator sort through the superfluous information and extract the essential elements of the allegation. The resulting information must then be applied to the law. Just because a complaining witness feels aggrieved does not necessarily mean the suspect's conduct is legally cognizable.

Without a legally cognizable claim, whether criminally or civilly, the investigator's efforts are essentially wasted. Although the complainants may feel good to have proven that the suspect in fact committed the alleged act, peace of mind will be of little solace when they realize that no legal action may be taken. Therefore, since the investigator's task is entirely results oriented, it is imperative to define the goal of the investigation in terms of legally cognizable actions. Stage I is an evaluation and a goal-setting stage.

Goal setting includes not only identification of the legal outcome of the case—whether civil prosecution, criminal prosecution, or perhaps administrative action is the goal—but also identification of the complainant's goals. For the fraud investigator in the criminal arena, this goal is often clearly defined. In most cases, the complaining party is seeking a combination of reimbursement and the proverbial pound-of-flesh—incarceration. Although from a goal-setting perspective this makes the investigator's job easier, in the customer expectation area it adds another dimension of complexity. For the civil fraud investigator, the goals may not be so clearly defined.

Although few readily admit it, crime victims are law enforcement's customers—they are involuntary customers but customers nonetheless. As customers, crime victims seek out the services of fraud investigators with certain preconceived notions about both obtainable results and acceptable outcomes. Where these expectations are reasonable and rational, the outcome is often satisfactory. However, when the customer arrives with unreasonable expectations, in terms of either obtainable results or acceptable outcomes, goal setting may be a bit trickier.

In this context, we will briefly define what we mean by obtainable results and acceptable outcomes.

An *obtainable result* is one that can be reasonably expected to be achieved in any given investigation, given the circumstances surrounding the allegation coupled with the current state of technology. In the context of financial investigations, it is necessary to redefine the term *current*. Here, current means not merely what is in cognizable existence now, but also what is foreseeable within the life cycle of the investigation in question. Currency must be defined in that way simply because financial crime investigations can, and frequently do, span periods of time in which technological discovery surpasses preconceived expectations. When that occurs, obtainable results shift.

An acceptable outcome in the arena of the criminal allegation is that final end product of the investigation that is reasonably expected given the current state of the law. In this context, the term *current* is in fact that period of time delimited by the actual criminal acts under scrutiny. This definition of currency is necessarily limited by constitutional constraints based on the prohibition against *ex post facto* laws. If we expanded our definition of currency to include the life span of the investigation, an accept-

122

able outcome might well include a punishment that was not in existence at the time the crime was committed. Not considering for the moment the notion of a course of ongoing criminal conduct, the customer might harbor an unreasonable expectation of a more severe punishment than allowed under the law.

Now that we have defined our terms, let us explain how they factor into the investigator's goal-setting objective of Stage I.

The effectiveness of every fraud investigator, in pursuing either criminal or civil fraud investigations, is ultimately judged by how closely—and consistently—she reaches or exceeds her investigative goals. In the criminal milieu, this effectiveness is often measured by the clearance or arrest rate—how often the bad guy is identified to a legal certainty. In the civil sector, effectiveness is much less easily determined. One measure of success is the depth and monetary value of the investigator's client list—investigators who consistently reach or exceed the customer's expectations generate greater volumes of business.

If the goal setting of Stage I occurred in a vacuum, there would be little, if any, need for further discussion. For example, if the investigator alone were responsible for setting the goals of the investigation, there would be very little chance that the goals would be poorly defined. This is because the trained investigator usually has an innate feel for both obtainable results and acceptable outcomes. But life abhors a vacuum, and customers' preconceived expectations complicate what would otherwise be a straightforward process.

Although less like investigative work and more like customer service, the fraud investigator's job during Stage I includes customer education. Education must include defining both obtainable results and acceptable outcomes. It is only through education that both investigator and client can reach common expectations about the result of the investigation. Once you have established common expectations, you must clearly identify the goals. These goals allow both the customer and the investigator to fairly and objectively assess the progress of the investigation as well as the acceptableness of the case's outcome.

The investigator's job at this stage is that of an educator; it is therefore vital that she possess the highest level of skill in the investigation of financial crimes, including strong working knowledge of investigative methods and technology. In addition, she must also have a thorough understanding not only of the rules of evidence, but also the legal burdens of proof necessary to successfully prosecute a case—criminally and civilly.

Armed with these tools, the fraud investigator is well equipped to clarify the customer's definition of obtainable results and acceptable outcomes. By clarifying and redefining where necessary, the investigator can help guide the customer in determining whether there is adequate justification to proceed further.

In criminal investigations, the end result of Stage I might be a determination that the conduct alleged by the victim is not in fact criminal. If you don't make this determination now—and clearly convey it to the victim—the victim will internalize unreasonable expectations about the acceptable outcome. This will become a source of dissatisfaction at future stages of the investigation. Conversely, if the fraud investigator clearly identifies the legal components of the allegation as falling below the threshold for criminal prosecution, the victim, though probably disenchanted with the announcement that the conduct is not criminally prosecutable, can explore other investigative options such as suing in civil court.

Aside from establishing reasonable customer expectations, the goal setting accomplished under Stage I provides a solid basis for the fraud investigator to build an investigative plan. These goals are the foundation of the investigation. If the investigative goals of the case are poorly designed or unsound, then the entire investigation suffers from a poor foundation. It may eventually fall under its own weight because the planning that you will do in Stage II is worthless without well-formed investigative goals.

Stage II

Investigative Planning

Once you have clearly established your goals, it is essential that you develop an investigative plan. In trying to stress the need for investigative planning, we are forced to borrow from the old adage, "no one plans to fails, they simply fail to plan." This is especially true in the area of financial investigations.

By their very nature, financial crimes often involve large volumes of information. This information quickly becomes unwieldy without a well-thought-out plan. When it does become unmanageable, it will bury you under a mountain of financial documents. By preparing a strong yet flexible investigative plan, it is possible to control the flow of the investigation, adapt the investigation to the inevitable changes that occur during its life cycle, and manage the massive sea of evidence on which all unsuccessful financial investigations founder.

A good investigative plan has three major goals: maintain focus, control growth, and promote adaptability.

- **Focus**: A strong investigative plan should focus your efforts in line with the goals of the investigation. A strong focus ensures that neither duplication of investigative effort nor oversight of leads hampers the progress of the case.
- **Control**: Financial crime investigations are living, breathing entities. Once they are brought to life, they take on a character of their own. If you let them, they will grow tendrils that crawl into every crevice of your office and attach themselves to every case file in your filing cabinet. They will give birth to other cases or marry themselves to operations throughout your office until they have taken over every inch of your life if you let them.

  A strong investigative plan recognizes this characteristic of fraud investigations and helps you manage it. It is not always preventable; however, careful management through planning can make its inevitable arrival less catastrophic to the underlying investigation.
- **Adaptability**: In keeping with their living nature, financial crime investigations evolve. They may grow (always) or they may shrink (rarely); however, they will change. For that reason, all good investigative plans must have some built-in adaptability. Without adaptability, slight changes in the circumstances surrounding the investigation will render the plan useless. Once this happens, the alternatives are to either operate ad hoc or take the time to reevaluate and re-plan. Either alternative is unfavorable. By ensuring that the investigative plan has built-in adaptability, changes in the course of the investigation do not necessarily require wholesale changes in the investigative plan.

Once you have mapped out the overall scope and direction of the investigation, it is much easier to predict the manpower needs and to assemble an investigative team designed to efficiently proceed with the investigation. Whether you anticipate that the investigation will be protracted or short, it is essential to identify key personnel requirements early. For long-term, complex cases this is imperative.

In today's high-tech world, the odds of encountering computer-based information are very high. It is unreasonable to expect that even the most well trained investigator will be capable of handling every possible scenario.

For that reason, it may be necessary to arrange for outside personnel to act as an investigative resource. Whether in the area of network topography, computer security, cryptography, or individual proprietary software, the investigator must often tap into the wealth of community resources.

These resources frequently come from outside law enforcement or security agencies. When that happens, depending on the sensitivity of the investigation and the nature of the support required, integrity concerns may arise. For example, if you anticipate encountering encrypted data, your case may require outside expertise in that area. This can lead to an operational concern about the integrity of the independent source. Without some assurance about the consultant's integrity, both the evidence and the investigation itself may be compromised beyond repair.

Preplanning cannot ensure against compromise, but it can relocate the task of assessing operational compromise to a time where study and deliberation may be made, avoiding the need for reactionary decision making. When you determine ahead of time what potential outside support you require, you reduce ad hoc decisions and overall integrity is increased. Decisions made under the pressure of time often lack the depth of vision that leisurely study affords. Therefore, to the extent that such decisions can be made in the comfort of the planning office, the investigation can proceed with fewer bumps in the road.

In addition to avoiding, or at least reducing, integrity concerns, preplanning for investigative resources is fiscally responsible. Regardless of the context of the investigation, whether undertaken at the behest of a private client or under the auspices of the local district attorney, money is always an issue. Regardless of the size of the investigation, there is rarely enough money to do the job in the way you would like. Therefore, like almost everything in an investigation, cost is a matter of compromise.

Identification of potentially expensive issues early in the investigation allows you to make key fiscal decisions at a time when alternative approaches can easily be considered. For example, although a phone tap might be the "perfect" investigative tool to achieve your overall investigative goal, failure to examine the "net cost" of that approach could be costly—both in terms of financial resources and in terms of wasted investigative man-hours.

If you undertake financial analysis during the planning phase, alternative techniques can be considered. Too many times perfectly viable investigations begin in the hope that money will eventually come through. When it does not, the investigation bogs down with no hope of achieving the initial objective. When you fail to identify alternatives to costly investigative procedures, the results are usually compromised outcomes—either failure to achieve the stated objective or expenditure of more funds than reasonable. Either outcome produces dissatisfaction and failure to achieve customer expectations.

At this stage, it is also important to consider the use of outside financial experts. Although you will be well prepared to handle almost any financial crime after reading this book, situations may arise in which financial transactions are beyond your investigative ability. In those situations, you need to enlist the help of financial professionals as either consultants or expert witnesses. In addition to accountants, the investigator should consider the use of experts in the area of stocks and securities transactions, corporate governance and structure, and international financial transactions, to name just a few.

Although none of these topics is beyond the ability of dedicated investigators who have studied the subject, utilizing outside expertise in these very technical areas can save valuable investigative time. In addition, if you contact these outside sources early, they can often provide sharper focus and stronger direction when planning your case.

One final thought on Stage II: Although careful planning is essential to the successful completion of a complex investigation, some investigations defy all attempts to map out their destiny. Murphy's Law is as active in the investigative realm as it is in everyday life and will invariably insinuate itself into your investigation at the most inopportune time. Even the most careful planning overlooks some eventualities. This is not to say that planning is helpless against Murphy's Law; it assuredly is not. By carefully planning the investigation, however, the eventual unforeseen detour will become the exception rather than the rule. You can eliminate the obvious hurdles in advance, and the investigator's best efforts can be directed at dealing with the inevitable unforeseen obstacles. In other words, planning will not prevent investigative obstacles, but it will make those inevitable hurdles much more manageable.

Stage III

Investigation

Once you have completed the planning, you may begin the investigation. This is traditionally where you perform the bread and butter of investigative work. You identify witnesses, collect documents, and analyze and assemble them into exhibits. Eventually, if all goes to plan, you will identify a suspect. This is the traditional venue of perseverance, legwork, and solid nuts-and-bolts police work—often backed by a healthy dose of intuition. Many facets of this stage are substantially similar to the investigative process for other types of crime. There are, however, some fundamental differences in investigative technique that mark financial crimes apart from other nonfinancial crimes. These areas—namely, interviewing financially savvy witnesses, documentary evidence in financial crimes, and analysis of financial evidence techniques—are addressed in Chapters 9, 10, and 11.

At this time you need only digest the fact that Stage III accounts for the lion's share of your job. You should also recognize that Stage III is both in a constant state of flux and inextricably intertwined with all other stages of the investigative life cycle—especially Stages I, II, and IV.

Regardless of how well the planning stage is undertaken, this constant change happens in large part because of the nature of the investigative process. It is a process founded in evolution. It begins with a preconception of a finite set of facts—a foundation for the entire set of what is known about the case and from which flows both cause and effect and theory and knowledge. As the investigation progresses, our knowledge about what happened evolves to include new facts, theories, and knowledge—your knowledge grows. And as knowledge grows, you must reevaluate hypotheses and theories of the case. With the learning of new facts, avenues of proof are either reinforced or weakened. Those that are bolstered rise in importance in the hierarchy of proof; those that are lessened get relegated to subtheories, alternative theories, or, if completely refuted, are discarded as disproved hypotheses. Indeed, knowledge is an ever-changing entity.

As knowledge changes and theories are modified, the investigative path changes. As a result, what was planned becomes obsolete, or at the very least altered. It is for that reason that Stage II and Stage III are inextricably intertwined. That is also why planning is never quite completed—hence the need for an adaptable plan.

Stage I is also intertwined with Stage IV. As documents, the essential evidence of all financial crime investigations is analyzed and collated, and the body of investigative knowledge expands and contracts.

Even after the investigator feels confident that all witnesses who have anything relevant to say have been interviewed, and even after all documents with relevant data have been collected, he cannot close the door on Stage III. Transposing analysis of what has been collected against what witnesses will say yields new theories. Even the most meticulous investigator will discover new potential witnesses and sources of documentary evidence as analysis takes place. This process of discovery often results in redirecting the planning stage. However, as long as you have undertaken goal setting properly in Stage I, these inevitable discoveries will require only slight modifications in the investigative plan.

Stage IV

Analysis

Financial crime investigations distinguish themselves from other investigations during Stage IV. At this stage you must collate, analyze, and digest the mountain of documents you have collected. Next, they must be transformed into simple charts, graphs, and demonstrative exhibits. What often makes prosecution of financial crimes so difficult is the fact that the evidence comes in the form of incomprehensible volumes of data. If left in raw form, this data, although the proverbial "smoking gun," will baffle the jury—and an occasional prosecutor—and will ultimately prove unpersuasive.

The key to selling a financial crime prosecution both to the prosecutor and to the jury is simplification. The underlying criminal conduct inherent in most financial crimes is often quite rudimentary. But the premise is masked by the overwhelming abundance of evidence. At this stage, it is essential to establish a powerful and efficient system of document tracking. Based on this document-tracking system, the eventual preparation of charts and demonstrative exhibits will become much easier and presentation of the evidence to both the prosecutor and the jury will be a much simpler matter.

Stage V

Presentation

At this stage you must assemble the case, marshal the evidence, and present it to the prosecuting authority. Whether the presentation is formal or informal, directed at the prosecuting attorney individually or as part of a grand jury proceeding, the task is greatly simplified if you have carefully followed Stages I through IV. Stage V is the decisional stage of the investigation.

At this stage you may have to reevaluate the investigative efforts. For example, if the prosecutor feels that prosecution of the case is unwarranted, you must make a decision about whether the desired goal (prosecution) can be reasonably attained. If the answer is no, you can officially close the case with no further investigation.

If, however, it is determined that further investigation will be fruitful and you decide to resubmit the case for prosecution, you reenter Stages II and III. In this way, the investigator continues to reevaluate and reinvestigate until the goal is either abandoned or reached.

If the prosecutor accepts the case, the investigation moves into Stage VI.

Stage VI

Trial

In this stage, the investigator takes a secondary, supporting, role to the prosecutor. If the documents and evidence have been properly tracked, you have already done the hardest work. This stage allows you to present your case to the jury. Your testimony will often be pivotal in securing a conviction. As the point man for the investigation, it is imperative that you present a professional, polished, and prepared image. Thorough preparation and proper courtroom demeanor are invaluable to a financial crime investigator. In addition, the ability to relate complex financial transactions in simple terms is essential if you want to secure a conviction.

Stage VII

Post-trial Critique

After the verdict is in, you must conduct a debriefing. The debriefing should include all members of the investigative team, as well as the supervisors. Every case contains mistaken assumptions, incorrect hypotheses, and missed goals. The objective of this stage is to identify these shortcomings and learn from your mistakes.

Although no two financial crimes are identical, most crimes have a significant number of similarities that make analysis of both successful ones and unsuccessful ones productive. It is possible to learn both effective and ineffective methods for conducting financial crime investigations by observing what went wrong and what went right. If you analyze what went right and why, those techniques and approaches that worked well may prove valuable in future cases. By the same token, careful analysis of what went wrong can provide the investigative team with the opportunity to refine or discard ineffective investigative methods.

Adding the methods and techniques you have identified as effective to the repertoire of available resources will benefit the planning of Stage II on the next complex financial crime. The key is learning from your mistakes.

SUMMARY

The investigative process has a seven-stage life cycle that carries the investigation from formation through conclusion. By recognizing that each stage of the process has unique characteristics, you can cope more effectively with the evolution of the case. The key to management of complex cases, especially in the financial crime area, is planning.

By using the investigative life-cycle model, you can segment the investigative process and efficiently plan for each stage. When you break the case down into its component stages, it becomes more manageable and successful, and rewarding results are much more likely.

NOTES

1. M.F. Brown, *Criminal Investigation: Law and Practice* (Newton, MA: Butterworth-Heinemann, 1998), pp. 11–13. See also J.E. Eck and W. Spelman "Problem Solving: Problem-Oriented Policing in Newport News," in R.G. Dunham and G.P. Alpert, eds., *Critical Issues in Policing*, 4th ed. Prospect Heights, IL: Waveland Press, pp. 541-555.
2. Lapping is a defalcation scheme whereby an employee with the responsibility of handling payments on customers' accounts skims money from one customer's account and then conceals the theft by crediting future payments by other customers to that account. In a typical lapping scheme, customer A makes a payment of $100 on his account. The dishonest accounts receivable clerk pockets the $100 payment (or some portion of it). To conceal the cash shortage, the employee then credits payment by customer B to customer A's account. This circular scheme of transactions continues as long as the employee continues to have access to the AR. Once the employee can no longer support the scheme, it collapses and the defalcation is discovered. See M.J. Comer, *Corporate Fraud Investigations and Compliance Programs* (Dobbs Ferry, NY: Oceana Publications, 1999), pp. 94–95.

SUGGESTED READINGS

Albrecht, W.S., and C.O. Albrecht. *Fraud Examination*. Mason, OH: Thomson South-Western, 2003.

Albrecht, W.S., K.R., Howe, and M.B. Romney. *Detecting Fraud: The Internal Auditor's Perspective*. Altamonte Springs, FL: Institute of Internal Auditors Research Foundation, 1984.

Albrecht, W.S., G.W. Wernz, and T.L. Williams. *Fraud: Bringing Light to the Dark Side of Business*. Burr Ridge, IL: Irwin Publishing, 1988.

Bintliff, R. *Complete Manual of White Collar Crime Detection and Prevention*. Englewood Cliffs, NJ: Prentice Hall, 1993.

Eck, J.E. "Rethinking Detective Management: Why Investigative Reforms Are Seldom Permanent or Effective." In D.J. Kenney and R. McNamara, eds., *Police and Policing*, 2nd ed. (pp. 171–186). Westport, CT: Praeger, 1999.

Hudzik, J.K. *Criminal Justice Manpower Planning: An Overview*. Washington, DC: U.S. Department of Justice, Law Enforcement Assistance Administration, 1981.

Propper, E.M. *Corporate Fraud Investigations and Compliance Programs*. Dobbs Ferry, NY: Oceana Publications, 1999.

9

INTERVIEWING FINANCIALLY SOPHISTICATED WITNESSES

INTRODUCTION

During the course of practically every case, it will become necessary for the investigator to sit down and interview a living, breathing person. Whether that person is an eyewitness, a records custodian, or, ideally, the suspect himself, you will embark on the task of attempting to elicit information using an interrogatory method of some type. Methods of questioning vary in complexity—depending on the subject and purpose of the interrogation—from simple question and answer to a veritable game of psychological survivor.

It has been said that an interview is essentially nothing more than a conversation with a purpose. Though true, this statement overlooks the fact that human dynamics intervene in the interview process to inhibit the parties' attempts to successfully realize their purpose. Regardless of whether the interview is being conducted with a suspect or merely a witness, there are many psychological barriers to the efficient communication necessary to reach the interview's goal.

It is the investigator's job to eliminate these barriers or at least to minimize them, to the greatest extent possible, and to open a clear channel of communication. It is no longer acceptable simply to approach a witness, notepad in hand, and implead in a monotone, "just the facts ma'am," expecting the minutia of observation to fall rolling off the witness's tongue. Even the most cooperative witness will generally have difficulty remembering details to the degree expected by most police officers.

In innumerable instances, police investigators resort to questioning witnesses by using prehistoric methods that are more reminiscent of Adam

12 than modern police procedure, only to throw up their arms in disgust when the befuddled witness fails to respond with the appropriate reply. Is it any wonder that interviewing officers fail to obtain decent accounts of crimes and accurate descriptions of suspects during a seven-minute-long canvassing interview done with all the finesse of a Bull Moose?

Human memory is a complex and labyrinthine system. Concrete answers to questions about how we store and access information continue to elude science, despite extensive psychological studies. It is still largely unknown how the human brain matches discrete observed events with instantly recallable memories.[1] This bewilderment as to memory accounts, in large part, for poor witness performance.

Beyond the psychological barriers, an interviewer must overcome social and environmental hurdles that impede the flow of information. Witnesses and victims often fail to provide candid interviews for a number of reasons. Some may not want to be involved in an adversarial process in which they may eventually need to testify against a neighbor, a loved-one, or other close acquaintance. Others may be reluctant because they themselves are hiding information to which they would rather the authorities remain oblivious. Yet others may be complicit in the crime—or perhaps they may fear reprisal from the suspect. There are as many reasons for reluctance as there are witnesses. Whatever the reason, however, interviews of both witnesses and suspects can be accurately characterized as a psychological tug-of-war.[2]

This does not mean that you should approach all interviews in a confrontational, accusatory manner under the assumption that the witness is hiding information or is intent on being uncooperative. Instead, you should be cognizant of the dynamics of human behavior and proceed in a non-confrontational way with the underlying recognition that natural barriers to a totally forthright exchange do exist.

As an investigator, it is ultimately your responsibility to break through these barriers and distill all the superfluous information down into a set of facts that can be used to prove or disprove the case.

Unfortunately, in addition to these natural barriers to a free flow of information, the financial crime investigator must confront another barrier—language. When interviewing a financially savvy witness, the witness is naturally going to speak in terms that are familiar to him. Often these terms define concepts that have both unique and unfamiliar meaning to people who are not proficient in the financial arena. In an ordinary conversation, the listener can merely edit out the data that is uninteresting or not understood, and continue the conversation with a moderate level of comprehension. Investigators, however, do not have that luxury. The data they edit out or misunderstand could be the key element in understanding the entire case.

In this chapter, we hope to provide a framework that the financial crime investigator can use to successfully build an effective interview process. Like all good models, it must be adapted to differing scenarios. However, it can help the investigator navigate the often choppy waters of interpersonal communication that is unique to this setting.

This chapter is divided into two sections. The first introduces the theory of cognitive interviewing techniques that are applicable to both suspect and nonsuspect interview modes. The second section provides the reader with financial crime-specific strategies for conducting successful and productive interviews in white-collar crime cases.

THE INTERVIEW PROCESS

Traditionally, interviews have been categorized as either suspect or witness.[3] Often these interviews are distinguished from each other by use of the terms *interview* and *interrogation*, with interview signifying nonsuspect and interrogation signifying suspect. Suspect interviews, usually called interrogations, are exactly as they sound—interviews with a person or persons who are suspected of committing some misdeed. Witness interviews are slightly different. The term *witness interview* encompasses witnesses, victims, and other people who are not *immediately* suspected of committing a misdeed. The reader should note the use of the term immediately in the preceding sentence. Much as a homicide investigator is trained to approach every death investigation with the assumption that there is foul play, every interview should be conducted with the subliminal notion that every witness may, at some point, mutate into a suspect. We don't mean to instill in the reader an "everyone is guilty" mentality; in fact, studies have shown that such bias leads to false determinations of deception.[4] We simply recommend that the financial crime investigator maintain a healthy level of professional skepticism. This attitude can prove invaluable when the comptroller, once believed to be nothing more than a reporting party, becomes ensnared in a web of his own deceit. If you approach every interview from a position of professional skepticism, it is much more likely you will avoid hasty supposition and incorrect assumptions—the bane of any good investigation.

Interviews are conducted for a myriad of reasons—scientific, psychological, journalistic, or investigative. But regardless of the purpose, certain dynamics exist between the interviewer and the respondent.

As stated earlier, the interview has been defined as a conversation with a purpose. This purpose, regardless of the reason for the interview, is to elicit information.[5] The process of eliciting this information requires verbal interaction. This interaction necessarily entails discourse. Discourse in turn is the exchange of a commodity. In the case of the interview, this commodity is language.

People exchange words to communicate. Communication is possible because words have shared meaning. However, words—components of the language—have culturally dependent value. This value, unique within the culture, signifies a specific meaning to members of that culture. The culture in this case is the financially astute community. The CPA, the comptroller, the bookkeeper, or the chief financial officer all speak a very unique dialect within their native language.

The interview may take many different forms, from open-ended to focused and predetermined.[6] The most common form in the investigational setting is the semistructured interview. This format allows the interviewer, guided by a set of basic questions and goals, to explore the issues as they arise within the broader context of the structure of the interview.

There are four stages for conducting a successful interview: (1) determining the interviewee (the respondent), (2) preparing for the interview, (3) conducting the interview, and (4) bringing closure to the interview. Though broad, these stages help to ensure that each interview is directed and productive.

Determining the Interviewee

Obviously, without this stage the interview will not take place. In the context of investigational interviewing, in contrast to scientific or research interviewing, these choices are usually fairly obvious. However, because financial crimes often involve witnesses and evidence that are not routinely encountered in other nonfinancial crimes, a brief discussion is in order.

In preparing a list of potential interview subjects, the investigator should keep in mind that there are relatively few eyewitnesses in financial crimes. There are two reasons for this. First, the overwhelming number of financial crimes are based on one variety of fraud or another. By definition, fraud is a surreptitious crime involving concealment and stealth. In contrast, nonfinancial crimes often involve an affront to a specific individual. Murder, robbery, assault, and even burglary—when unsuccessful—involve witnesses who theoretically can provide a description of the suspect and a more or less detailed account of what happened. The secrecy with which fraudsters ply their trade is designed to avoid eyewitness accounts.

Second, to the extent that a person may witness a discrete act by the suspect, they will likely regard the person's actions as falling within the bounds of routine business activity. The problem of a witness's inability to identify aberrant behavior stems from the fact that successful embezzlers attempt to mimic as closely as possible the patterns and activities of legitimate business. When they are successful, their activities are often indistinguishable from routine daily operations—even to a well-trained observer.

For those reasons, the list of interview candidates should include a much wider range of potential information-holders.

Although a witness who can actually place the CFO's hand in the proverbial cookie jar is ideal, it is much more likely that the investigator will have to reconstruct that visual image using circumstantial documentary evidence. In which case, people with very little or no direct contact with the suspect may provide some of the most powerful and damning evidence. Exactly who these people are, and what their role within the investigation is, will vary wildly from investigation to investigation and by type of crime. However, you should never overlook such potential witnesses as external auditors, accountants, banking personnel (including tellers and branch managers), mortgage and loan brokers, and business consultants. In short, any individual or firm that may have information about how the business is running, or should be running, is a potential source of information. This fact holds true regardless of the nearness of the witness to the suspect or his business history. It should not be necessary at this point to present a laundry list of potential witnesses; it should be sufficient to remind the reader to use both creativity and logic when selecting candidates to be interviewed.

Preparing for the Interview

After identifying those individuals with whom you would like to speak, you must prepare yourself for each interview.[7] If you fail to prepare, you will be unequipped to control the flow of the interview, and its goal will likely remain unrealized. When planning, you should:

- Review all available information.
- Attempt to conduct the interview as soon as the witness is able.
- Select an environment that is private and minimizes distractions.
- Ensure that proper resources are available (pens, notepads, recorders, interview room, etc.).
- Keep witnesses separated.

Conducting the Interview

For many years, police interviewers were trained, when trained at all, in a classical, question-and-answer style of witness interviewing. This procedure consisted of an interviewer-controlled session of closed-ended questions often requiring yes or no answers. The interviewer, in this case the police officer, asked the witness a series of pointed questions designed to elicit a specific factual response relating directly to a relevant fact in the investigation. "What color was the suspect's hair?" "Did he have a gun?" "What was the license plate number?" These are all questions one would reasonably expect to hear in a classical police interview scenario.[8]

Often these questions resulted in inaccurate answers or an inability for the witness to recall the details of the event. Unfortunately, after such an exchange, the witness was left feeling unhelpful, and the investigator was left feeling appalled at the witness's poor observational skills. What is more disheartening is that the officer was left with little hope of developing further investigative leads based on the witness's observations. Any information the witness was able to give was likely to be only marginally accurate.

Fortunately, advances have been made in the study of cognitive behavior and applied psychology.[9] These advances, relating to the manner in which humans store and retrieve information, have direct correlation to how witnesses store and recall observed events. One of the most promising advances in this area is the development of a memory facilitation technique known as the cognitive interview.[10]

The Cognitive Interview

In 1984, Dr. R. Edward Geiselman, a professor of psychology at UCLA, his associate, Dr. Ronald P. Fisher, and several colleagues developed the theory behind cognitive interviewing. This new approach to questioning provided a breakthrough in interview technique and was based in part on a concept known at the time as the structured interview (SI). The cognitive interview expanded the SI paradigm and added a number of strategies designed to enhance the efficiency of witness recall.[11]

The strategies that underpin the cognitive interview have several theoretical bases. First, it is hypothesized that remembered (referred to as encoded) information is stored in "records" or discrete units containing event-relevant data. These records are indexed by headings and may be searched using descriptions until the matching record is found. It is believed that information about context, the environment in which the event was recorded, is part of this description information. The reinstatement of the context, or re-creation of the environment, therefore aids the individual in accessing the description information and the record.[12]

Second, it is theorized alternatively that, instead of discrete units, our memories are comprised of a network of associations. As a result, it is possible to access the memories from several different places. For instance, it may be possible to trigger recall of an event by shifting the temporal perspective such as starting in the middle or end of the event and regressing.[13]

The last model incorporated into the cognitive interview process is known as the schema theory. This theory holds that familiar events have a script that guides how they are encoded in our brain. If we observe a familiar event, that event is organized into a hierarchy of slots according to this script. New events are stored in slots based on the familiar slots already scripted by the brain. This allows the brain to encode information based on prior expectations and to fill in slots with default information.[14]

The cognitive interview is essentially a systemized approach to exploiting these models of information encoding and retrieval in order to enhance witness recall of event information. Although it has its detractors, the cognitive interview has met with statistical success and has been shown in several studies to increase correctly recalled details by as much as 45 percent over noncognitive interview formats.[15]

Procedurally, the cognitive interview is a multiphased approach incorporating communication facilitation techniques. Phase one consists of free report; phase two is questioning; and phase three is known as second retrieval. Within this procedural context, the interviewer utilizes memory recall techniques that are consistent with the cognitive approach.[16]

During phase one, it is crucial that the interviewer emotionally transfer control of the interview to the witness. In the reporting phase, the witness is encouraged to do the majority of the talking. This may be accomplished by the use of open-ended questions that allow the witness to dictate the pace of the interview. At this point, it is important that the interviewer avoid interrupting the witness's narrative by timing their comments and any necessary questions carefully.

During phase two, the interviewer can begin basic questioning based on the witness's free report recollection of the event. This form of questioning differs substantially from the standard police interview in which the interviewer approaches the interview with a specific, script-like list of questions designed to fill-in-the-blanks on the report. Although some structure is desirable and necessary to ensure that the "who, what, where, why, when, and how" are covered, the bulk of this phase should be determined on the fly as the witness re-creates the event in her own narrative.

Finally, in phase three, once the interviewer's basic questions have been covered, the witness is directed to make a second attempt to retrieve the information she could not recall during the initial free report.[17]

While proceeding through all three phases of this model, the interviewer should employ several cognitive techniques that will help to jog the witness's memory. By encouraging the witness to re-create the scene in her mind, visually picturing the event, you are helping her to re-create the context. This retrieval-enhancement cue conforms to the first model of memory encoding; it helps to increase the overlap between the event and the recall context, and it may also help the witness to recall hidden details of the event or episode.[18]

Once the witness has re-created the scene, question the witness about specific aspects of the image. You can ask her to describe specific details of the room, persons in the room, or physical sensations she feels. By probing the image for details, you may elicit further recalled images. At this stage, you should encourage the witness to report even partial information, regardless of how unimportant she perceives it to be. This may be effective both because the witness misperceives the importance of the information and because the act of remembering the seemingly inconsequential details triggers further recall.[19]

While guiding the witness through this recall process, explore other memory access routes. This technique exploits the multiple trace and schema models of memory retrieval and requires the witness to approach the event from an alternative perspective. Consider guiding the witness to rearrange the event temporally. For example, ask the witness to recall the event from the middle or some other nonchronological point. The reader should note that some research indicates that accessing the event in strict reverse chronological order may be counterproductive with the context reconstruction technique. It is theorized that this is the case because the context reconstruction technique encourages the witness to re-create an exact image of the event in her head—both visually and temporally. By instructing the witness to access the memory in reverse chronological order, the benefits of context reconstruction may be lost.[20]

As successful as these techniques may be, you should be aware that there is the increased possibility of error in recall.[21] It is inevitable that any technique that increases the amount of information recalled will necessarily also increase the number of errors in recollection. This is true of any interview technique that is designed to enhance a witness's ability to remember. It is the interviewer's responsibility, then, to lessen the impact of this phenomenon.[22] One way to do this is to use this technique only as an investigative tool. As with any evidence developed during an investigation, the officer must make every effort to develop additional corroborating evidence. In the context of financial crime, corroboration can most likely be effected through the use of documentary evidence.

While discussing the topic of recall error, you should note that two types of error are generally associated with memory recall: errors in recall and confabulations. Errors in recall—simply called *errors*—are mistakes of fact about something that actually occurred. For example, if a witness reported that the vehicle was blue when in reality it was brown, it would be termed an error.

Conversely, a confabulation is an instance where the witness constructed a memory that did not exist in the first place. An example would be that of the witness who reported that the suspect carried a gun when in reality he did not. Confabulations are often seen, or suspected, in cases of repressed childhood sexual abuse reports. It is interesting to note that the research appears to indicate that cognitive interview techniques may increase errors as opposed to confabulations.

Research has also shown that the use of the cognitive interview on children under the age of eight may produce a higher rate of error.[23] In the context of financial crime investigation, the frequency of witnesses in that category providing relevant details in a case is small. However, as with any investigative technique, the investigator should be aware of its potential for misapplication and govern himself appropriately.

As we stated earlier, the most effective interview strategy is the combination of the cognitive interview with communication facilitation techniques. To a large degree, the free report phase of this three-phase process is a communications facilitation technique. Because it transfers control to the witness, it empowers the witness and encourages her to participate in the process. More importantly it begins to establish a rapport.

Although often viewed as nothing more than idle "chit chat" or a luxurious nicety, preliminary questioning can be the key to building rapport and getting everything you need from a witness.

Often an interviewer's job can be likened to that of a clinical psychologist where an intimate bond must first be developed before intimate secrets can be shared. In the case of the interview, those intimate secrets might just be the details of the criminal enterprise you are seeking to uncover. Once the interviewer establishes rapport, barriers disappear, trust grows, and a free exchange of information follows.

During the rapport-building phase of the interview, the interviewer must build trust between himself and the witness. During this phase, two things must happen: (1) the interviewer must assess both the verbal and nonverbal cues to a witness's behavior patterns; and (2) the witness must become familiar with the investigator and develop a comfort level on which to build the tone of the conversation.[24] Often this may be accomplished through application of techniques from a communications model known as NeuroLinguistic Programming (NLP).

NeuroLinguistic Programming

NeuroLinguistic Programming is a communications model that was developed by John Grinder, an assistant professor of linguistics at the University of California at Santa Cruz, and Richard Bandler, a student of psychology, in the early 1970s.[25] The technique is premised on the idea that all communication originates from the processes of seeing, hearing, tasting, feeling, and smelling. Our experiences are filtered through our sensory perceptions. However, because human beings are essentially verbal communicators, we must translate our thoughts and ideas into language—that is where linguistics enters the equation.[26]

According to Grinder and Bandler, each person uniquely decides how to organize ideas internally in order to access them and produce results. The main premise of NLP, therefore, is that people use their senses to perceive the world, and internally the filter of these senses determines how they will representationally access them. In essence, people can be classified as visual (seeing), auditory (hearing), or kinesthetic (feeling),[27] and, to a lesser degree, gustatory (tasting) and olfactory (smelling), based on how they perceive, store, and reaccess their thoughts and memories. Therefore, when people communicate, they access their thoughts by mentally accessing the sights, sounds, or feelings—and to a lesser degree tastes and smells—associated with the experience or memory. This is their representational system.[28]

We advocate the study and use of NLP models for building rapport and maintaining a productive informational flow during your interviews. By utilizing the information provided by NLP, an investigator can successfully create an environment where the witness or suspect feels much more inclined to speak freely.

The most effective approach to building rapport with an interviewee occurs on three levels: the kinesic, the language, and the paralanguage. The kinesic, perhaps the most obvious level, involves the mirroring of the person's body language. The language technique involves using words with bases in similar representational systems, and the paralanguage involves the mimicking of the interviewee's speech patterns.

Kinesic Mirroring

A person's kinesic[29] behavior includes things such as gestures, body posture, leg, hand, and arm position, and other subtle body movements. When an interviewer adopts similar body positions and subtly mirrors the interviewee's movements, a greater chance for rapport is realized.[30]

Please note the use of the term *subtle*. This technique, although quite powerful as a rapport-building tool, can, when overdone, lead to offense—exactly the opposite of the desired effect. There is a difference between matching a person's body language and mimicry. Matching involves very subtle adoption over a period of time. The process must be used cautiously and developed slowly. Otherwise, all hopes of a good rapport between the investigator and the subject are lost.

Small gestures, such as adopting a similar rate and depth of breathing pattern, and adopting a similar posture, head position, hand position, or seating arrangement all have a strong influence on the witness's subconscious defense system. Over time, like partners in an elaborate dance, the interviewer and interviewee will respond to each other's movements in unison. This mirroring of actions lays the foundation for building a strong rapport and ideal interview environment.

Language Matching

People use language to communicate. They relate their thoughts and experiences through the veil of their individual sensory perceptions. This is the foundation of the entire structure of the NLP model. Language matching utilizes the knowledge that people's words provide in order to establish a subconscious connection.[31]

Language matching is not, however, simply the use of the same words as the interviewee. Although it may often involve using similar words, the theory is not meant to convey a notion that the interviewer is supposed to use street language if he is dealing with a person of that demographic origin. In fact, much like mimicry, if the investigator's use of slang terms and words is incongruous with her background, it will likely be interpreted as a mocking gesture—another definite killer of rapport.

Instead, language matching looks deeper into the theory of linguistic communication to the sensory processing that people undertake when storing memories. As we indicated earlier, people process information through a sensory filter: visual, auditory, kinesthetic, gustatory, and olfactory. It is this sensory filter that dictates the language people select in order to communicate. Visual people will communicate visually, kinesic people will communicate kinesically, and so on.[32]

These tendencies to communicate through the veil of sensory processing often exhibit themselves in subtle ways. For example, a person whose predominant representational system is auditory will speak in terms of auditory sensation. "I hear what you are saying," "that rings true," or "that sounds about right to me," are all examples of phrasings an auditory person may use.[33]

Visual people, on the other hand, speak in terms of sight. "Do you see what I mean?" "I can't see my way clear to speak to you now." Or "I get the picture," are probably much more likely to be used by visually centered people. Similar linguistic patterns are found in people centered in other processing paradigms.

In terms of rapport building, these linguistic cues into the person's representational system can be adopted. Respond to the interviewee's comments or questions with similarly centered answers. Phrase your questions in a way that the interviewee can relate himself to representationally. At first, this technique may be difficult. If you, as an interviewer, are predominantly an auditory person attempting to interview a visually representational person, you may have to carefully rephrase your questions in a visually centered form. It will take practice. Given the value of information to most investigations, however, the rewards are well worth it.[34]

In conjunction with the subject's choice of words, NLP provides other, nonlinguistic, cues to a person's representational orientation. According to Grinder and Bandler, eye movements, referred to in NLP parlance as "eye-accessing cues," reflect a person's data processing orientation. It follows from this tenet that people's eyes move to specific spatial areas when accessing information, dependent on their preferred mode of representation.[35]

For example, people typically move their eyes up at an angle when remembering pictures, they typically look to the side when recalling past sounds, and they look down at an angle when recalling kinesthetic, or felt, sensations. These visual cues can unlock the key to a subject's method of accessing information.

If your subject consistently looks up and to the left when accessing information, he is "seeing" a picture. If the witness is looking down and to the right, he is probably accessing information in a kinesthetic manner. Similarly, if he looks consistently to the side, he is probably an auditorily oriented thinker. These cues to the subject's preferred representational system can be used to the interviewer's benefit.[36]

When asking questions of a subject who is visual, attempt to stimulate the witness's visual recall. Ask for information based on how things appeared to the witness, how the scene looked, how the defendant appeared, or how things appear in her mind. By asking the witness to access the information in a manner that is internally consistent with her representational system, there is a much greater likelihood that her recall will be fruitful.[37]

By the same token, by asking a visually centered subject to recall things based on an auditory representational system, you are asking the witness to remember in a way that is both foreign and uncomfortable. That is not to say that a witness who is auditory cannot recall visual images. It simply means that by speaking with a witness in her "native language," a rapport is more likely to develop.

Claims have been made that interviewers can act as "human lie detectors" based upon an advanced application of NLP. This technique has often been taught in kinesic interviewing seminars. However, it is widely disputed as a technique for detecting deception, and significant research has shown that factors other than deception often influence a subject's method of accessing information.[38]

The principle of this technique is based on an NLP model constructed in the late 1970s, which postulated that people access remembered and "constructed" (false) information from different spatial areas. For example, it is believed that a constructed cue is accessed with a rightward eye movement. Regardless of whether or not constructed cues are accessed in this manner, and whether this NLP model is predictably accurate regarding the spatial relationship of constructed cues, there are other difficulties associated with using this communications model as a predictor of deception. People construct mental images and sounds for many reasons. For example, Grinder and Bandler explain that many people reconstruct their memories. This reconstruction would then show a "construct" eye-accessing cue, even though the information related was factual and not fabricated. When dealing with such critical matters as truth and deception correlating directly to guilt and innocence, this margin of error, in our opinion, is too great. There are much better nonverbal cues to deception that are more easily calibrated by the layperson. Therefore, we believe that this use of NLP is unreliable.[39]

Paralanguage Matching

Paralanguage refers to the optional vocal effects, such as rate, tone, and volume, that accompany or modify human speech patterns and often communicate subtle meaning. Although an investigator should be cognizant of changes in volume, tone, or inflection in a witness's voice, paralanguage matching goes beyond mere observation.

Paralanguage matching requires the interviewer to adopt similar speech patterns as those of the witness. If a witness speaks slowly in a low volume, an investigator should attempt to adopt a similarly slow and low pattern of speech. In this way, the investigator and the witness are allowed to get in "sync." This mirroring technique does not have to be an exact match. It should, however, closely resemble the speaker's cadence and volume to be effective. When done properly, it is perhaps the most powerful rapport-building technique available to the investigator.[40]

BRINGING CLOSURE TO THE INTERVIEW

During the interview process, it is imperative that the investigator properly and accurately document the interview. Although a videotape recording is preferable, an audio recording, a stenographer's notes, or the witness's own handwriting will suffice.

Once the interviewer is confident that no further information will be developed during that interview, the interviewer should continue the rapport building by ensuring that the witness feels like a stakeholder in the process and should signify that the interview is being concluded.

When bringing the interview to a close, it is important to assure the witness that if he recalls anything else, he should feel free to contact you and relay the information. In addition, it is important to establish that you may wish to speak to the witness again at a later time for further questioning. Clearly explain that this occurs frequently as new information surfaces and as various other witnesses provide their account of the incident. You should therefore reassure the witness that this happens all the time and is simply a matter of routine.

By closing the interview in this rapport mode, you will likely have a much easier time if you actually do need to reinterview that particular witness. Once the interview is closed, it is imperative to accurately document in your report the content of the witness' statement.

INTERVIEWS IN FINANCIAL CRIMES

Although there is no methodological difference when interviewing a financially savvy witness, a language barrier is an added aspect of such an interview. Hopefully, you have carefully read the first section of this book and feel comfortable in your knowledge of the basic concepts of the accounting equation. If not, feel free to do so now. Understanding the language and reasoning used by accountants and other financial professionals will substantially reduce the communications barrier. Once this barrier is lessened, the interview becomes a matter of attention to details. The greatest difference between conducting an interview in financial crimes over other crimes, in our opinion, is the need for preparation. In other crimes, for example, murder, complication is seldom involved. Often, it is a smoking gun homicide, and you are questioning witnesses about personal observations.

Financial crimes are quite different. Many times in complex corporate structures, nominee owners and offshore transactions are involved that tend to blur or completely obliterate true ownership. There are complex financial transactions that, though perfectly legal, seem somehow illegitimate. Financial crime interviews are all about the details—unfortunately, as the saying goes, the devil is in the details. Because these types of witnesses will often recount complicated transactions, simple yes-and-no questioning, or "tell me what happened," open-ended questions will yield nothing. Therefore, preparation is of paramount importance.

When interviewing witnesses in financial crimes, the most critical time is before the interview even begins. Sometimes, the opportunity to interview a particular witness will present itself only once. This may be true in the case of a witness who later becomes a suspect, or perhaps, the witness unfortunately passes away before the case can be completed. Because you may get only one shot, it is imperative that you plan carefully before you step into the interview room.

Begin this planning by carefully studying the business operation that is the subject of the investigation. By understanding the day-to-day operations of the firm and knowing the normal flow of funds, you will be prepared to recognize answers that provide either keys to new lines of questioning or perhaps cues that the witness may be withholding information. It is important to understand the normal flow of funds within the firm.

If possible, request that the witness provide, in advance, copies of any documents that he will be referring to in his interview. This allows you time to study the documents and make detailed notes concerning what questions you wish to ask. Too often, an investigator examines the financial documents while also attempting to interview the witness. This poses two problems. First, because you are unfamiliar with the documents, you may not notice inconsistencies. Second, by dividing your attention between formulating your next question and examining a complex document, neither task receives its requisite attention.

Summarize the information. When time allows, you should create a summary, even if it's just a brief handwritten synopsis, of the financial information the witness will be expected to know based on your examination of the documents. Draw a flow chart of funds, transactions, or deposits. Visual aids can be an indispensable part of your brainstorming session. If you can understand the information well enough to create a one-page summary or chart, you likely will have a strong enough grasp of the financial picture to thoroughly question the witness. In addition, if you have a chart or summary of the information with you while conducting the interview, staying on track is much easier—simply follow the summary.

Do not be afraid to ask the witness to look at your flowchart or diagram. Have the witness tell you exactly where you are mistaken. Let him make the corrections. Or ask the witness to draw a chart of his own. By following along visually as the witness explains the flow of transactions, what once was blurred in your mind may become clear.

When preparing for the interview, conduct research on similar enterprises within that industry. For example, if you are preparing to interview the comptroller for a medium-sized import-export firm, know what a similar firm looks like. What sort of yearly revenue can you expect to see?

Regardless of the industry, there are likely several journals and trade organizations that can provide detailed information about standard operating procedures and financial ratios within the industry. Often, a simple telephone call or Internet visit will yield enough information to keep you busy for several days.

Examining industry-specific information and making detailed notes allows you to assess the validity of the answers to your interview questions. For example, if the industry average for bad debt write-offs is 1 percent of gross sales, a figure wildly over that should signal that further inquiry should be made into accounts receivables.

Interview the witness with the most general information first. For example, the comptroller has a great deal of knowledge regarding the overall operations of the business. However, it is unlikely, at least in a large operation, that he would be able to answer specific questions about any particular account within the company's receivables department. By interviewing this person first, you can often obtain a much broader picture of the operation, which may help you formalize a more specific tactical approach to the remainder of the investigation. Obviously, if you suspect the comptroller or other high-ranking financial officer as being complicit, you may wish to use an alternative strategy.

By starting at the top and working your way down, you will be increasing your knowledge base about the business while you are narrowing the focus of your questions until you have reached the point where specific pointed questions will elicit the detailed evidence necessary.

Finally, be prepared to enlist help. Although you will have a much better handle on most financial crimes after reading this book, you will invariably run across scenarios that put you out of your league. Hopefully, these will be few and far between—and fewer as you expand your experience. They are inevitable nonetheless. When an unfamiliar scenario arises, set aside your pride and seek the assistance of an expert in that particular field. Whether you spend an hour trying to absorb as much information as possible, or whether you enlist experts' help in preparing your preinterview analysis, don't be afraid to use them. Literally hundreds of financial professionals would be eager to assist in a little "cloak and dagger" work. Be careful though: their assistance often comes at a price.

SUMMARY

Although interviews with witnesses in financial crimes differ from interviews with witnesses in other types of crimes, certain key interview techniques can help you as an investigator develop as much information as possible. First, the use of cognitive interview skills, though designed to enhance the recall of eyewitnesses to crimes, can be used effectively to enhance the recall of witnesses in financial crimes as well. Any inquiry that requires the recollection of details can benefit from these techniques. Financial crimes, because they are won and lost based on the details, are just these types of crimes.

Second, preparation is the key to properly and effectively interviewing a financially knowledgeable witness. Although there is no magical list of questions that an investigator must ask, the skills you have developed reading the first section of this book should suggest a logical sequence and some general questions to use in certain financial crime interviews. Beyond that, there is nothing magical about interviewing financially bright people. Preparation will give you the edge, which will allow you to elicit the most detailed and accurate statement possible. "Be prepared" should be the motto of the financial crime interviewer, not just that of the Boy Scouts.

NOTES

1. R. Milne and R. Bull, *Investigative Interviewing: Psychology and Practice* (Chichester, England: John Wiley & Sons, 1999), pp. 34–39.
2. C.L. Yeschke, *The Art of Investigative Interviewing*, 2nd ed. (Burlington, MA: Butterworth-Heinemann, 2003), pp. 15–21.
3. A.S. Aubry Jr. and R.R. Caputo, *Criminal Interrogation*, 2nd ed. (Springfield, IL: Charles C. Thomas, 1972), pp. 21–40. See also R.W. Shuy, *The Language of Confession, Interrogation and Deception* (Thousand Oaks, CA: Sage Publications, 1998), p. 12.
4. C.A. Meissner and S.M. Kassin, " 'He's Guilty!' Investigator Bias in Judgments of Truth Deception," *Law and Human Behavior*, 26, no. 5 (2002): 469–480.

5. Shuy, *The Language of Confession*, p. 13.
6. Ibid.
7. D.E. Zulawski and D.E. Wicklander. *Practical Aspects of Interview and Interrogation* (CRC Press, 1993), pp. 7, 13–29.
8. M.R. Kebbell and G.F. Wagstaff, "The Effectiveness of the Cognitive Interview." In D. Canter and L. Alison, eds., *Interviewing and Deception* (Aldershot, Hauts, England: Ashgate, 1999), pp. 26–30.
9. Ibid., p. 25.
10. Ibid., 25–26.
11. Ibid., 25. See also Milne and Bull, *Investigative Interviewing*, pp. 33–34.
12. Milne and Bull, *Investigative Interviewing*, pp. 34–39.
13. Ibid., p. 36.
14. Ibid., p. 38.
15. Ibid., 33–34.
16. Kebbell and Wagstaff, "The Effectiveness of the Cognitive Interview." pp. 30–33.
17. Milne and Bull, *Investigative Interviewing*, pp. 39–47.
18. Ibid.
19. Ibid.
20. Ibid.
21. Ibid., pp. 184–187.
22. Ibid.
23. Ibid., pp. 136–139, 143.
24. Ibid., pp. 40–41.
25. S. B. Walter, *Principles of Kinesic Interview and Interrogation,* 2nd ed. (Boca Raton, FL: CRC Press, 2003), p. 139.
26. Ibid., pp. 139–140.
27. Ibid.
28. Ibid. See also R. Bandler and J. Grinder, *Frogs into Princes* (Moab, UT: Real People Press, 1979), pp. 5–8.
29. The terms Kinesic and Kinesthetic, while closely related, refer to two different areas of study. The term kinesic refers to the study of the relationship between body motions such as blushing or eye movement and human communication. Kinesthetics, on the other hand, refers to the relationship between human sensory experience and memory. When we discuss kinesics, we are referring to techniques for reading nonlinguistic cues in communications. When we are discussing kinesthetics, we

are talking about the influence that human sensory experience has upon the way in which people encode and access their memories.
30. Zulawski and Wicklander, *Practical Aspects of Interview and Interrogation*, pp. 143–146.
31. Ibid., pp. 146–147.
32. Ibid.
33. Ibid.
34. Ibid.
35. Walter, *Principles of Kinesic Interview and Interrogation*, pp. 140–142.
36. Ibid.
37. Zulawski and Wicklander, *Practical Aspects of Interview and Interrogation*, pp. 143–146.
38. Walter, *Principles of Kinesic Interview and Interrogation*, pp. 141–146.
39. Ibid.
40. Zulawski and Wicklander, *Practical Aspects of Interview and Interrogation*, pp. 147–149.

SUGGESTED READINGS

Buckhout, R. "Eyewitness Testimony." *Scientific American*, 231. no 6 (1974): 23–31.
Crombag, H.F., W.A. Wagenaar, and P.J. Van Koppen. "Crashing Memories and the Problem of 'Source Monitoring.'" *Applied Cognitive Psychology*, 10 (1996): 95–104.
Fisher, R. P., and R. E. Geiselman. *Memory-Enhancing Techniques for Investigative Interviewing*. Springfield, IL: Charles C. Thomas, 1992.
Geiselman R.E., R.P. Fisher, G. Cohen, H. Holland, and L. Surtes "Eyewitness Responses to Leading and Misleading Questions Under the Cognitive Interview." *Journal of Police Science and Administration*, 14, no. 1 (1986): 31–39.
Gudjonsson, G.H. *The Psychology of Interrogations Confessions and Testimony*. Chichester, England: John Wiley & Sons, 1992.
Hall, J.A., and M.L. Knapp. "Nonverbal Communication." In *Human Interaction*. Forth Worth, TX: Harcourt Brace Jovanovich, 1992.
Kohnken, G., E. Scimossek, E. Aschermann, and E. Hofer. "The Cognitive Interview and the Assessment of the Credibility of Adults' Statements." *Journal of Applied Psychology*, 80 (1995): 671–684.

Laborde, G.Z. *Influencing with Integrity*. Palo Alto, CA: Syntory Publishing, 1987.

Mann, S., A. Vrij, and R. Bull. "Suspects, Lies and Videotape: An Analysis of Authentic High-Stakes Liars." *Law and Human Behavior*, 26, no. 3: 365–374.

Mantwill, M., G. Kohnken, and E. Aschermann. "Effects of the Cognitive Interview on the Recall of Familiar and Unfamiliar Events." *Journal of Applied Psychology*, 80 (1995): 68–78.

Memon, A., and D.B. Wright. "Eyewitness Testimony and the Oklahoma Bombing." *The Psychologist*, 12, no. 6 (1999): 292–295.

Memon, A., A. Vrij, and R. Bull, eds. *Psychology and Law: Truthfulness, Accuracy and Credibility* New York: McGraw-Hill, 1998.

O'Connor, J., and J. Seymour. *Introducing Neuro-Linguistic Programming*. London, England: HarperCollins, 1990.

Parker, A.D., and J. Brown. "Detection of Deception: Statement Validity Analysis as a Means of Determining Truthfulness or Falsity of Rape Allegations." *Legal and Criminological Psychology*, 5 (2000): 239–259.

Rassin, E. "Criteria Based Content Analysis: The Less Scientific Road to Truth." *Expert Evidence* 7 , no. 4 (2000): 265–278.

Sporer, S., R. Malpass, and G. Kohnken, eds. *Psychological Issues in Eyewitness Identification*. Mahwah, NJ: LEA, 1996.

United States Department of Justice, Office of Justice Programs. *Eyewitness Evidence: A Guide for Law Enforcement*. Washington, DC: National Institute of Justice, 1999.

Vrij, A. "Detective Deceit via Analysis of Verbal and Nonverbal Behavior." *Journal of Nonverbal Behavior*, 24, no. 4 (2000): 239–263.

Vrij, A. *Detective Lies and Deceit: The Psychology of Lying and the Implications for Professional Practice*. Chichester, England: John Wiley & Sons, 2000.

Vrij, A., and M. Baxter. "Accuracy and Confidence in Detecting Truths and Lies in Elaborations and Denials: Truth Bias, Lie Bias and Individual Differences." *Expert Evidence*, 7, no. 1 (1999): 25–36.

Vrij, A., and S.K. Lochun. Neuro-Linguistic Programming and the Police: Worthwhile or Not?" *Journal of Police and Criminal Psychology*, 12, no. 1 (1997).

——— 10 ———

ANALYTICAL TECHNIQUES FOR FINANCIAL CRIME INVESTIGATION

INTRODUCTION

As we have cautioned the reader throughout this text, financial crime investigations are unlike most any other types of criminal investigations. They are fraught with complexity and they are by nature information intensive. Whether you are following the paper trail of a money-laundering organization or attempting to find the assets siphoned from the corporate bank account, you must follow the paper trail—a trail that often contains checks, bank statements, wire transfers, money orders, stock certificates, receipts, purchase orders, letters of credit, and possibly thousands more individual documents.

If you are lucky, your subpoenas, search warrants, and other documentary fishing expeditions will yield a plethora of information—so much so that your office will be filled with boxes of papers (perhaps even the offices of your colleagues). This is, to put it mildly, a double-edged sword. Although everything you need to prove your case is contained in those boxes, they are worthless pieces of paper, unless you can find exactly what you need when you need it. They are also worthless unless the documents can be made to tell a compelling, persuasive story. Sitting in the boxes, they offer nothing to your case.

The average nonfinancial crime probably has several hundred pieces of physical or documentary evidence (not considering major homicides, conspiracies, and organized crimes). These pieces of evidence, though cumbersome, can be tracked effectively without an overly complex system.

On the other hand, many complex financial crimes have thousands of pieces of physical and documentary evidence. Managing evidence of this magnitude is possible only through effective organization, and effective organization is possible only when the system in use allows the investigator—and subsequently the prosecutor—to move the case forward through presentation of evidence. Forward, in this case, means toward some ultimate proposition—and in the case of criminal prosecution, guilt.

In other words, the goal of any good organizational system is to marshal the evidence in a way that tends to prove the ultimate theory of your case. As a result, it is imperative that you not only know what you must prove, but also where the documents are that propel your case in that direction. The system that we present in the remainder of this chapter is just such a system. It combines elements of the science of judicial proof with a system of visual analysis that sorts, classifies, and catalogs every piece of relevant evidence moving toward the ultimate goal. A key advantage of this system is the ability to adapt the format to any size prosecution. Regardless of whether the inventory of evidence contains 1,000 documents or 10,000, the system is equally adept at organizing your case.

GETTING ORGANIZED

As we stated earlier, this system is based in part on the scientific theory of judicial proof. Therefore, it is important to understand this concept. Whether you are working toward preparation of a civil complaint or criminal indictment, the bottom line remains the same. As an investigator, you are an extension of the legal process. Unfortunately, many investigators, and some lawyers, often forget this fact. As a result, investigators may tend to conduct preliminary fact investigations in a vacuum. Although all good investigators are cognizant of the elements of the particular offense they seek to prove, few, if any, investigate, collate, and present their cases like lawyers.

Investigators, as a rule, do not build their cases like lawyers; perhaps they should. If investigators can be trained to think like lawyers (at least in terms of how to prepare and prosecute a case), a stronger case will be built from the ground up. By investigating financial crime cases in this manner, you will not only present a more compelling case for prosecution, but you will also reduce the amount of superfluous work that tends to insinuate itself into the investigative process. The process of thinking like a lawyer begins with understanding how cases are built.

Everyone knows that in order to prove a case the lawyer must prove that the defendant committed certain acts. These acts, or elements, are defined with relative clarity by codified law and legal precedent. In the case of criminal accusations, the elements of the offenses are codified in statutory form. In the case of civil accusations, the elements of the offenses are uncodified and generally based on common law principles of *stare decisis* and judicial precedent. However, knowing the elements of the offense is only half the battle: knowing how to reach that burden is the other half.

THE PROCESS OF PROOF

Inference

Great lawyers (remember we are trying to teach investigators to think like lawyers), as distinguished from good ones, never forget that guilt is based upon inference. Inference, in turn, relies on a chain of logic that must be forged one link at a time. Like proof of scientific theories, the inferences on which guilt is based must be linked together in a logical, linear way. Unlike scientific discovery, however, legal proof must conform to a narrow framework of rigorously enforced rules. These rules, for the purpose of this text, revolve around relevance.

If this tome were written for lawyers (real lawyers, not investigators thinking like lawyers), we would depart at this point and discuss the niceties of the rules of evidence and their admissibility. Because it is not, it will suffice to expound upon the rules of evidence only far enough to say that evidence must be confined to those things that are relevant. Of course, this does not mean that the investigator can totally disregard the bright line rules of admissibility. Collateral uncharged crimes evidence and other highly prejudicial facts, as well as illegally obtained evidence, are inadmissible (under most circumstances) and should not be the object of your pursuit. However, the finer details of these legal principles should be left up to the prosecutor—a highly trained legal practitioner.

Relevance

In short, evidence is relevant if it tends either to prove or disprove an issue in contention. For example, if the question of whether or not the sun is shining, were the ultimate question, the fact that it is 10:00 o'clock in the morning would appear highly relevant. The fact that it is January 17, 2003 would not.

The confusion over relevance versus irrelevance arises because cases are rarely proven under a singular line of logic. What first appears to be a singular question—did the suspect take the money—is ultimately misleading. Instead, each ultimate question contains subquestions. Collateral lines of logic can work together to blur the issue of relevance. A fact may not immediately appear to be relevant to the ultimate question in issue, however, when the ultimate question is broken down into its component subquestions, the relevance of the fact becomes clearer.

In our sun-is-shining hypothetical, the parenthetical reference to date may have at first appeared obtuse. However, if we reformulate the question into its subquestions, date might be more important. Implicit in this question is the assumption that we are referring to an observation at our current location. If our current geographic reference point is Nome, Alaska, date suddenly becomes important since Nome's hemispheric location limits the dates on which the sun is shining at 10:00 o'clock in the morning: from irrelevant to relevant in one easy step. Clearly, this is a simplistic example. No doubt many of our readers instinctively saw the relevance of the date fact; however, legal questions are rarely so transparent.

To fully understand how to effectively build this chain of logic, the investigator must grasp the nature of the logic underpinning legal argument. There are several forms of logical argument; the two that we are most concerned with in the context of legal proof are deductive and inductive.

THE LOGIC OF ARGUMENT

The Deductive Argument

Deductive reasoning is a form of argument that works from the general to the more specific; it is often referred to as "top-down" logic. Inductive reasoning on the other hand, works from specific observations to the broader and more general; it is sometimes called "bottom-up" reasoning.[1]

An argument stated deductively offers two or more rules or assertions that lead automatically to a conclusion. This syllogistic form of argument, first propounded by Aristotle, is designed to produce mathematical certainty. The use of syllogisms, or mathematical statements, ensures that the lines of argument lead logically to the conclusion.[2]

A deductive argument has, as a minimum, three statements: the major premise, the minor premise, and the conclusion. The first statement, or the major premise, is a statement of general truth dealing with categories rather than finite objects. Contained within the major premise are two sections: the antecedent and the consequent.[3]

The antecedent phrase is the subject phrase, and the consequent phrase is the predicate. For example, the statement "all men are mortal" contains the antecedent phrase, "all men" (the general category), and the consequent phrase, "are mortal."

The second statement, the minor premise, is a statement about a specific instance encompassed by the major premise. For example, the phrase, "Socrates is a man," is a statement of truth dealing with a specific instance governed by the major premise.[4]

The third statement, the conclusion, must follow naturally from the relationship of the major and minor premises to one another. If no deductive fallacies exist, this statement will be the inescapable result of the first two statements. In the above example, "Socrates is mortal" is the natural and inescapable conclusion to the major and minor premise.[5]

In forming deductive arguments, the minor premise can be related to the major premise in four different ways. Only two produce sound logical arguments; the other two produce deductive fallacies.

The structure in our illustration is an example of affirming the antecedent. In this form, the minor premise asserts that a particular instance is an example of the major premise's antecedent. In our example, we are asserting that Socrates is indeed a man. We are affirming that Socrates and the state of being a man are equal.

The converse of this form is known as denying the consequent. In order to construct a deductive syllogism in which the consequent is denied, we must assert that a particular instance does not equal the consequent. Our major premise, "all men are mortal," may remain the same. However, the minor premise must change.

If, instead of asserting that Socrates is a man, as we did in affirming the antecedent form, we deny that a specific object is mortal—"my car is not mortal"—we have constructed the second sound syllogistic argument. From this minor premise logically follows the conclusion that "my car is not a man."[6]

The strength, or soundness, of a deductive argument rests upon the truth of the major and minor premise. If the first two statements are true, the conclusion must be correct. However, a sound argument does not necessarily guarantee the truth of the conclusion. If either the major or minor premise is false, an incorrect conclusion may be reached using sound syllogistic logic.

The Inductive Argument

In contrast to the mathematical precision of deductive reasoning, inductive reasoning is not designed to produce certainty. This form of logical argument uses a series of observations in order to reach a conclusion. These observations, often referred to as a chain of observations, are combined with previous observations to reach a defensible conclusion.[7]

Of the three basic forms of inductive reasoning, induction by enumeration, or generalization, is the most common.[8] In this form, you make a general statement regarding some predicted outcome based on observations of a specific instance of a class. For example, the statement, "all lawyers are sleazy," when based on your observation of the last three lawyers you have come into contact with, would be induction by enumeration.

Because inductive logic is less precise than deductive logic, fallacies are often less easily identified. The fallacy most commonly associated with inductive reasoning is the hasty generalization.[9] When an argument fails as a hasty generalization, the inductive leap that the proponent asks the decision maker to make is too remote. It is not supported by sufficient evidence. The following statement suffers from the fallacy of hasty generalization:

- XYZ Company is involved in money laundering. It is an import-export company operating from Miami, Florida.

This statement may or may not be true. There is insufficient evidence based on these statements to draw the conclusion. It is possible that the statement is true, but the leap from XYZ Company's existence as an import-export business in Miami to the conclusion that it is laundering money is much too broad to make with any certainty.

A second common fallacy associated with generalization is exclusion. Exclusion occurs when important pieces of information are omitted from the chain. Put simply, alternative explanations for reaching the conclusion have been excluded.[10] For example, consider the following argument:

- The police found a dead body with three bullet wounds.

It would be a safe, albeit not mathematically certain, conclusion that the person found by the police died as a result of his gunshot wounds—that is, unless we also knew that the body was missing its head.

Although it is still possible that the victim died of gunshot wounds and that the decapitation was inflicted postmortem, it is equally possible that the manner of his death was decapitation and the bullet wounds were administered for some other purpose. The fallacy of exclusion forces the decision maker into reaching a false conclusion owing to lack of relevant alternative evidence.

Induction versus Deduction in Case Proof

As you can see, inductive and deductive reasoning is very similar, the greatest difference being the manner in which the argument is expressed. When you argue from the general to the specific, deductive reasoning is in play. When you reason from the specific observation to broader generalizations, inductive logic is in play. It is important to note that all inductive arguments may be recast as deductive syllogisms and vice versa.

As an investigator, you will encounter both forms of logical reasoning. However, the offering of evidence in the legal system will most often expose you to inductive logic. In the process of proof, it is common to allege and prove specific isolated facts and build to a general conclusion. Therefore, the inductive process of moving from the specific observation to the general conclusion just seems to feel right.

We should note that some readers may argue that deductive reasoning, being the more mathematically certain, should be the more favored logical form in legal proceedings. Keep in mind that the law, and the system for legal resolution of disputes, is concerned with probabilities, not certainties. It is not absolute proof that we seek; it is proof beyond a reasonable doubt. Because inductive reasoning is ideally suited to reason from specific facts (evidence) toward broad generalizations (guilt or culpability), induction is the more natural form of legal argument. In truth, it doesn't matter greatly which form the argument takes. All arguments may be formulated as either inductive or deductive premises.

That is not to say that deductive reasoning is useless in the legal context. Quite the opposite is true. When we choose the deductive over the inductive, the inferential focus shifts. There are still inferential leaps that you must make; they are simply made in a different location.

For example, our argument regarding XYZ Company's activities can be formulated either way. To state the argument inductively: XYZ Company is involved in money laundering since it is an import-export company operating in Miami, Florida.

Stated as syllogisms: (1) All import-export companies operating in Miami, Florida, are involved in money laundering. (2) XYZ Company is an import-export company located in Miami, Florida. (3) Therefore, XYZ, Company is involved in money laundering (deductive).

Obviously, these examples are oversimplified, exposing the fallacies of logic quite quickly. In reality, the inferential links in a logical chain will be much more subtle, and the fallacies of logic that can cripple the argument will be heavily obscured by the facts.

Both arguments, as they stand, are legally indefensible. In the inductive example, the inferential leap may not be as clearly evident as in the deductive, requiring the reader to infer that all import-export companies operating in Miami, Florida, are engaged in money laundering. Although the reader undoubtedly intuits that something is not quite right, specifically pinpointing the source of the illogicality may be difficult.

In the deductive example, the breadth of the inferential leap required of the reader is much more apparent. By breaking the proposition down into deductive form, the fallacies of logic inherent in the inductive process are more easily exposed.

Based on our previous discussion and the fact that the process of legal determination revolves primarily around inductive logic, your job as investigator requires you to guard against the fallacies associated with its use. The danger of the two most common fallacies, hasty generalization and exclusion, can be reduced by carefully analyzing the line of argument transposed over the specific legal elements.

THE INFERENTIAL NATURE OF PROOF

As noted above, all legal arguments are built on inference. However, it is rare for a legal argument to be based on one single inference. Instead, many inferences are piled one upon the other until the ultimate proposition—usually guilt or innocence—is the inescapable conclusion. This chain of inferences is referred to as *compound,* or *catenate, inferences.*[11] The strength, or weakness, of the legal argument is determined by the granularity of this chain of inferences. The finer the grain is (shorter inferential leap), the more powerful, and persuasive, the argument becomes. Understanding the complexities and dynamics of inferential logic is essential to properly investigating a case. During the investigative stage, the investigator must remain cognizant of the intermediate inferential steps between the evidence that exists and the ultimate issue. Only by careful dissection of the intermediate inferences within the chain can we determine the location of the possibility of doubt. This explicit analysis of the catenate inferences is the greatest safeguard against fallacious reasoning an investigator possesses. The use of inference networks to visually depict and explicitly analyze the lines of argument toward the ultimate proposition—guilt/liability—is invaluable.

Inference Networks

Inference networks are graphic representations of complex probabilistic reasoning tasks based on masses of mixed evidence. Although the concept of the inference network is neither new nor originally applied to the subject of financial investigation, the technique's facility for organizing and analyzing a large mass of data makes it well suited to such a task. Chapters 11 and 12 are an adaptation of an inference network model originally propounded by John H. Wigmore, an early twentieth-century legal scholar, for use in legal analysis of complex cases.[12] Because it is a system based on the science of judicial proof, in combination with the analytical functionality of an inference network, we find it invaluable for identifying the weaknesses in investigations that involve a mass of mixed evidence—financial crimes.

Although, in our opinion, a tremendous benefit of this technique's usefulness is its graphical depiction of the lines of logic, its true power stems from the preliminary work necessary to construct the chart. We should offer a word of caution to the reader at this point. Although this technique is very effective, it is both laborious and somewhat complicated. As such, it would be overkill to consider its application—in undiluted form—in every financial investigation. Instead, we urge the reader to carefully digest the information that follows and build upon the principles contained in the system. Great benefits can be realized by applying some of the techniques from each stage of the process without full-scale analysis and charting.

The true strength of the analytical techniques introduced in this chapter lies in their ability to synthesize and organize a large mass of evidence. However, even in smaller, less complex cases, by engaging in the thinking process involved in each individual step to a greater or lesser degree, you will develop a much stronger grasp of the strengths and weaknesses of the case. Any time you are forced to critically examine the logical underpinning of your case, it can only be beneficial.

The Inferential Network Analysis Process

There are eight steps in the inferential network analysis process: (1) formulation of the ultimate probandum and penultimate probanda; (2) evaluation of existing evidence; (3) formulation of theories, themes, and stories of the case; (4) preparation of the master chronology; (5) formulation of the working narrative; (6) gathering of supporting data and evidence; (7) plotting of the inferential network chart; (8) completion of the analysis.[13]

Formulation of the Ultimate Probandum

In terms of legal argument, the ultimate *probandum* is that ultimate proposition that you must prove.[14] In the criminal context, it is the actual charge that must be proven, whereas in civil cases, it is the legal cause of action under which your client wishes to proceed.

This is a crucial preliminary step that provides the focus for the entire case. Without a properly formulated ultimate probandum there is no guidepost for relevance. If we formulate it too loosely, our investigation will falter for lack of a solid direction. If we define it too narrowly, our investigation will fail to reach its ultimate objective because our lines of reasoning will be too narrowly focused to uncover valuable collateral evidence.

In order to properly formulate the ultimate probandum, you must identify the controlling propositions of law. These controlling propositions are derived from the substantive law and the major premise of a deductive syllogism.

For example, if we are contemplating an investigation into alleged defalcations by a pension plan administrator under Title 18, Chapter 31, Section 664 of the United States Code, the syllogism could be stated as follows:[15]

Major Premise: Any person who steals the premiums of any employee pension benefit plan is guilty of theft from an employee benefit plan.

Minor Premise: The defendant stole premiums of an employee pension benefit plan.

Conclusion: Therefore, the defendant is guilty of theft from an employee benefit plan.

These propositions of law, however, are rather abstract. They don't really tell us much about our case, so we must make the syllogism more specific to our facts. Our syllogism thus becomes:

Major Premise: If John Smith stole premiums from an employee pension benefit plan, he is guilty of theft from an employee benefit plan.

Minor Premise: John Smith took checks made payable to Southern Trust Pension fund and deposited them into an account held in his name personally.

Conclusion: Therefore, John Smith is guilty of theft from an employee benefit plan.

In order to prove the federal crime of theft or embezzlement from an employee benefit plan, the ultimate probandum could be phrased like this: "John Smith did unlawfully and willfully convert to his own use, premiums of Plan B, an employee pension benefit plan."

In this case, the source of the ultimate probandum is Title 18, United States Code, Chapter 31, Section 664, which reads, "Any person who embezzles, steals, or unlawfully and willfully abstracts or converts to his own use or to the use of another, any of the moneys, funds, securities, premiums, credits, property, or other assets of any employee welfare benefit plan or employee pension benefit plan, or of any fund connected therewith." Clearly, this statute encompasses a great deal more conduct than we would like to have to prove.

In our example, we do not anticipate that we will be trying to prove that the defendant, John Smith, took property or other assets, only premiums. Therefore, when formulating the ultimate probandum, we must eliminate those optional or conditional elements of proof that do not pertain to the case at hand. However, if we believe that we will be trying to prove the defendant took multiple things, such as premiums and properties, the additional element would be inserted into the probandum—being mindful of the conjunction employed.

In the case of this statute, the language makes it clear that in order to succeed we must prove either property or premiums. If either burden is reached, the elements of the statute have been met. Conversely, if we used the conjunction *and*, we would have to prove that the defendant took both property and premiums. Both constructions create an entirely different line of logical argument. This is a very important aspect of how we formulate our ultimate probandum—it defines how our investigation will proceed.

If the ultimate probandum—John Smith did unlawfully and willfully convert to his own use premiums of Plan B, an employee pension benefit plan—then the penultimate probandum is the minor premise of our syllogism.[16] In this case, John Smith took checks made payable to Southern Trust Pension fund and deposited them into an account held in his name personally. In other words, the penultimate probandum consists of the constituent elements of the offense. Now that we have defined the ultimate and penultimate probanda for our case, we can leave them for a moment, but first a word of caution.

Although the exercise in which we have just engaged may seem very pedantic, perhaps even simple-minded, it is a crucial step toward really understanding what we are trying to prove. In the statute used for an example, there are relatively few elements we must prove. We must prove that premiums were taken, that it was John Smith who took them, and that the pension plan was in fact entitled to them. This is a relatively straightforward prosecution. However, if, instead of this relatively simple prosecution, we substitute Title 18 Chapter 96—RICO—as our ultimate probandum, the scenario instantly becomes much more difficult to manage efficiently.

Some of the complexity associated with mounting a prosecution under RICO stems in part from the fact that, in order to prove the case, the prosecutor must first prove that the defendant engaged in a series of predicate acts. These predicate acts, defined under Section 1961, are crimes in and of themselves. In essence, the prosecutor must prove many crimes in order to prove that the defendant engaged in the pattern of "racketeering activity."

In addition, what initially appear to be four singular elements, on closer inspection require a much more complex line of logic. Paragraph "c" of section 1962 reads, "It shall be unlawful for any person employed by or associated with any enterprise engaged in, or the activities of which affect, interstate or foreign commerce, to conduct or participate, directly or indirectly, in the conduct of such enterprise's affairs through a pattern of racketeering activity or collection of unlawful debt.[17]

By deconstructing this paragraph, the following elements of our penultimate probandum become evident. We must prove that (1) the defendant was either employed by, or associated with, an enterprise; (2) the enterprise was engaged in activities which affect interstate or foreign commerce; (3) the defendant did either conduct, or participate directly or indirectly in the conduct of, the enterprise's activities; (4) by engaging in a pattern of racketeering activity or collection of unlawful debts.

As complex as these penultimate probanda appear to be, they are still deceptively simple. We can unpack these elements further. Implicit in each element are other more subtle lines that will ultimately appear in our inferential analysis network. For example, implicit in our definition is the necessity to prove the existence of a legal "enterprise" as defined by the statute. In addition, we must allege—and prove, of course—that the enterprise engaged in activities that affected interstate or foreign commerce. Although not necessarily difficult tasks, there are hidden elements to the crime that cannot be overlooked when formulating the ultimate probandum and penultimate probanda.

In short, the formulation of the ultimate and in turn the penultimate probanda is a process of defining, based on the exact language of the statute, what we must prove. The ultimate criminal charge becomes the ultimate probandum made finite to the facts at hand. The penultimate probanda then become the constituent elements of that crime. And, as we will see later in this chapter, we will break those constituent elements down further as we prepare to construct our inference chart. For now, however, let us focus on the next step in our inferential network analysis process.

Evaluation of the Existing Evidence

In this step, the investigator is required to assess all the evidence that is currently known. This may be as simple as reading the complaining witnesses' statement, or it may be as complicated as collating and organizing a year's worth of bank statements. Most often, during the early stages of an investigation the investigator will have few substantial leads—perhaps a police report, intelligence data, or other broadly defined facts. These facts, however, do paint a picture. Indeed, if they did not, there would not be any way to formulate some notion about what law was allegedly being broken. There will be facts, sometimes scant few, but they must be organized into a comprehensible format based on the category into which the known evidence falls. It is essential that the investigator catalog the evidence in terms of which element of the penultimate probanda it tends to support.

During this step, you must be careful not to overlook exculpatory evidence. Sometimes investigators tend to overlook, or even disregard, evidence that does not fit conveniently into their preconceived line of argument. This cripples the ability to critically examine the strength of the case.

For this very reason it is essential to catalog exculpatory evidence, or evidence that may be interpreted in an exculpatory manner. At this stage, generally separating the evidence into lines of argument serves two purposes. First, you can assess the progress of the case—where you are in relation to where you may wish to go. Second, this visual representation of your evidence is very likely to point out new or not fully explored lines of inquiry. Like most activities associated with the investigative science, this process is reflexive.

Even though you have already formulated your ultimate probanda and penultimate probandum, you cannot pack that step into a box and forget about it. Instead, it is necessary, even up to the time of trial, to think of these probanda as *provisional*. They are provisional in the sense that each successive step in the analysis process may render them inaccurate. Because your ultimate proposition is the terminal set of facts you hope to prove, the unfolding picture painted by your evidence may shift the proposition. If it does, you cannot be afraid to reformulate or recast your penultimate or even ultimate probandum. This reflexive endeavor, much like the planning process outlined in Chapter 8, remains a work-in-progress. It is imperative that as new facts come to light and new lines of inquiry surface, the ultimate proposition of your argument must adapt to meet the actual picture being assembled. Do not adapt the facts to paint the picture you have presupposed exists, but instead, paint the picture that the facts naturally form.

At this stage, preparation of an outline of the available evidence is a helpful heuristic device. The outline should organize the available evidence according to each penultimate probandum. One format is not necessarily preferable to another; however, it is essential that the outline serve as a precise index. It should identify each element under the provisional theory that has been adopted and also name each witness or exhibit that the investigator believes is directly relevant to that element—including a brief synopsis of the testimony each witness is expected to render. The outline must be an adaptable tool so that new information and evidence can be inserted as it arises.

At this stage, it is helpful for the investigator to ask, "what evidence do I have that supports this element?" If you continuously do this for each of the elements that comprise the provisional penultimate probandum, weaknesses in your lines of inference will show themselves. These exposed weaknesses in the logic of the case point out the areas where further investigative efforts must be directed.

At first, the weaknesses will, most likely, far outstrip the lines of solid logic leading to an inescapable conclusion of guilt. However, as the investigative process moves forward, you will patch the holes in the logic dike and eventually build the necessary unbroken line of inferential links necessary to prosecute the case.

When you marshal the facts and evidence, not only will the weaknesses become apparent, but also you will more clearly see opportunities for developing new lines of argument. Sources become obvious once the weaknesses surface. If it becomes apparent that evidence to document spending habits is lacking, several sources immediately spring to mind—bank records and credit card statements, to name just two.

The initial marshaling phase serves the tripartite purposes of organizing the evidence, exposing the weaknesses in logic, and providing direction to the remainder of the investigation. In order to serve its purpose well, it must remain a reflexive process acting as an adaptable guide to the entire investigative process. If time is productively invested here, the results will reveal themselves tenfold as the complexity of the case grows.

Formulation of Theories, Themes, and Stories

Lawyers have known for years the value of a good story.[18] Similarly, the interrelated notions of theory and theme have served successful litigators well throughout legal history. What is not often considered is the role of theory, theme, and story in the prosecution of criminal cases. After all, the story of the case is simply the scenario presented to the jury. Although this is true, little, if any, emphasis has been placed on formulation and implementation of a coherent theme that synthesizes theory and story into a criminal prosecution. Much less has there been the suggestion that story, theory, and theme might provide assistance at the investigative stage of a case.

In order to appreciate the benefit you may derive from attention to theory, theme, and story, it is necessary to introduce you, the uninitiated investigator, to the differences among the three, their relationship, and the role of each in the judicial process.

Theory

Theory, simply stated, is a logical statement that defines the case as a whole.[19] It should be a statement of the case that may be expressed as a series of concise syllogisms that elucidate the controlling legal elements of the prosecution that compel the inference that the desired conclusion is true—the defendant is guilty. This is a compelling explanation of the factual scenario that shows, *logically*, why the defendant should be convicted. In the criminal case, the theory often parallels the elements of the particular indictment. However, it is important to note that consideration must be given to situations in which alternative theories of the case may be supported.

In our RICO example, there are several combinations of factual scenarios in which a jury could be compelled to find guilt. This is apparent based on the use of the coordinating conjunction *or* in the statute. We have our choice of which illegal conduct we wish to prove. In some circumstances, some theories of the case may be more easily supported than others. What is more important is that an investigative theory must not be developed in a vacuum.

Because theory, theme, and story are so closely related in the legal context, formulation of a theory independent of consideration of its sister elements of theme and story will most likely produce a less salable case. And, as we have already examined, the key to getting the case to court is selling the merits of the investigative efforts to the prosecutor or client.

Story

Story, in the legal context, has been defined loosely as a narrative account of the events in chronological order. A story must be a narration of the facts, abstracted from the evidence arranged and presented as a cohesive, purposeful whole. As simple as this definition is, it is deceptively so. Assembling the sequence of events in chronological order is not a difficult task for an investigator. Humans tend to think chronologically and, as such, our natural tendency is to find order in such a construction. However, this definition overlooks one key consideration—there is never simply one construction of the story that will be adequately supported by the available assemblage of facts.[20]

"Get the judge's gut" is a phrase that is repeated countless times amid the dusty volumes of cases and stuffy rhetoric that pervade the legal classroom. It is classic and classical, yet its simplistic truth remains today. Cases are won and lost based on story. Lest the uninitiated believe we mean disservice to the legal system, some elucidation is in order.

In most if not all cases, there are equally compelling legal bases for a verdict on either side. Rarely is the case so cut-and-dried that no doubt remains as to the verdict when the judge or jury retires to deliberate. Therefore, when faced with equally persuasive legal arguments, how must a finder-of-fact reach a reasonable conclusion? We must rely on what we believe. And to a great extent, what we believe is focused through the prism of our emotions.

Judges, and juries to an even greater degree, suffer from the human condition. That condition is the fact that we are creatures of both reason and emotion. Reason, though based on finite logical principles, is as much influenced by emotion and past experience as it is by calculated thought. As such, when rendering difficult and important decisions, we unavoidably tend to rely on emotion.

Therefore, he who creates the most compelling and most believable story supported by the facts will usually win. Accordingly, the role of story in legal argument and strategy is a major, even though often overlooked, element of pretrial preparation.

As an investigator, your ability to formulate a story of the case is somewhat limited by the subordinate role you will play to the prosecutor. However, if you begin your investigation with an eye toward building a compelling story—that must be supported by the facts—the prosecutor will be predisposed to accept the case. After all, contrary to popular opinion, prosecutors also suffer from the human condition.

When we speak of story construction, the eloquence of Shakespeare is not necessary. What matters is finding a scenario within the facts that paints a compelling picture of the victim as being desperately in need of the unwavering impartiality of the justice system. The only conscionable result in the case must be that the sword-of-justice avenge the victim.

A word of caution is in order. It is important to keep in mind that you are acting as an arm of the court, and as an officer of the court you must adhere to the tenets of honesty and integrity. When constructing your story of the case, there is a decided difference between painting a compelling picture that cries out for the result you seek and fabricating or concocting a scenario that, though compelling, is also unsupported by the evidence.

As we stated earlier, story is defined as a narration of the facts, abstracted from the evidence. As such, the facts must support the story. The manner in which the story is told simply must compel the finder-of-fact that it is the most plausible account of what "really happened" that can be constructed from the evidence.

Conventional teaching in most investigative courses ignores the role of story telling in investigative activity. This, we believe, is a disservice to both the investigator and the victim. So many times, by the time the case wends its way through the hallowed halls of justice, the victim's story is merely a footnote within the reams of evidence on the prosecutor's desk. At the investigative stage, you have the opportunity to amplify the story behind the facts and ensure that they remain the focal point of the case. After all, every case in fact has a story; it is not merely a random assembly of facts.

Theme

Theme is directly related to theory.[21] As an investigator, you will have much less influence on the theme than on either story or theory. Theme has been defined as the framework on which to hang the case. It is the underlying moral force of your case. If the theory of the case is the explanation of the facts that show logically why the defendant is guilty, then the theme of the case is the explanation of the facts that shows, morally, why the defendant is guilty. It is also within the context of theme that the investigator must often deal with anticipated defenses, or possible inculpatory or contributory conduct on the part of the victim. It is within this framework that the investigator must attempt to build the most sympathetic case for the victim.

In the area of financial crime investigation, this task may prove challenging. Your victim may not always come across as helpless. More than likely, the defendant's counsel will create a theme and story that paint the theft of trade secrets from your corporate victim as a David versus Goliath struggle. This characterization, though not a legal defense, is surely aimed at rationalizing the defendant's actions in the face of oppressive, intolerant big business. If the defendant succeeds, the jury will likely have an emotional predisposition to find his version of the story more compelling.

A great deal of progress can be made toward defeating this strategy by recognizing this potential in your case from the outset and using this knowledge to guide the formation of your story and theory.

By acknowledging that these decidedly *lawyerly* endeavors exist and influence the outcome of your case, you can actively participate in shaping its course. Although the investigative role in the legal arena is limited to pre-trial (pre-indictment usually), it need not be helpless in the pre-trial process. By maintaining a constant awareness of the interaction of legal theory, compelling story, and morally supported theme, the case in which you have invested the better part of your recent waking life will offer a greater intrinsic and extrinsic reward.

These three elements, loosely termed case strategy, cannot be developed at too early a stage in any case. Historically, case strategy has been the exclusive province of the lawyers. This is neither necessary nor logical.

If it is generally accepted that development of a cohesive case strategy at the earliest possible time is favorable, then participation in case strategy development by the investigative arm is ideal. Since no earlier moment exists in a case—save the moment the crime is committed—than when the investigator first endeavors to ferret out the facts, no one is more perfectly poised to develop a sound case strategy than the investigator.

Preparation of the Master Chronology

When dealing with historical events (which crimes always are), the use of a master chronology, often called a timeline, is a powerful analytical tool. As we discussed earlier, the human brain tends toward chronological thinking. Anything else tends to confuse and confound the logical process.

As an example, recall any of the popular movies in recent years that have departed from the Hollywood formulaic approach to storytelling—chronological sequence. Of these, *Pulp Fiction* comes to mind first. Among the most striking characteristics of this movie (aside from the graphic detail with which the violence of society was portrayed) was Quentin Tarantino's adroit rearrangement of chronological order. His anachronous technique produced an intricate story that required constant vigilance to follow the plot.

Personal taste and aesthetics aside, the use of anachronistic story telling obscures clarity and disorients listeners by skewing their normal frame of reference—the normal progression of time. Events occur in sequence. When events are presented out of sequence, our brain must work that much harder to "cut and paste" them into the proper order. In the mission-critical world of investigation and prosecution, anachronistic stories prevent effective investigation.

For this reason, a master chronology can do wondrous things. In the course of most investigations, information is collected and analyzed in anachronistic fashion. Evidence is collected from different points in the sequence of events. If we collected evidence in a chronological manner, the use of the master chronology would prove less valuable.

The role of the master chronology is to reassemble the shards of evidence that have been collected into a chronological sequence. Such a chronology accomplishes two goals: It assists us in constructing stories people can follow by ordering the events in a normalized fashion, and it makes gaps and conflicts in the sequence of events more readily identifiable. By allowing us to graphically see where time gaps exist, our investigation can focus on sources from which to draw additional evidence to fill them.

Beyond the master chronology, other graphic devices can prove useful in ordering the sequence of events in our case. Although usually of limited use in financial crimes, scene diagrams and charts may be of assistance in following the flow of events. Of more substantial use, however, is a flow diagram.

In financial cases, the investigator is often confronted with complex, unfamiliar accounting processes. These processes or, more accurately, the weaknesses in them, hold the key to uncovering the point of loss. A process that may appear simplistic to the chief financial officer who implemented it will probably befuddle that investigator tasked to understand it.

By using simple flowcharting principles, a graphic representation of the normal progress of funds or transactions can be created. By breaking the process down into its constituent stages, two things are accomplished.

First, analysis forces the investigator to become intimately acquainted with the process in order to accurately chart the flow. Second, the graphic representation of the process summarizes each step and can be used in an analysis of each questioned transaction.

Regardless of the techniques that are employed, there is one underlying premise. The goal of the technique must be to fix the alleged events in time and space and make them concrete and amenable to analysis and presentation.

Formulation of the Working Narrative

The working narrative stage gives the investigator the opportunity to reformulate the progress of the case to this point in a format that can be analyzed in terms of story. Can the facts available at this point be organized into a coherent, believable form that present a compelling argument for a verdict of guilty-as-charged?

Although we advocate no particular method of narrative preparation, the process is indispensable. This process over form approach acknowledges that each individual investigator has a particular manner in which he creates narratives of the investigative efforts. We do not want to change that. What we do advocate is early involvement in the narrative process.

At the outset it is important to define what we mean by narrative. This is not the investigative report narrative that is a chronological blow-by-blow account of every investigative step. Instead, it is a rough draft of the synthesis of theory, theme, and story. Using the facts collected to this point, the investigator must assemble a rough draft of the narrative of the case. In so doing, the plausibility or implausibility of the "story" becomes apparent.

By creating a narrative version of the master chronology blended with the story and filtered through the combined prism of the theory and theme of the case, the investigation's focus can be assessed and redirected if necessary. The narrative will help to illustrate the weaknesses of the case and the gaps in both the evidence and the timeline. It will help move the case forward.

Gathering of Supporting Data and Evidence

Although appearing late in the process, this step comprises the lion's share of the investigative effort. Although its importance cannot be overstated, its value should not overshadow the importance of the steps that come before it.

This step is truly the investigative phase. Documents are collected, collated, analyzed, and reanalyzed. It is here that you are the investigator. You employ all manner of investigative techniques such as search warrants and subpoenas to produce evidence tending to support your ultimate probandum.

The key component of this stage is its interrelationship with the previous five stages. As we have stated, this entire process is a reflexive endeavor. Because the landscape of what is known and unknown is constantly shifting, we must carefully evaluate every shred of evidence through the lens of our ultimate and penultimate probanda.

For this very reason, the sequence of steps matters. We have formulated our penultimate probanda early simply because it guides our inquiry concerning relevance. Nowhere is our notion of relevance more significant than here. Our search for evidence is guided by this notion of relevance, which has been defined by the work done in step one.

Our notion of what we are seeking to prove, as defined in step one, must also be influenced and guided by our efforts in this step. As new evidence is uncovered, new sources of inquiry will be opened and others will be foreclosed. Perhaps entire lines of logic will collapse, while others will spring up from nothingness. The collection of evidence guides our quest to solidify our penultimate probanda and reify our theory and theme of the case.

Plotting of the Inferential Network Chart

This step synthesizes the first six steps into a graphical representation of the case. It is effective in pointing out faulty lines of argument and gaps in the inferential chain necessary to produce a conviction. It is by far the most laborious of the steps, yet it can produce the greatest yield in clarity and focus for your case.

Along with being the most laborious, this step is also the most in need of detailed explanation. Therefore, the intricacies of the charting process will be reserved for Chapters 11 and 12. Suffice it to say here that the charting process combines the theoretical values of steps one, two, and three with the practical activity of step six into a living document capable of lending clarity to a chaotic mass of evidence.

Completion of the Analysis

Like every step along the way, the charting step is not a finite step. Through careful analysis of the lines of argument and their supporting evidence, the investigator can determine where further investigation is necessary (refocus the attack) or assess whether there is probable cause to arrest or indict. Because analysis of the chart is closely tied to its actual plotting, it will be covered in detail in Chapter 12.

SUMMARY

The process of proof involved in investigating and proving financial crimes hinges on your ability to compel the finder of fact to draw a series of inferences based on the evidence. Several factors influence your ability to powerfully influence the jury. These factors include the strength from inferential step to inferential step. It is imperative that you carefully evaluate each implicit inference made during your navigation from link to link in your inferential chain. In order to properly evaluate the inferences in your argument, we have suggested an analytical tool known as the inference network.

As you proceed through the remaining chapters of this book, we will define and implement an inference. As we do, we hope to make its value in the investigative science clearer to you.

NOTES

1. D. Kuhn, *The Skills of Argument*. (Cambridge, MA: Cambridge University Press, 1991), pp. 7–9.
2. W. Schaeken, G. De Vooght, A. Vandierendonck, and G. d'Ydewalle, eds., *Deductive Reasoning and Strategies* (Mahwah, NJ: Lawrence Erlbaum, 2000), pp. 9–15.

3. Ibid.
4. R. M. Johnson, *Fundamentals of Reasoning*, 4th ed. (Belmont, CA: Wadsworth/Thomas Learning, 2002), pp. 37–41.
5. Ibid.
6. Ibid.
7. T. Anderson, and W. Twining, *Analysis of Evidence: How to Do Things with Facts Based on Wigmore's Science of Judicial Proof* (Evanston, IL: Northwestern University Press, 1991), pp. 63–65.
8. Ibid. See also Deductive and Inductive Arguments (February 8, 2003), retrieved February 8, 2003, from Shepherd College, Rhetoric Department website: *http://webpages.shepherd.edu/maustin/rhetoric/deductiv.htm.*
9. Ibid.
10. Ibid.
11. Anderson and Twining, *Analysis of Evidence*, pp. 57–59.
12. Ibid., pp. 108–118. See generally, J.H. Wigmore, *The Principles of Judicial Proof: As Given by Logic, Psychology, and General Experience and Illustrated in Judicial Trials* (Littleton, CO: Fred B. Rothman & Co., 1988).
13. This inference model is an adaptation and expansion of a theory first set out by J.H. Wigmore to the area of criminal investigation. The authors make no claim to having originated the use of an inference model in organizing legal proof; however, its application to the area of pre-arrest investigation seems to be new.
14. Anderson and Twining, *Analysis of Evidence*, pp. 45, 54–55.
15. Title 18 U.S. Code Chapter 31, Section 664 (2001).
16. Anderson and Twining, *Analysis of Evidence*, pp. 54–55.
17. Title 18 U.S. Code Chapter 96 §1962 (2001).
18. Ibid., pp. 166–167.
19. Ibid., pp. 165–166.
20. Ibid., pp. 166–167.
21. Ibid., pp. 167–168.

SUGGESTED READINGS

Abimbola, K. "Abductive Reasoning in Law: Taxonomy and Inference to the Best Explanation." *Cardozo Law Review*, 22 (2001): 1683–1689.

Abimbola, K. "The Logic of Preliminary Fact Investigation." *The Journal of Law and Society*, 29 (2002): 533–59.

Arthur, W.B. "Inductive Reasoning and Bounded Reality." *American Economic Review*, 84 (1994): 406–411.

Binder, D., and P. Bergman. *Fact Investigation: From Hypothesis to Proof*. St. Paul, Minn.: West Publishing, 1999.

Eco, U. *Semiotics and the Philosophy of Language*. Bloomington: Indiana University Press, 1984.

Eco, U. *A Theory of Semiotics*. Bloomington: Indiana University Press, 1976.

Eco, U., and T. Sebok, eds. *The Sign of Three: Dupin, Holmes & Pierce*. Bloomington: Indiana University Press, 1983.

Josephson, J., and S.G. Josephson. *Abductive Inference Computation, Philosophy, and Technology*. New York: Cambridge University Press, 1994.

Kadane, J., and D.A. Schum. *A Probabilistic Analysis of the Sacco and Vanzetti Evidence*. New York: John Wiley & Sons, 1996.

Ketner, K.L., ed. *Pierce and Contemporary Thought: Philosophical Inquiries*. New York: Fordham University Press, 1995.

Oldroyd, D.R. *The Arch of Knowledge: An Introductory Study of the History of the Philosophy and Methodology of Science*. London: Routledge Kegan & Paul, 1986.

Pierce, C. S. Reasoning and Logic of Things. In K. L. Ketner, ed., *Reasoning and Logic of Things: The Cambridge Conference Lectures of 1898*. Cambridge, MA: Harvard University Press, 1993.

Robertson, B., and G. A. Vignaux. *Interpreting Evidence: Evaluating Forensic Science in the Courtroom*. New York: John Wiley & Sons, 1995.

Schum, D.A. *The Evidential Foundations of Probabilistic Reasoning*. New York: John Wiley & Sons, 1994.

Schum, D.A. "Marshaling Thoughts and Evidence During Fact Investigation." *Southern Texas Law Review*, 40 (2001): 401–454.

Schum, D.A. "Species of Abductive Reasoning in Fact Investigation." *Cardozo Law Review*, 22, 1645-81.

Schum, D.A., and P. Tillers. "Marshaling Evidence for Adversary Litigation." *Cardozo Law Review*, 13 (1991): 657–704.

Schum, D.A., and P. Tillers. "A Theory of Preliminary Fact Investigation." *University of California at Davis Law Review*, 24 (1991): 931–1012.

Schum, D.A., and P. Tillers. "Alternative Views of Argument Construction from a Mass of Evidence." *Cardozo Law Review*, 22 (2001): 1461–1502.

Thagard, P. *Computational Philosophy of Science*. Cambridge, MA: MIT Press, 1993.

Thagard, P., and C. Shelley. "Abductive Reasoning: Logic, Visual Thinking, and Coherence." In M.D. Chiara, K. Doets, D. Mundici, and J. van Benthem, eds., *Logic and Scientific Methods. Volume One of the Tenth International Congress of Logic, Methodology and Philosophy of Science, Florence*. Dordrecht: Kluwer Academic Publishers, 1997, pp. 413–427.

Tillers, P. "Webs of Things in the Mind: A New Science of Evidence." *Michigan Law Review*, 87 (1989): 1225–1226.

Tillers, P., and D. Schum. "Charting New Territory in Judicial Proof Beyond Wigmore." *Cardozo Law Review*, 9 (1993): 907–950.

11

INFERENCE NETWORK ANALYSIS

INTRODUCTION

As introduced in Chapter 10, legal cases are proved through inferences. These inferences, built in chains, must lead logically from point A to point B. It is the strength, or weakness, of these inferences that determines the strength or weakness of the case.

In legal argument, inference is the persuasive effect of each individual piece of evidence. From the existence of the evidentiary item it may be inferred that some ultimate fact exists. Proof, then, can be thought of as the total net effect of the inferences that have been drawn. In other words, from evidence flow inferences, and from combined inferences flow conclusions. In the legal context, conclusions amount to proof.

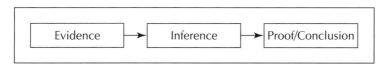

Exhibit 11.1 The Role of Inference in Proof

As Exhibit 11.1 demonstrates, the ability to prove an ultimate fact rests solely on the strength of the inferences, not the evidence itself. This is true because regardless of the nature or volume of the evidence presented, if the inferences drawn are either incorrect or weak, the desired conclusion cannot be reached.

This notion may be new to some investigators. The difference is subtle, yet crucial. By bringing this critical distinction to your conscious thought, we hope to help you develop a better understanding of how to prove your case. The end result will be better, more focused investigations.

LINKING INFERENCES

The inferential weight of evidence can range from weak to strong, depending on how clearly the inference may be drawn from the existence of the evidence. Weak inferences exist when the leap from evidence to conclusion is great. Conversely, strong inferences are generated when the leap from the evidence to the conclusion is short. A weak inferential relationship exists between the evidentiary statement, "The defendant and his ex-wife were hostile toward each other," and the conclusion that the defendant killed his ex-wife. A strong inferential relationship exists between the statement, "I saw the defendant stab his ex-wife," and the conclusion that the defendant killed his ex-wife.

In the first case, there is too great a leap between the statement and the conclusion—there are too many intervening steps. In the second case, there are no, or at least very few, intervening steps between the evidentiary statement and the conclusion. The goal of the investigator is to reduce the distance between intervening steps between the defendant and the conclusion.

Chain of Inferences

We reduce this distance by creating a chain of inferences referred to as concatenate inferences.[1] Concatenate inferences build, one upon the other, until ultimately, the chasm between the defendant and the conclusion is reduced to a manageable distance. We are not shortening the overall distance human reasoning must travel; rather, we are merely breaking it up into smaller steps.

We can illustrate this process by concocting a hypothetical situation. Assume we wish to link the defendant to the murder of his ex-wife. Initially, the connection—the inferential relationship—between the defendant and the victim is weak, as shown in Exhibit 11.2.

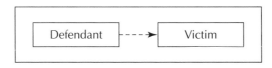

Exhibit 11.2 Initial Relationship of Defendant to Victim

We may argue for the inference that because the defendant and the victim were known to each other and divorced, the defendant had a motive to kill her. It is a plausible theory, yet not very strong—certainly not strong enough to proceed to trial. How can we strengthen this inferential relationship? We must build our chain.

Our investigation has uncovered a bloody glove at the crime scene. Immediately, there is an inference that the glove is somehow involved in the murder. If we later learn that the DNA from the blood on the glove matches that of the victim, the inferential relationship between the glove and the murder becomes very strong, as shown in Exhibit 11.3.

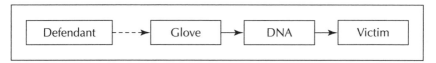

Exhibit 11.3 Building the Inference Chain

Although the connection between the defendant and the victim is still tenuous—as indicated by the dashed line in Exhibit 11.3—the connection between the victim and the glove is strong. Obviously, we are not satisfied. Our investigation continues.

The forensic examiners at the crime lab have determined that the gloves are in fact a very expensive brand sold only in exclusive up-scale department stores. They are so unique that only 25 pairs have been sold in the past year. This information alone does not necessarily strengthen the inferential relationship to the defendant. However, taken in combination with the fact that department store records show that a pair of these gloves was purchased using the defendant's credit card two months earlier, we are slowly strengthening our chain.

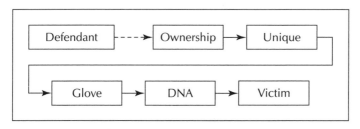

Exhibit 11.4 Strengthening the Chain

Exhibit 11.4 illustrates the evolving inferential relationship. We have still depicted the link between the gloves and the defendant in a dashed line. Although there is a fairly good connection between the two, there are 24 other people who have a connection to the gloves—at least hypothetically.

Finally, our forensic experts compare the DNA from skin cells found in the glove's lining with those of the defendant—they match. This final piece of evidence is the link we have been waiting for. Up until now we could link the defendant inferentially as an owner of similar gloves. Now, we can link him as the owner of *these* gloves. Exhibit 11.5 illustrates the completed inferential chain.

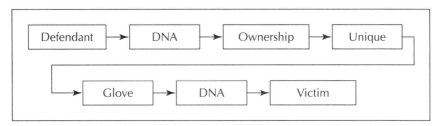

Exhibit 11.5 Completed Inferential Chain

We can now depict the relationship between the defendant and the victim with solid lines. Does this mean that we have proven that the defendant murdered the victim? No, of course not; all it proves is that there is a strong inference that a pair of gloves owned by the defendant were found at the scene of the murder with the victim's blood on them. Such is the nature of inferential proof. Is this chain of inferences strong enough to convict the defendant of murder? That is a question only the jury can answer.

As you can see by this simplistic example, the job of the investigator is not to *prove* that the defendant committed the crime. The investigator's job is to construct a chain of inferences sufficiently strong enough to convince a fact-finder that the desired conclusion is the most *plausible* sequence of events. In order to do that, you must internalize the distinction between evidence and inference.

Hidden Inferences

Until now, we have been discussing only explicit inferences—those inferences that are directly urged by the investigator. For example, the inference that the gloves were involved in the murder is an explicit inference because the investigator has asserted the fact that DNA belonging to the victim was found on the gloves. There are, however, other inferences that are of concern to the criminal investigator—they are hidden, or implicit, inferences. An implicit inference is not directly urged by the evidence; instead, implicit inferences tag along as baggage. An example of an implicit inference that the investigator expects the jury to draw involves the ownership of the gloves. Before introducing evidence that the defendant's DNA was found inside the gloves, we drew an ownership inference based on the credit card purchase.

The inference was a reasonable one. However, implicit in that inference was the assumption that the defendant, not someone using his credit card, had purchased the gloves. If we lay bare this implicit inference, a weakness in our inferential chain becomes apparent. Our link between the defendant and the murder, absent the DNA-glove evidence, weakens when we consider the alternative possibility that someone using the defendant's credit card purchased the gloves. By ignoring the implicit inference, we leave the flank of our logical line of argument open for counterattack.

Closely related to the implicit inference is the generalization. A generalization is merely an implicit inference that is generally recognized by a majority of people. For example, the generalization that dropped objects fall is universally accepted as being true. Therefore, an eyewitness account of the victim being pushed from a tall building, coupled with the recovery of the body at the base of the building, will urge the jury to conclude that the defendant died as the result of the fall. Implicit in this conclusion are the hidden inference that there were no intervening causes of death (the victim was not shot on the way down) and the generalization that gravity acted upon the body, propelling it downward. Both implicit inferences in this scenario are quite reasonable and in fact relatively safe from attack; not all generalizations are so bulletproof.

Generalizations become especially dangerous when they are made by trained investigators. This is true because investigators draw very specific conclusions from random facts based on their experience and training. Juries in general do not possess the same training and experience and may not draw the same generalized conclusion. It is the nature of generalizations that makes them so dangerous.

A generalization might also be called an assumption based upon experience. The key, then, is the fact that people have a broad range of experiences and may or may not make the same assumption given the facts. As Lawrence Lessig put it, facts derive their meanings from "frameworks of understanding within which individuals live."[2] It is this diversity of

185

experience that makes ignorance of the existence of implicit generalization, or reliance on common sense, so dangerous to the process of logical proof. Like it or not, common sense plays an integral role in judicial determination. The legal rules guide the formation of our original legal hypothesis. However, these hypotheses are ultimately grounded in our common-sense understanding of the world. Common sense, however, may be problematic. Not all common-sense assumptions are legitimate grounds for the interpretation of evidence.

Common sense, though implicit in any legal context, can cause inferential errors. For example, common sense can be culturally specific. Assumptions, based on culturally specific common-sense principles, can cause grave inferential errors. One result of common sense inferential logic is tunnel vision in police investigations.

This does not necessarily mean that a single generalization in your line of argument will doom it to failure. It does mean that broad generalizations may leave your otherwise airtight logical chain vulnerable.

As an investigator, it is imperative that you guard against assuming that the jury will draw implicit inferences and generalizations. The only way to guard against them is to recognize them. The only way to recognize them is to carefully analyze the entire logic of the case. And to analyze the logic of your case, you must first understand how it fits together. This is where inference network analysis comes in.

Inference

In our rudimentary example, the line of logic is simple. A glove owned by the defendant was found at the scene with the victim's blood on it. The logic of the argument seems to compel the conclusion that the defendant committed the murder. It is rare that the logic of a case is so simple. It is even more rare that the logic of a financial crime case is that simple. On the contrary, most financial crime cases suffer from a double curse. First, the sheer mass of evidence is incomprehensible. Second, the logic necessary to prove the case is often composed of several interlocking and conjunctive lines of argument formed in a proposition of alternatives.

This form of allegation can confound the investigator and can bog down an investigation that lacks a strong focus. To avoid this miring effect, the investigation must be both organized and constructed in the simplest logic possible.

Deconstructing the legal theory of the case into the ultimate and penultimate probanda is the first step (for an introduction to defining the ultimate and penultimate probanda, please refer to Chapter 10). The second step is focusing the efforts of the investigative team, and the lines of argument leading up to the ultimate probandum should dictate this focus. If your lines of argument are weak, so is your focus.

By organizing the lines of argument of your case into an inference network, you can analyze both the explicit and implicit inferences that must be drawn in order to reach the ultimate conclusion (guilt). As a graphic representation of both the lines of logic and how the evidence fits within them, an inference network visually alerts the investigative team to areas in need of support, areas that lack logical basis, and areas of potential attack.

Inference networks make implicit inferences more obvious and allow you to see those sneaky generalizations more clearly. The hope and purpose of the inference network are to point out your folly and allow you to react before the prosecutor (or defendant) does. After you have recognized the weakness, your effort can be reorganized in a more directed, purposeful way.

What Is an Inference?

An inference network is a graphic representation of an inferential relationship. Graphical models provide a natural tool for dealing with uncertainty and complexity. They provide us with an intuitively appealing interface by which we can understand highly interactive sets of variables. Often used for problems in applied mathematics and engineering, graphical models provide a natural framework with which to examine the multivariate nature of legal proof and logical argument.

Bayesian Networks

Graphical models offer us a way to view all the variables in our reasoning problem, express assumptions, and facilitate making inferences from observed data. In the context of legal investigation, an inference model can allow us to simultaneously assess all our variables—evidence—and follow the flow of our argument in a logical fashion.[3]

Many forms of graphical models for representing inference networks exist, from Bayesian[4] networks to Markov networks.[5] Generally, however, all inference networks consist of nodes, often called vertices, and links known as edges. In a traditional Bayesian inference network, the vertices in the graph will correspond to variables within the problem to be modeled. Similarly, the edges correspond to relationships that exist between pairs of variables.

In Exhibit 11.6, the nodes, *A*, *B*, *C*, and *D* represent variables in a causal relationship. For example, if *D* represents an event—my car won't start—the vertices *A*, *B*, and *C* may represent possible causes for the event. Like most "real-world" situations, the event "my car won't start" is not a binary relationship.

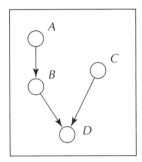

Exhibit 11.6 Variables in a Causal Relationship

Instead, the event *D* may be caused by more than one variable. If we allow *B* to represent the condition "I am out of gas" and *C* to represent the condition "my battery is dead," our model becomes a more accurate representation of a real-life problem. Our model tells us, graphically, that there are two possible causes of our event—either *B* or *C*. Bayesian networks of this type are helpful both in diagnostic reasoning, known as "bottom up" since it works from event to causation, and in causal or "top-down" reasoning because it helps compute the probability that an event will occur given a predecessor event.

Diagnostic Models

Diagnostic models often incorporate Bayesian techniques to help choose from among several competing hypotheses. For example, using Bayesian decision-making techniques, Microsoft® has created its infamous anthropomorphic Office Assistant™ paperclip. Using Bayesian decision-making techniques, the paperclip offers context-sensitive advice to users based on the program in use and other real-time data.[6] Similarly, Microsoft's® new Mobile Manager™ takes a vast amount of information about the nature and content of incoming e-mail into account in order to sort, filter, and forward the message based on Bayesian decision theory.[7]

In much the same way that Bayesian diagrams and inference networks can be used to reason through statistically difficult and voluminous problems, they can, with some adaptation, be used to reason through complex legal and investigative problems. This adaptation entails revision of the terminology of Bayesian theory, as well as elimination of the theory of probability and statistics that accompanies its use in mathematic and scientific problems. We are left then with a skeleton framework on which we can build an inference network. One such framework was developed by John Henry Wigmore and bears his namesake as the Wigmorean Chart.[8]

Wigmore's Chart Method

John Henry Wigmore, an early twentieth-century legal scholar in the field of evidence and proof, devised a graphical model for proceeding from point A to point B in terms of legal proof. Based loosely on probability theory combined with notions of the science of judicial proof, Wigmore's method was a study in exposing the underlying logic of each thread of legal argument.[9] His approach and perspective, and the approach of those who have followed, were decidedly lawyerly. To the extent that his method has received notice in terms of investigative potential, it has been from the standpoint of a lawyer conducting fact investigation during the pre-trial discovery process.

Admittedly, lawyers in trial preparation and criminal investigators have divergent methods and differing roles, but at its heart, their goal is very similar. Both the criminal investigator and the lawyer in the pre-trial discovery, fact investigation phase must uncover as much evidence, both inculpatory and exculpatory, as possible and marshal it into a working hypothesis that supports their theory of what happened. Often, these are a decidedly parallel set of tasks. Wigmore's method, with some adaptation, is very well suited to this task.

As with all graphical models, Wigmore's chart method of analysis presents a structured approach to a complex problem. In Wigmore's case, the problem we face is reasoning from a mixed mass of evidence to some ultimate fact in issue. In other words, we are faced with a mixture of evidence, which varies in both type and probative force, and we are tasked with organizing that mass into a coherent, hopefully forceful, explanation of a real-world event. In broad terms, our graphical inference network is a communication medium—it allows us to convey meaning. Underlying this communication medium, like all forms of communication, is a language. Although Wigmore's method is well suited to visualize the legal arguments necessary to prove a case in court, there are some minor limitations to its application and effectiveness in analyzing a complex investigative process. For that reason, we have borrowed Wigmore's theory underlying his method and adapted it slightly to more accurately reflect the investigative process. This investigative inference will aid criminal and civil investigators in their pursuit of legal proof much like Wigmore's chart method, but using a slightly different perspective—in Wigmore's words, the "standpoint" of an investigator as opposed to a lawyer during case preparation.[10]

THE INVESTIGATIVE INFERENCE MODEL

The Language

The first task in designing our inference model is the definition and explication of language. In this case, the "language" derives from a palette of standard graphic symbols, combined with syntax for ordering them. In a way no different from traditional language systems, our inference network language must provide the words as well as the punctuation that gives them meaning. Also in a way only slightly different from traditional language, our system can benefit from some broad general rules as a starting point. In this case, we may begin by discussing the nature of a mixed mass of evidence.

The term *mixed mass of evidence* refers to the notion that cases are proven through evidence that is heterogeneous, not homogeneous.[11] In other words, a case is built on evidence of different types and probative value. Though not a difficult concept to understand, it is important to define for the reader exactly what the distinction between type and probative value, in the context of this system, is.

In general, we shall use the term *type* to refer to the extrinsic quality of evidence. For example, fingerprints, documentary evidence, trace fibers, and DNA evidence are all different "types" of evidence for our purposes. The term *probative value*, on the other hand, will be used to discuss the inferential weight of an item of evidence.

In the legal context, probative force refers to cogency, or the weight and impact the evidence will exert on the finder of fact—the jury. Although our definition of probative force is nearly identical, since we are after all ultimately trying to convince the jury of the defendant's guilt, we shall think of it in a slightly different way. We will think of it in terms of its inductive and deductive qualities. We will think of probative force in terms of how strongly it supports or defeats the logical steps in our inferential chain. Probative value, then, may be thought of in terms of the mode in which the evidence endeavors to prove the ultimate fact. For our purposes, we are speaking of the difference between direct and circumstantial evidence.

The term *direct evidence* is used to describe evidence that directly proves the ultimate fact in issue, with no intervening inferential steps in between.[12] Because direct evidence comes in the form of testimony from an eyewitness who actually heard, saw, or touched some thing or event, its probative value is high. If an eyewitness takes the stand and testifies that on Friday morning he observed the defendant take out a gun and shoot the victim, he has given direct evidence, which, if believed, directly proves that the defendant did in fact kill the victim. As such, the inferential value is high and should be accorded appropriate weight within our system of analysis.

Conversely, circumstantial evidence is evidence that indirectly proves the ultimate fact in question.[13] Circumstantial evidence consists of evidence that builds up inferences tending to show that the ultimate fact occurred. It is evidence from which the finder of fact can infer other facts based on the circumstances. Clearly, then, circumstantial evidence requires more inferential steps between subordinate facts and the ultimate fact in question. It is important to caution the reader at this point not to confuse issues of credibility and corroboration with the probative value of evidence in this context.

Normally, probative value is the sum of both credibility and the nature of the evidence, either circumstantial or direct. However, for the purposes of constructing our graphical inference, issues of credibility will be addressed separately. For now, we want the reader to focus on the differences inherent in the two forms of evidence. If, for the sake of argument, we assume that the credibility and reliability of both witnesses—the one providing testimony regarding the ultimate fact and the other providing testimony regarding circumstances from which inferences about the ultimate fact may be drawn—is equal, the probative value of their testimony becomes easier to evaluate. In turn, the discrete inferential steps between our evidence and our ultimate probandum become more easily definable.

Introduction to the Symbols

The first symbols in our language palette, then, must represent the difference between circumstantial and direct evidence. This is true because the key to organizing our argument is in being able to graphically see where the weakest and strongest links are being made. Circumstantial arguments, which are by definition weaker, must be readily distinguishable from direct arguments.

Circumstantial Evidence   Direct Evidence

Exhibit 11.7 Symbols for Circumstantial and Direct Evidence

Exhibit 11.7 introduces the first two symbols our system uses: the circle, to represent circumstantial evidence, and the square, to represent direct evidence. To this limited palette we must add a few more basic symbols.

First, in order to represent real evidence, evidence that the fact-finder will physically perceive, we will use the symbol for *infinity*—∞. This symbol may be used to represent both testimonial assertions and tangible physical evidence. For example, eyewitness testimony regarding the location of a weapon, or the actual weapon itself, could be represented using this symbol.

Next, we must assign a symbol to represent propositions that will be either stipulated to by the defense or taken as judicially noticed by the fact-finder. For example, in a divorce case it is necessary to prove that a legal marriage exists at the time of the action. If this fact were uncontested, it would be helpful to have a way to represent this in the chart. Similarly, in the criminal arena, certain facts may be subject to judicial notice without extensive proof. Scientific facts, foreign laws, and other uncontroversial matters are often subject to such notice. By providing a symbol to depict this condition, immediately we graphically identify areas of the investigation where no further, or at least very little further, investigation must be done. We will use the proofreader's paragraph symbol to represent this condition—¶.

As we discussed earlier in reference to the need for graphic analysis, generalizations often play crucial roles in the proof process. As we stated, they are often hidden and sometimes the center of uncertainty in our investigative logic. Because generalizations are based on common-sense assumptions, they are often not supported by evidential proof, so representation by other evidentiary symbols would lead to confusion. However, they are clearly circumstantial arguments by their very definition, and it is imperative that we identify them so that their role in our investigation becomes clear. We will depict generalizations within the chart using the symbol ¥.

This rudimentary set of symbols will allow us to depict certain nodes within the investigative chain—in other words, individual propositions within the overall flow of proof. These nodes of evidence are worthless, in terms of the overall picture, unless we can represent their interrelationship to one another. After all, the power of Bayesian networks and their offspring is in their ability to make visually clear the influence each node has upon the others within the problem space. Enter the simple directional arrow.

Using directionally oriented arrows, we can easily and clearly represent the flow of the theory of proof from one proposition to another. These symbols give us the ability to logically order, graphically, the propositions within our investigative chain. Finally, to our growing basic palette of symbols we will add two final signs.

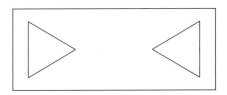

The right- and left-facing vertical triangles will be used to represent lines of logic that detract from our main theory and corroborating lines of logic, respectively. The use and flexibility of these final two symbols will be discussed in more detail later, but for now their introduction to the reader will suffice.

Exhibit 11.8 is a summary of our basic symbol palette.

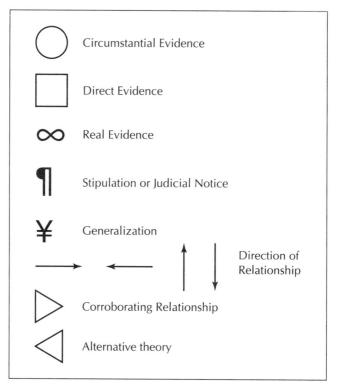

Exhibit 11.8 Basic Symbol Palette

A Word About Supplemental Symbols

One of the most powerful aspects of inferential models is their ability to deal with a variety of different situations. As such, our basic inferential model with its basic symbol palette should be more than adequate to deal with any investigative situation that arises. However, inferential models in general lend themselves well to adaptability. This intrinsic adaptability provides even more flexibility because the basic system can be modified so that new or unique relationships can be illustrated, and their cause, effect, and influence can be graphically plotted.

Given that unique situations might arise in the course of real-world application of investigative inference models, additions and modifications to the basic palette of symbols can be made at any time. For example, certain applications may call for a more well-defined, or specialized, way of representing an alternative theory or explanation. In that case, a new symbol can be introduced to succinctly represent perhaps an alibi, a defendant's argument or affirmative defense, or any other condition that needs greater clarity.

The introduction of the new symbol gives the model more visual impact because it allows the users to immediately recognize lines of argument or investigative flows that relate to that particular condition. A new symbol must meet three requirements: (1) the symbol must be well defined; (2) the symbol must be unique; and (3) its use must be consistent.

If a symbol is introduced without a universally agreed upon definition, confusion instead of clarity will ensue. Similarly, if each symbol represents more than one condition, say circumstantial corroborating evidence and alibi evidence, its visual impact and logical clarity will be lost. Finally, related to uniqueness is consistency.

Consistency allows the user to immediately recognize, from argument to argument, that certain logical propositions are being pursued. By representing each similar logical investigative proposition with the same symbol, immediate recognition will result. Otherwise, the user of the chart will spend needless time examining definitions and symbols trying to internalize a labyrinthine set of variables with no coherent similarity.

Finally, although not a requirement, we highly recommend that any adaptation or expansion of inference models strive for simplicity. The beauty of the graphical representation of complex relationships is lost when the model becomes nearly as complicated as the relationship itself. For that reason, the fewer symbols your system contains, the easier it will be to clearly see the relationship and evaluate their influence upon each other. The goal then, as we see it, should be to accurately represent each unique fact pattern with as few symbols as possible. Avoid superfluity.

SUMMARY

As we have seen in this chapter, our first task, definition of our language, must necessarily set the tone for the analysis process that follows.

Simplicity is the watchword. As we delve deeper into the investigation of inference models as tools for investigators, we ask the reader to bear in mind that the purpose of our newly acquired language is simplification. However, with simplification comes compression. We are, after all, trying to construct a model of a complex, real-world event with eight or nine "words." This is equivalent to attempting to paint a sunset in black and white.

Capturing nuance and subtlety will be difficult, but like anything in life this is a trade-off. We are trading verbosity for clarification of logic. Because our vocabulary is intentionally limited, we must pay careful attention to what we wish to say with our words. A man of limited vocabulary, as long as they are some key, carefully chosen words, can communicate very effectively, albeit less eloquently, as long as he thinks logically and plans his speech carefully. It is this planning and choice of phrasing that we will encounter in the next chapter.

As you will hopefully see in the next chapter, clarification of logic depends on how well we can deconstruct our phrases. As we encounter complex causal theories and long chains of inference, we must strive to decompose them into simple statements capable of expression with our limited vocabulary. The process of deconstruction and restatement enables us to both think critically about the legitimacy of our logical propositions and to visualize the natural flow of the investigative process. These by-products of the investigative inference model alone make the investment of time worthwhile.

The concept of the key list underpins the implementation process. By carefully constructing a key list comprised of simple propositions and inferences broken down into their most rudimentary elements, the actual charting phase becomes simply a matter of plotting symbols following the defined syntax of our new language. It is the mechanical translation of simple phrases into our new language. The analysis therefore predominantly occurs during the key list preparation phase since the task of preparation necessarily forces the investigator to completely digest the premise of the case and think through exactly what it is that is being said.

The power of the chart becomes evident when it becomes clear that the investigator has not exactly said what he has set out to do either, because his logic is faulty or, if his logic is sound, because the distance between the inferential steps is weak and the conclusion does not necessarily follow from the premise. Either way, the investigative stage is the optimal stage in which to identify and correct both types of error.

NOTES

1. T. Anderson and W. Twining, *Analysis of Evidence: How to Do Things with Facts Based on Wigmore's Science of Judicial Proof* (Evanston, IL: Northwestern University Press, 1991), pp. 57–59, 89–91.
2. L. Lessig, "The Regulation of Social Meaning," *University of Chicago Law Review* 62(1995): 952.
3. K. Murphy, *A Brief Introduction to Graphical Models and Bayesian Networks*. Retrieved February 3, 2003, from the University of California, Berkeley, Computer Science Division Website: *www.cs.berkeley, edu/~murphyk/Bayes/bayes.html*.
4. Despite the name, not all Bayesian networks necessarily adhere strictly to the principles of Bayes's theory. Bayes's theory is a mathematical technique that allows scientists to combine and test data with prior hypotheses and observations to arrive at a new probabilistic prediction of cause and effect. It was first propounded by Thomas Bayes, an eighteenth-century Presbyterian minister.
5. Murphy, *A Brief Introduction to Graphical Models and Bayesian Networks*.
6. Unfortunately for users, the decision-making framework for *when* the paperclip appears is not based upon Bayesian theory, but instead upon a relaxed, non-Bayesian algorithm that allows the paperclip to pop up with more frequency—and concomitant annoyance to most users.
7. "Son of Paperclip," *The Economist* (electronic version), March 22, 2001.
8. See, generally, J.H. Wigmore, *The Principles of Judicial Proof: As Given by Logic, Psychology, and General Experience and Illustrated in Judicial Trials* (Littleton, CO: Fred B. Rothman & Co., 1988).
9. Anderson and Twining, *Analysis of Evidence*, pp. 47–48.
10. Ibid., pp. 120–21.
11. Ibid., pp. 50–51.
12. Ibid., pp. 56–57.
13. Ibid., p. 57

SUGGESTED READINGS

Allen, R.J. "The Nature of Juridical Proof." *Cardozo Law Review*, 13 (1991); 373–401.

Allen, R.J., and A. Carriquiry. "Factual Ambiguity and a Theory of Evidence Reconsidered: A Dialogue Between a Statistician and a Law Professor." *Israel Law Review*, vol. 31, nos. 1–3 (1997): 464.

Binder, D., and P. Bergman. *Fact Investigation: From Hypothesis to Proof.* St. Paul, Minn.: West Publishing, 1999.

Cohen, L.J. *The Introduction to the Philosophy of Induction and Probability.* New York: Oxford University Press, 1989.

Finkelstein, M., and W. Fairly. "A Bayesian Approach to Identification Evidence." *Harvard Law Review*, 83 (1970): 489–517.

Franklin, J. *The Science of Conjecture: Evidence and Probability Before Pascal.* Baltimore, MD: Johns Hopkins University Press, 2001.

Hastie, R., and N. Pennington. "The O.J. Simpson Stories: Behavioral Scientists' Reflections on *The People of the State of California v. Orenthal James Simpson,*." *University of Colorado Law Review*, 67 (1996): 957–976.

Huygen, P.E.M. "Use of Bayesian Belief Networks in Legal Reasoning." Presented at 17th BILETA Annual Conference, Amsterdam: Computer Law Institute, 2002.

"In Praise of Bayes." Retrieved March 25, 2003, from the University of California, Berkeley, Computer Science Division website, September 30, 2000: *www.ai.mit.edu/~murphyk/Bayes/economist.html.*

Josephson, J., and S.G. Josephson. *Abductive Inference Computation, Philosophy, and Technology.* New York: Cambridge University Press, 1994.

Kadane, J., and D.A. Schum. *A Probabilistic Analysis of the Sacco and Vanzetti Evidence.* New York: John Wiley & Sons, 1996.

Kaye, D.H. "Bayes, Burdens and Base Rates." *International Journal of Evidence and Proof*, 4, no. 4 (2000): 260–267.

Kaye, D.H., and J.J. Koehler. "Can Jurors Understand Probabilistic Evidence?" *Journal of the Royal Statistical Society*, Series A, 154, part 1 (1991): 75–81.

Koehler, J.J. "The Base Rate Fallacy Myth." *Psycoloquy*, 4, Article 93.4.49. Retrieved March 13, 2003, from *www.monash.edu.au/journals/psycoloquy/volume_4/psyc.93.4.49.base-rate.1.koehler.*

Lempert, R., S. Gross, and J. Liebman. *A Modern Approach to Evidence.* St. Paul, Minn.: West Publishing, 2000.

Leonhardt, D. "Adding Art to the Rigor of Statistical Science." *The New York Times* (electronic version), April 28, 2001.

MacCrimmon, M. "What Is "Common" About Common Sense?: Cautionary Tales for Travelers Crossing Disciplinary Boundaries." *Cardozo Law Review*, 22 (2001): 1433–1460.

Pennington, N., and R. Hastie. "A Cognitive Theory of Juror Decision Making: The Story Model." *Cardozo Law Review*, 13 (1991): 519–530.

Robertson, B., and G.A. Vignaux. *Interpreting Evidence: Evaluating Forensic Science in the Courtroom.* New York: John Wiley & Sons, 1995.

Saks, M.J., and R.F. Kidd. "Human Information Processing and Adjudication: Trial by Heuristics." *Law and Society Review*, 15 (1980): 123–160.

Schafer, G. *The Art of Causal Conjecture.* Cambridge, MA: MIT Press, 1996.

Schum, D.A. "Alternative Views of Argument Construction from a Mass of Evidence." *Cardozo Law Review*, 22 (2001): 1461–1502.

Schum, D.A. *Evidential Foundations of Probabilistic Reasoning.* New York: John Wiley & Sons, 1994.

Schum, D.A. *The Evidential Foundations of Probabilistic Reasoning.* Evanston, IL: Northwestern University Press, 2001.

Schum, D.A. "Marshaling Thoughts and Evidence During Fact Investigation." *Southern Texas Law Review*, 40 (2001): 401–454.

Schum, D.A. "Species of Abductive Reasoning in Fact Investigation." *Cardozo Law Review*, 22 (2001): 1645–1681.

Schum, D.A., and P. Tillers. "Marshaling Evidence for Adversary Litigation." *Cardozo Law Review*, 12 (1991): 657–704.

Thagard, P. "Probabilistic Networks and Explanatory Coherence." In P. O'Rourke and J. Josephson, eds., *Automated Abduction: Inference to the Best Explanation.* Menlo Park: AAAI Press, 1997.

Tillers, P. "Webs of Things in the Mind: A New Science of Evidence." *Michigan Law Review*, 87 (1989): 1225–1265.

Tillers, P., and D. Schum. "Charting New Territory in Judicial Proof Beyond Wigmore." *Cardozo Law Review*, 9 (1988): 907–950.

Wagenaar, W.A. "The Proper Seat: A Bayesian Discussion of the Position of Expert Witnesses." *Law and Human Behavior*, 12 (1988): 499–510.

Walker, V. R. "Theories of Uncertainty: Explaining the Possible Sources of Error in Inferences." *Cardozo Law Review*, 22 (2001): 1523–1570.

12

IMPLEMENTING THE INVESTIGATIVE INFERENCE MODEL

INTRODUCTION

As we noted in Chapter 11, the key to the investigative inference model is careful definition of our language, coupled with a detailed examination of what we wish to say. In this chapter, the reader will discover that every proposition or conclusion must be a natural inference from the previous proposition. This rule holds true even where generalizations are concerned. Shortly, we will explore a hypothetical case that will hopefully point out the devious way that generalizations creep into even the simplest conclusions.

We will also discover that the implementation of the investigative inference is a reflexive and intuitive process. This is both the nature of the beast and one of its strengths. By constantly reevaluating the status of the investigation while preparing the key list and plotting the chart, the investigator is forced to reexamine each and every underlying assumption and logical conclusion. The process of examination, formulation, reevaluation, and restatement must occur from beginning to end in order to have a functional and helpful model. We begin our implementation by creating our key list.

THE KEY LIST

As we have said, the beauty of graphic models lies in their simplicity. This simplicity is lost when the model contains more information than is absolutely necessary. For this reason, the key to effective investigative management with inference models is the "key list." The key list is a list or database, depending on the complexity of the case, that contains a numerically indexed list of propositions and evidence. Each entry in the key list, therefore, corresponds to an individual node in the model.

By using the key list and model in tandem, every proposition is cross-referenced and represented on the chart. Later, as we will see in the next chapter, the key list may be used to organize and order your evidence for presentation to whoever must be persuaded.

Although we have introduced the concept of the key list after introducing the model itself, in reality, key list preparation comes first. It is from the key list that the actual model is constructed and the propositions are charted.

The process of developing the key list and organizing its elements is both reflexive and somewhat intuitive. It is reflexive in that it requires constant revision. It is intuitive in that each element in the key list should be relevant to the ultimate proposition to be proven. This task is not always easy, since deciding what is relevant is sometimes the product of inductive and deductive reasoning. Because these are the very processes we are striving to pin down, there is the constant risk that your key list will be either overly inclusive or overly restrictive.

Given the choice between the two, it is preferred that, at least during the initial phases of the investigation, you err on the side of over inclusiveness. It is much easier to redact superfluous references on the key list later after their irrelevance becomes clear than it is to follow nonexistent lines of logic that your under-inclusive key list has eliminated early on. An under-inclusive key list will obscure productive lines of inquiry and is the graphic equivalent of tunnel vision in investigations.

What then do we include on our key list? Simply, anything that tends to prove or disprove the ultimate fact in issue. This is precisely where the ultimate and penultimate probanda we introduced in Chapter 10 becomes crucial. Our key list has a direct relationship between the ultimate probandum and the investigation. Using the ultimate probandum, we examine the evidence that is in existence and organize it into lines of argument leading up to the final ultimate probandum. Let's examine the creation of a key list using a hypothetical crime as follows:

A Hypothetical

Frank's landlady entered Frank's apartment to collect the rent and found him lying in a pool of blood on the floor of his bathroom with a single gunshot wound to the head. A .38 caliber revolver was lying 3 feet from Frank's body. A neighbor observed Frank's girlfriend, JoAnn, enter Frank's apartment at 4:00 P.M. on the day of the murder. The UPS driver observed a woman matching Frank's girlfriend's description leave his apartment at 5:30 P.M. that same day. A gun shot was heard in the area of Frank's apartment at 5:10 P.M. JoAnn's best friend stated that JoAnn was planning to break up with Frank after she found out that Frank had slept with another woman. Responding officers located an apparent handwritten suicide note, covered in blood and signed in Frank's name.

As discussed in Chapter 10, our ultimate probandum is the ultimate fact that we are attempting to prove. The penultimate probanda are, therefore, the component sub-facts that must be proven in order to prove the ultimate fact. As an example, we will construct an ultimate probandum as follows: "JoAnn murdered Frank." We must break this ultimate fact down further, however. The penultimate probandum for this scenario could be stated as three sub-facts as follows: "Frank is dead;" "Frank did not die of natural causes," and "it was JoAnn who killed him". Now, using our first four statements, we can begin to assemble our key list.

Beginning the Construction of Our Key List

The first statement in our key list is "JoAnn murdered Frank." This statement is assigned no. 1, since it is the starting point of our inquiry. We follow this statement with our penultimate probanda, "Frank is dead," "Frank was murdered," and "it was JoAnn who killed him," nos. 2, 3, and 4, respectively. Next, our intuitive abilities and our deductive and inductive reasoning skills get a workout.

It will most likely be easiest to begin by analyzing the supporting propositions underlying probandum no. 2. (We have syntactically switched the structure of the sentence to place "Frank is dead," grammatically before "JoAnn murdered him," since arguably[1] it will be easier to prove that Frank is in fact dead than to prove that JoAnn killed him. This allows us to logically assign Frank's death to proposition no. 2 in our key list—not a requirement but as a matter of housekeeping, more orderly.) Using this proposition, we must look for the supporting evidence to prove it.

Since there is a body, we will likely have a wealth of evidence from which we can support our proposition. The medical examiner will likely have responded, or at least conducted a subsequent *post mortem* examination of Frank. Given that, she will be in a position to testify regarding Frank's state of health. We now have proposition no. 5, "Medical examiner Jones reports that Frank is dead." In creating our key list, it is important that trivial steps such as making explicit the medical examiner's testimony not be overlooked. Similarly, it is important to make distinctions between various forms of evidentiary support. For example, although the medical examiner will undoubtedly testify at trial, the basis for her testimony will be her report on the autopsy. Therefore, it is imperative that we include in our key list an entry for the autopsy report. Attention to detail in this regard can make the difference between productive analysis and time-wasting exercises.

After making this adjustment, we renumber our key list (an example of the reflexive nature of this type of analysis). Medical examiner Jones's testimony is now no. 6, and the autopsy report is no. 5. Given this simple scenario, the line of logic is easy to visualize in our heads. If all cases were this simple, an investigative inference would be unnecessary. After all, "Frank is dead" is proven by the autopsy report, which is authenticated by Dr. Jones's testimonial evidence. This is a short, straight—as opposed to a bifurcated—line of logic, with very little room for inferential error. As you will see, not all lines of exploration in our simple example will be so straightforward.

Having "proven," or at least built a chain of inferences that tends to convince us that Frank is in fact dead, we can turn our attention to the more difficult task of proving that he was both murdered and that JoAnn did it. But first, here is our key list as it looks now (Exhibit 12.1):

```
#1  -  JoAnn murdered Frank.
#2  -  Frank is dead.
#3  -  Frank was murdered.
#4  -  JoAnn did it.
#5  -  Autopsy report—Frank is dead.
#6  -  Dr. Jones's testimony "Frank is dead."
```

Exhibit 12.1 Initial Key List

Because we have phrased proposition no. 3, "he did not die of natural causes," proposition no. 7 becomes "Frank died of a gunshot wound."

Again, given the evidence with which we are confronted, we may or may not be more certain than not that Frank was murdered. If there is uncertainty, as here, then both propositions must be charted in order to avoid tunnel vision and false conclusions. The problem with this is that the propositions, "Frank was shot by someone else" and "Frank committed suicide," appear to be irreconcilable propositions; they cannot coexist in a logical world. How, then, do we represent them in our key list?

At this stage, we do not have to worry about dealing with this polemic. We simply list both opposing propositions in the key list and address it later during the charting phase. The two propositions become no. 8, "Frank was shot," and no. 9, "The gunshot wound is self-inflicted."

Expanding Our Key List

We have now listed the ultimate and penultimate probanda in our scenario. Next, we must scour the hypothetical, or in the real world evaluate our evidence, and extract from it the remaining evidentiary propositions that naturally flow from the facts—including generalizations. In compiling our key list, the remaining order, or the initial order for that matter, is not of great consequence. However, for cosmetic purposes and for purposes of readability, deconstructing the ultimate and penultimate probanda and assigning them numbers first are usually best.

From the remaining facts of our hypothetical we can cull the following additional evidentiary points:

10. Landlady discovered body in bathroom.
11. Body was in bathroom.
12. Landlady's testimony.
13. Frank was killed in the bathroom.
14. Frank was killed with a gun.
15. Witness no. 1 saw JoAnn enter the apartment at 4:00 P.M. on day of murder.
16. Witness no. 1's testimony.
17. Witness no. 2 heard a gunshot in the area at about 5:10 P.M.
18. Witness no. 2's testimony.
19. Witness no. 3 saw a woman matching JoAnn's description leave Frank's apartment around 5:30 P.M.
20. Witness no. 3's testimony.
21. JoAnn was at Frank's apartment at 5:10 P.M.
22. Frank died at 5:10 P.M.
23. People who have strong motives act on them.

24. Jealousy is a strong motive.

25. JoAnn was jealous.

26. Frank was cheating on JoAnn.

27. Witness no. 4's testimony about Frank's cheating and plans to break it off with JoAnn.

28. Frank was planning to break up with JoAnn.

Invariably, the reader has picked out some propositions and generalizations that we may have overlooked or excluded from this list. Although thoroughness is important, at this stage an exhaustive listing is not necessary. As you will see, there is room for addition, refinement, and deletion as our hypothesis is tested during our investigation.

Speaking of hypothesis, it is clear from the facts that a hypothesis emerges that may explain the sequence of events that led up to Frank's untimely demise. In fact, two competing hypotheses emerge with relatively equal strength. The first implicates JoAnn, and the second exonerates her.

The Role of the Key List in Hypothesis Formulation

All experienced investigators formulate working hypotheses at very early stages of the investigation. The formation of a hypothesis allows us to explain observations, test theories, and propose cause and affect relationships based on the two forms of reasoning. For example, in our scenario our primary hypothesis is probably that on the date in question, JoAnn came to Frank's apartment to confront him about his philandering ways. Unhappy with his infidelity and in a fit of jealous rage, she shot him with a .38 caliber revolver. Realizing the consequences of her action, she hastily scribbled a suicide note and fled the apartment shortly thereafter. This is a believable theory, fully supported by the evidence. Our job during the investigative process will be to test this hypothesis using the reasoning process and our inference model. But first, we must construct our model using the evidence we have gathered so far.

PLOTTING THE CHART

If you have carefully crafted your ultimate and penultimate probanda, and diligently constructed your key list, the plotting of the inference chart should be largely a straightforward matter. However, if you have not given enough consideration to the formulation of your penultimate probanda, or you have slighted the compilation of your key list, plotting the chart will become very tedious and cumbersome.

Because in our example we have carefully considered our ultimate and penultimate probanda, we can chart, at least the top level, with relative ease. It is here that we combine the language of our system with the logic of our hypothesis.

Plotting the Ultimate and Penultimate Probanda

Using our symbols, we must represent each numbered item in our key list and connect them, logically, with each other in order to form a logical chain proceeding to the conclusion that JoAnn murdered Frank.

We start with our ultimate probandum—"JoAnn murdered Frank." This must be proven circumstantially. After all, there is no eyewitness that links JoAnn to the actual act of killing Frank. Therefore, we represent the ultimate probanda, no. 1 on our key list, with a circle from our symbol palette.

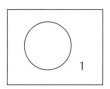

Next, we plot the relationship between the ultimate probanda and the penultimate probandum—numbers 2, 3, and 4—as shown in Exhibit 12.2.

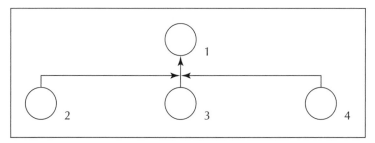

Exhibit 12.2 Relationship of Ultimate and Penultimate Probanda

Ultimately, if we can prove nos. 2, 3, and 4, we can prove no. 1.

Plotting Supporting Probanda

As we discussed earlier, proving no. 2 depends on testimony from Dr. Jones relating to her autopsy of Frank and the resulting autopsy report. The underlying propositions for this node of the chart would look like the illustration in Exhibit 12.3.

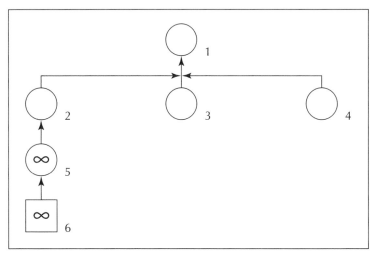

Exhibit 12.3 Underlying Propositions

In Exhibit 12.3, nodes no. 5 and no. 6 represent Dr. Jones' s autopsy report and her testimony, respectively. As such, the symbol depicting real evidence is placed inside the nodes. This makes it clear that some physical evidence exists that supports that inference. In node no. 5, it is the actual autopsy report. In node no. 6, it is Dr. Jones's testimony. Similarly, Dr. Jones's testimony is depicted using the direct evidence symbol. Although Dr. Jones is not a witness to the murder itself, she is a direct witness who will testify to the ultimate fact relative to Frank's state of health, that is, his death. Inasmuch as the analysis of our case reveals that no further decomposition of this line of argument is necessary, our charting for node no. 2 is complete.

Charting Alternative Theories

Charting the relationship of the sub-facts to probandum no. 3 is very similar.

The reader should note the use of the alternative theory symbol (>) in Exhibit 12.4. As we stated earlier, Frank's death could have been caused by a self-inflicted gunshot wound.

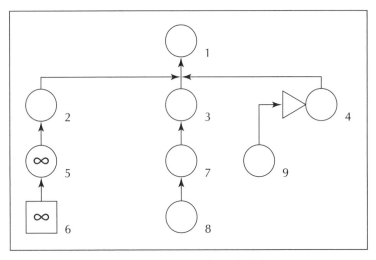

Exhibit 12.4 Relationship of Subfacts

Since proposition no. 4 stands for the assertion that Frank's unnatural death was caused by JoAnn, we need to represent the competing hypotheses that would explain the origin of the gunshot wound as self-inflicted. Proposition no. 9 (Frank's wound was self-inflicted) offers an alternative theory, as such. We can chart this possibility using the ">" sign to denote an alternative cause of the gunshot wound. As we uncover new evidence and test new subhypotheses, we can add nodes onto either chain until one or the other appears the more likely of the two explanations.

Charting the Remainder of Our Hypothetical

Charting the relationships between the evidence and our hypothesis continues until all the items in our key list have been worked into our inference model. As we proceed down the key list, we determine which probandum the evidence tends to support—which ultimate fact in question it is most relevant to proving or disproving—and then plot it in the logical chain leading up to that fact. Appendix A shows the completed key list and inference chart for this hypothetical.

We urge the reader to examine the chart in the Appendix and note the use of the various symbols and how we charted each proposition within the key list. For example, note that many propositions listed in the key list might, at first, appear overly simplistic, such as the two statements "Frank was killed with a gun" and "Frank died of other than natural causes." These two statements seem redundant and an almost simpleton-like statement of the obvious. In our example, these two statements are so naturally obvious that charting them seems somehow obsessive. It is precisely this type of attention to detail and deconstruction of the logic of argument and reasoning that makes inference models effective tools for investigative tasks. Because the proposition "Frank died of other than natural causes" is a natural inference flowing from the proof that he was killed with a gun, our example seems obvious. If the logic were faulty, or the premise were not so universally accepted, our chart would point it out.

An example of this may be seen when we begin to examine the underlying generalizations in our chart. When we examine the underlying logic of proposition no. 4 (JoAnn killed Frank), we see that inferences no. 21, 20, and 25 are fairly straightforward—JoAnn was at Frank's apartment at 5:10 P.M., Frank was killed at 5:10 P.M., and Frank was killed in his apartment, respectively. Inference no. 22, however, is less obvious but just as necessary to prove in order to develop probable cause to believe that JoAnn did it.

We have charted no. 22 as the proposition that "People who have a strong motive to act, usually act." This proposition goes directly to JoAnn's motive for killing Frank (jealousy) and, though not an element of the crime, certainly constitutes relevant evidence of intent. Wouldn't it have been just as easy, and required two fewer inferential steps, to simply list proposition no. 24, JoAnn killed Frank out of jealousy, alongside no. 25? This answer is easier, but not as accurate.

Simply stated, the beauty of the inference model is contained in its ability to help identify fallacies of logic. This requires recognition of *all* underlying generalizations—step by step. Propositions no. 22 and 23 are broad generalizations regarding jealousy and their effect on human behavior. If either generalization in this case does not hold true, the force of our evidentiary chain leading up to JoAnn is destroyed. If the generalization that jealousy is a strong enough motive to make someone murder is not universally accepted—at least by the universe that comprises our fact finding world—then all propositions and inferences that flow from it crumble.

When we conflate the logical steps into one sweeping statement such as JoAnn killed Frank out of jealousy, we are stating what we wish to prove. We are, however, glossing over what we must ultimately convince the jury of—the fact that human jealousy is a sufficient motive for murder—in order to make our larger proposition believable.

In obvious arguments such as this one, the damage may be minimal. In this case, fortunately, there are several remaining inferences that seem to point equally toward JoAnn as the guilty party. The reader, however, could easily imagine a situation in which this is not the case. Getting into the habit of carefully deconstructing each proposition into its component generalizations is good practice and can serve the investigator well when truly tenuous leaps of logic are encountered.

Ultimately, we may be faced with a situation where an item in the key list may tend to support or disprove more than one penultimate probanda. For example, no. 5, the autopsy report, would logically be valuable in both establishing that Frank was dead as well as the cause of Frank's death. Similarly, Dr. Jones will likely be a necessary witness to both elements of our penultimate probanda. This is not a problem. The flexibility of our model allows for this type of redundancy. In fact, the ability for a proposition to appear in more than one place is a crucial element in this model's flexibility. We simply re-plot that item in its proper place within the inferential chain in which it is a support element.

As we stated, plotting is a relatively intuitive process. As such, individual investigators will often develop charts with different lines of logic reaching the same conclusion. Neither investigator is necessarily more correct nor more accurately describes the investigative effort more clearly—it is simply a matter of approaching the same problem from different perspectives.

In fact, if you were to plot our key list independent of this chapter, you would likely arrive at the same destination through an alternative route. As long as the logic that underlies the inferential steps within each segment of the chart is sound, there are a large number of "correct" charts.

SOME TIPS FOR CHARTING SUCCESS

Charting the model is an inherently personal process exhibiting a great deal about the reasoning process of each individual investigator. And, as we stated above, successful conclusions may be reached via any number of routes. However, a few key notions need to be considered when charting the investigation—especially where the investigation is complex.

Top Down

First, try and chart from the top down. Although there is no hard and fast rule governing the best pattern to use, top-down charting offers some advantages. It has a more intuitive feel because you are thinking from general to specific. You are working from the general statement about who killed Frank, down to the most minute detail such as the gun was found 3 feet from the body.

Top-down charting also allows you to visually plan the chart more efficiently. By using top-down methodology, your physical layout of the chart becomes more apparent. Invariably, you will end up squeezing new probanda into tight spaces in the end, but using the top-down paradigm tends to reduce the necessity of squeezing in new probanda.

Modular Charting

Second, plot the chart in segments. Using a modular approach to plotting makes organization, layout, and planning much easier. For example, in plotting our chart it would be a perfectly legitimate strategy to plot inferences no. 1, 2, 3, and 9 on page one. Under inference no. 2, the remaining two inferences could be listed; however, under no. 3, 4, and 9 a cross-reference would point us to pages 2, 3, and 4. On page 2 we can plot all the inferences leading up to conclusion no. 3, on page 3 we plot all the inferences leading up to inference no. 4, and similarly, on page 4 we can plot the inference leading up to the counter-probandum (Frank committed suicide) no. 9. Modularity makes for a less crowded, simpler looking chart. After all, simplicity and ease of visual reference are our goals.

Finally, as we have seen in our example, charting complex investigative problems often requires duplication of nodes. In our hypothetical, both Dr. Jones's autopsy report (and attendant testimony) are valuable to proving more than one proposition. Similarly, the responding officer's observations and crime scene search are necessary to prove some physical aspects of the scene. As such, these items will necessarily appear in more than one area of the chart. It is, therefore, imperative that a common number apply to all instances of that witness's testimony appearing on the chart. In other words, do not switch numbers on the same witness in the middle of the chart. If Dr. Jones appears under no. 6 in segment 1 of the chart, she must, for clarity's sake, remain no. 6 for the remainder of the chart.

APPLYING THE CHART TO THE INVESTIGATIVE PROCESS

Once the chart is completed, or at least the initial chart is completed, the focus turns to how we synthesize it into the overall investigative process. As a reasoning tool, the chart can be used to help clarify where your case is and where it needs to go.

Using our model, we can test our assumptions about how the events unfolded. For example, in our hypothetical, if we wish to explore the possibility that Frank committed suicide, we could examine the inferences leading up to node no. 9 in order to test our logic. The self-inflicted gunshot wound and the evidence of a suicide note logically lead us to deduce that Frank may have killed himself. Reasoning from the evidence to the conclusion is common in investigating a crime. Abductively, however, our model can offer us other avenues of assistance, avenues that may in the long run help us uncover more clues or eliminate one of several competing hypotheses.

Instead of following the logic from the bottom to the top, we select a proposition or inference, and we propose underlying logic to support it. For example, in inference no. 9 we propose that Frank's death was suicide. In this mode, we ask ourselves if, in fact, Frank committed suicide, what would we expect to find? Our example already identifies a fair number of evidentiary facts that support suicide. However, if it did not, we would be forced to think about what *should* have been found.

One such undiscovered item might be gunshot residue (GSR). Under normal conditions, any person who fires a handgun deposits trace amounts of metals on their hands and clothing. The explosive nature of a bullet's discharge causes burning particles to embed themselves in the surrounding soft tissue and cloth. These deposits are often undetectable with the human eye and the shooter is rarely ever cognizant of their existence. Nonetheless, chemical tests can conclusively demonstrate the existence of GSR.[2]

In our hypothetical, if Frank had inflicted his own gunshot wound, logically we should find GSR on his hands, his clothing, or both. Taking this process one step further, we would also be forced to examine and propose an evidentiary proposition concerning Frank's "handedness." Was Frank left-handed or right-handed?

Depending on the trajectory and entry angle of the bullet, Frank's natural proclivity to one hand or the other could prove significant. If we lack evidence regarding this line of logic, the reasoning process, assisted by our inference model, will urge us into an evidence search and recovery mode. If we find evidence to support this proposition, we chart the outcome as a corroborating factor—or at least as an additional supporting inference alongside proposition no. 44.

Conversely, if we fail to find evidence where logic tells us we should, we can chart that as either an alternative proposition (suicide as an alternative explanation for Frank's unnatural death) or as a corroborating factor supporting an alternative proposition.

Either way, we have laid bare the underlying logic of our case, examined what we know critically, and tested the hypothesis. In the process, we have discovered new evidence and moved the case forward drastically.

In the investigative stages of a case, the inference model proves an invaluable tool in directing and organizing the efforts of one or more investigators. Its assistance does not end there. As the reader will see in the next chapter, the inference model's life cycle does not end once the case has been solved and an arrest has been made: quite the opposite in fact.

As we have said repeatedly—and the reader is no doubt tired of hearing—the power of graphic inferences lies in their ability to organize large volumes of mixed evidence. As indispensable as this characteristic is during an investigation, it is even more so while documenting the investigation.

As we proceed to Chapter 13, which deals with documenting the investigation, and Chapter 14, which focuses on courtroom presentation, we hope that the value of the inference model as a reference tool, demonstrative exhibit, and debriefing tool will become more obvious. For now, we trust that the reader's curiosity and appetite have been piqued.

SUMMARY

At this point, the reader may be thinking that our inference model was all well and good for proving that JoAnn killed Frank. Or perhaps the more astute reader is thinking that we have not proven that JoAnn killed Frank, but have merely built a chain of inferences that leads us to believe that it is at least more likely than not that JoAnn killed Frank. But this is a text on economic crime, so how can this model possibly apply?

We have used the case of JoAnn and Frank to illustrate the effectiveness of inference models simply because the fact pattern is very straightforward and easily adaptable to our purposes and limited space. Simply stated, we used murder as our crime of choice based on the simplicity of the act and the fact that murder is, unfortunately, a crime with which most people are familiar. We could have detailed the process of constructing a key list and inference model for an act of embezzlement from company XYZ. However, to adapt that fact pattern would have required a longer chapter and more complex logical propositions. Instead, we have left that task up to you, the reader.

As you digest the theories and techniques to which you have been introduced, attempt to apply them to your own knowledge of economic crime. Experiment with the elements of the economic crime with which you are most familiar. State the crime in the form of a simple ultimate probandum and work at breaking it down into its component propositions. We believe that, as you do, your understanding of the concepts introduced will rapidly gel, and you will soon realize the power you now possess for detailed analysis and deconstruction of even the most complex scheme: Instead of listing the medical examiner, you will list the records custodian or the bank teller, but the underlying principles remain the same.

As this seedling of knowledge grows, you will come to appreciate the power of the concept of modularity and segmented charting as it applies to complex economic crimes involving large masses of documentary evidence. By charting discrete propositions and their supporting inferences and documentation as individual charts and cross-referencing them, the organization of your case will rapidly improve; and along with it your ability to succinctly summarize and oversee your case will also be enhanced.

NOTES

1. We say "arguably" because prosecutions for murder have been known to proceed, more or less successfully, lacking a *corpus dilecti*. In that case, proving Frank's death would be a matter of proving, largely through circumstantial evidence, that he is in fact deceased, which might be difficult to do without a body.
2. S.H. James and J.J. Norby, eds., *Forensic Science: An Introduction to Scientific and Investigative Techniques* (Boca Raton, FL: CRC Press, 2003), pp. 272–273, 344–347.

SUGGESTED READINGS

Anderson, T., and W. Twining. *Analysis of Evidence: How to Do Things with Facts Based on Wigmore's Science of Judicial Proof.* Evanston, IL: Northwestern University Press, 1991.

Murphy, K. *A Brief Introduction to Graphical Models and Bayesian Networks.* 2001. Retrieved February 3, 2003, from the University of California, Berkeley, Computer Science Division Web Site: *http://www.cs.berkeley.edu/~murphyk/Bayes/bayes.html.*

Schum, D.A. "Alternative Views of Argument Construction from a Mass of Evidence." *Cardozo Law Review,* 22 (2001): 1461–1502.

Schum, D.A. "Marshaling Thoughts and Evidence During Fact Investigation." *Southern Texas Law Review,* 40 (2001): 401–454.

Schum, D.A., and P. Tillers. "Marshaling Evidence for Adversary Litigation." *Cardozo Law Review,* 13 (1991: 657–704.

Wigmore, J.H. *The Principles of Judicial Proof As Given by Logic, Psychology, and General Experience and Illustrated in Judicial Trials.* Littleton, CO: Fred B. Rothman & Co., 1988.

13

DOCUMENTING THE
INVESTIGATION

INTRODUCTION

In the last few chapters we introduced the reader to a powerful organization and analysis tool—the investigative inference model. The model's utility, however, is limited by the investigator's ability to quickly and accurately retrieve the underlying facts and data on which the key list and chart are based. Without the ability to put your hands on the evidence supporting the conclusion, or to identify the witness who will testify for a particular proposition, the model is nothing more than an elaborate flowchart. To be effective, it must be related directly to the process of prosecution. The most efficient model in the world will be useless to us if we have to wade through several stacks of paper on our desk in order to find the specific document necessary to prove a particular proposition. We must have ease of retrieval.

To achieve this ease of retrieval, we must integrate our inference model with an organizational system. The organizational system must fulfill some basic requirements. First, the system must have a direct correlation between the underlying data and the model. In other words, we must be able to directly reference each node within our chart from our system and vice versa. Second, the system must be easy to implement. With ease of implementation, consistent use of an organization tool becomes more likely. Third, the system must be flexible—it must be able to expand or contract in complexity according to the nature of the case at hand. Rigidity limits the application of the system to only those particular types of cases for which it was originally designed. It is important that the system be just as applicable to drug investigations as it is to murder investigations. And fourth, the system must be scalable.

Scalability, much like flexibility, allows our system some degree of portability. What flexibility is to various *types* of cases, scalability is to the size and complexity of cases. Implementation of our system must be as easy for a complicated racketeering scheme as it is for a small employee theft.

Keeping these four primary requirements in mind, we have borrowed from the toolkit of experienced trial lawyers and adapted the casebook system to the investigative arena.

THE CASEBOOK SYSTEM

Like investigation, trial preparation is fluid, often complicated, and always a time-consuming endeavor. For this reason, lawyers have searched for tools in order to minimize the time necessary to prepare for trial and prosecute a case. Behind this search has always been the principle that coherence must be assembled from chaos, and immediate access to coherent information must be maintained. The transition from trial preparation to prosecution must be seamless. The product of this search is the trial book, sometimes referred to as the casebook.[1]

Basically, the casebook is nothing more than an organizational tool. It is a central repository for everything that is known about your case. From preliminary reports through final disposition, the casebook catalogues and organizes everything in the life cycle of the investigation. It is both the index to, and the body of work resulting from, your ongoing investigative efforts.

In practice, the trial book[2] is often prepared during the final stage of pre-trial preparation. It is often seen as a way to pull everything together into a coherent unit and organize the evidence in a logical way, given the anticipated needs of a trial. As such, it is introduced relatively late in the life cycle of the case—that is not to say that the experienced litigator ignores the trial book until the last minute, but simply that the book itself is often compiled late in the case.

From an investigative standpoint, this approach is inefficient. Instead, initiating the casebook system at the time the initial case report is received will organize your investigation into a much more efficient and focused undertaking. Every investigation, of course, could benefit from a greater focus at the outset. If nothing else, beginning your casebook preparation at the outset forces you to examine the case closely and helps identify goals early on (for goal setting in investigations, please refer to Chapter 8).

Direct Correlation

As we have stated, the first requirement of our organization system is relatedness. In other words, we must have a direct, easily identifiable link between our model and our information. At the heart of this correlative capacity is a robust cross-reference capability. Everything within the purview of the case is indexed and cross-referenced in a way that allows immediate and intuitive access to it.

For example, if a witness appears on our inference chart, it is imperative that the casebook contains an entry that both summarizes the witness's involvement and directs the investigator to additional contributions or follow-up requirements. Therefore, we must develop a consistent system of indexing and cross-reference.

Ease of Implementation

From the beginning, the casebook is a filing system. Implementation of the filing system will occur immediately. Once you recognize that your case has the potential to benefit from greater organization, you should establish the casebook as the main source of investigative documentation. Because this method is essentially nothing more than a filing system, implementing it should be fairly straightforward. The most difficult facet of implementation will probably be to discipline oneself constantly to maintain the system.

The casebook system does not contain any complicated strategies, nor does it require a lengthy "learning curve" in order to comprehend the method behind the madness. Instead, it is quite straightforward and requires no more effort than any other system for maintaining a group of files.

Flexibility

Flexibility is built into the system. Because it is nothing more than a filing system that is diligently indexed, it may contain any number of different types of evidentiary matter. From a filing and indexing standpoint, there is no material difference between a murder weapon and a canceled check. Both must be indexed, and both qualify as evidentiary items. The only difference is what they tend to prove—or disprove—and where our charting process may place them within our investigative framework.

For this reason, the casebook system contains all the flexibility necessary for cross-disciplinary application. Whether you are investigating traditional Organized Crime Network (OCN) activity, or a phantom employee payroll scam, the casebook system will efficiently track and organize all the evidence necessary to plan and complete your investigation.

Scalability

The casebook system of investigative organization is not a commercial product. Nor is it the brainchild of any particular individual or group. It is really nothing more than the application of a concept to the process of problem solution. In this case, the problem is concise organization of a large mass of evidence and information. Because we are not advocating a particular product or device, scalability is inherent in the method.

Our system scales from one defendant to 100 simply by expanding the size and method of file maintenance. There are no additional "modules" to buy, nor are there more user licenses to acquire. Simply expand the filing system to include a larger number of participants—suspects, victims, or witnesses.

Because the system is merely the implementation of a concept, it is effective on many scales. The casebook system has been used effectively in situations as simple as an indexed notebook and as complex as several filing cabinets. The difference between the two is in volume, not in additional effort to adapt the system. An inherent beauty in the system is its innate ability to grow with the investigation.[3]

Having said all this, we would like to note that what follows is nothing more than an illustration of the casebook concept. As such, it is no more or less "correct" than any similar—or different for that matter—filing system that the reader may develop or currently use. In addition, we make no claim as to the originality of the concept, nor do we hope to inspire a revolution in investigative technique.

What we do hope to accomplish is to illustrate how the concept can add greater value to the investigative inference model that we already find so valuable a tool in the investigative arsenal. We encourage the reader to digest the information, reformulate it, and apply it to whichever situation he or she desires. There is nothing particularly special surrounding our method; it is simply something that the test of time has validated. We hope that the reader will also benefit from the insight that clear organization can provide amidst a voluminous mass of mixed evidence.

COMPONENTS OF THE SYSTEM

Typically, a casebook will contain a number of documents and checklists ranging from initial reports to probable cause affidavits and to-do lists. What you choose to include in your casebook will largely be dictated by the nature of your case, combined with personal preference.

Generally speaking, however, every casebook should contain certain basic elements. First, regardless of the scale of your investigation, every casebook should have an actual book. This consists of a three-ring binder ranging in thickness from 1 inch to 3 or more inches, depending on the size of your investigation. In small investigations, the book might in fact comprise the entirety of the system. In larger, more complicated cases, the book will act as the index and cross-reference system between the inference model, the narrative content, and the documentary content, logically linking the three.

The role of the book is to coordinate those three elements. The casebook, then, will have a many-to-many relationship (to borrow from relational database parlance) between the inference chart and the supporting evidentiary material. In other words, each node on the inference model will point to an entry in the book, which will in turn point to each individual item of evidence necessary to support the inferential proposition.

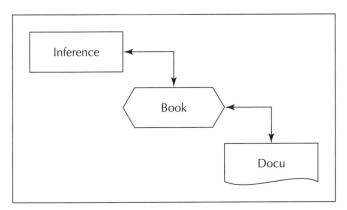

Exhibit 13.1 Relational Quality between Inference Model, Book, and Documentation

Exhibit 13.1 illustrates the relational quality between the inference model, the book, and the supporting evidentiary documents. As you can see, a relationship also exists between the underlying documentation, the book, and the model. In other words, given a specific item of evidentiary support, by using the book it should be possible to locate the proposition it supports on the model. The existence of this two-way relationship gives the casebook system its robustness.

The book is composed of three sections: administrative, investigative, and evidentiary.

The Administrative Section

The administrative section contains important documentation about the case itself, such as the underlying legal premise on which the case is based. If the investigation is based on an allegation of racketeering, a restatement of the racketeering law and the elements underlying it must be made. By restating the crime alleged, in terms of specific elements relative to the actual facts of your case, you can ground the investigation in the reality of the situation.

In terms of specificity, the restatement should indicate the identity of the defendant, the actual conduct alleged to constitute a violation, and any specific defenses anticipated. For example, if our initial report alleges that JoAnn has killed Frank, our restatement should restate the crime of murder through the prism of the facts alleged as follows:

On or about April 1, 2003 at approximately 5:10 P.M., JoAnn entered Frank's apartment and did, with premeditated design, shoot Frank with a deadly weapon, to-wit; a .38 caliber revolver, and as a result of JoAnn's intentional act Frank sustained a fatal injury and did in fact die as the result of said injury, contrary to Florida Statutes.

Not only does this statement clearly outline the elements that you must prove, but it also begins the all-important process of story telling. (For a discussion of the importance of story telling in criminal investigation and litigation please, see Chapter 10.)

Eventually, this statement, to the extent that your investigation supports it, will become the basis for the probable cause affidavit and subsequent charges.

The administrative section should also contain a synopsis of the facts being alleged in the original complaint. The synopsis should be written based solely on what is being alleged, not on what you believe you can prove. If it were done the other way around, there would be a danger that tunnel vision might occur. In other words, if you limit the synopsis of the facts to what seems easily provable at the time, you will begin to foreclose lines of inquiry and limit your creativity with regard to alternative explanations of factual events.

If there is no allegation, perhaps this case is self-initiated based on suspicion of wrongdoing you observed; then create a synopsis of the facts based on what you believe has occurred. You should be mindful that narrowing the field of inquiry too quickly might result in a similarly over-narrow view of the facts, precluding the ability to quickly recognize alternative explanations. In short, this section of the casebook should contain basic documentation of an administrative nature.

The Investigative Section

The investigative section should contain all paperwork that pertains directly to the investigation. Items such as the original initiating report, all supplemental reports, and all investigative narratives should be filed in this section.

The task of report writing, especially in the area of investigations, is largely controlled by departmental policy and personal preference. Departmental policy is often rather inflexible. Personal preference, on the other hand, is open to influence.

Our experience shows that there are two schools of thought regarding report writing. The first, which we shall refer to as the minimalist school, favors an austere approach advocating sparse detail and brevity—all this, it is supposed, in the name of fewer attack points for the lawyers.

The second approach, which we refer to as the kitchen sink approach, comes at the problem from the opposite angle; here one should include every possible detail, leaving out nothing. The reasoning behind this approach is obviously that fading memories require significant bolstering. Which approach is most reasonable? The truth, as usual, probably lies somewhere in between.

As a practical matter, an investigative report should include as much significant detail as necessary to accurately document the investigator's actions without being overly burdensome. How much is too much? That is a difficult question to answer—especially in the abstract. It is imperative that your investigation report achieve its goal. It must both enable third parties to discern what actions have been taken in a case, and it must help in jogging your memory at some future point in time. Often, this future point in time could be years later. After many years of conducting investigations, the facts of innumerable cases often blend together to form a montage of disjointed images. Culling from that montage specific facts during strenuous cross-examination could be a difficult task, leaving you looking rather foolish on the stand.

As for the minimalist school of report writing, we think it treads dangerously close to malpractice (if such a thing existed in the investigative context). As the adherents are quick to point out, when there are fewer details in a report, a defense attorney will have fewer details to attack during cross-examination. Although the truth of this statement is indisputable, the logic behind it is fallible.

First, having the benefit both of years of trial testimony and an extensive legal education, we can assure the reader that a sufficiently skilled defense attorney can effectively cross-examine an investigator regardless of the detail contained in the report. Second, the lack of detail in the report hinders, not helps, the investigator at trial time.

As we stated earlier, trials often occur months, or perhaps years, after the investigative action took place. Given the fact that most investigators have difficulty recalling with total accuracy what they had for breakfast two weeks ago, recalling the minutiae of a criminal investigation after years of intervening cases is an exercise in futility rife with inaccuracy. This inaccuracy will come across during testimony as either deception or ineptitude, qualities neither of which juries find particularly endearing in a witness. At best you will appear to be a buffoon, at worst a liar.

We recommend, as you contemplate how detailed you wish to make your report, that you consider two things. First, and foremost, consider the purpose of your job in the big picture. Your task, whether you are a criminal investigator or a civil investigator, is to discover the truth. Sometimes, this duty becomes obscured by the rhetoric of the pursuit of the bad guys. Whether obscured or not, this is job one. Therefore, accuracy should be the goal of every investigative report—regardless of where the facts point you.

Whether your investigation points you in the direction you anticipate (i.e., the suspect is guilty) or in a different direction altogether, the report should reflect exactly what your inquiry revealed. This ensures that, ultimately, the truth regarding the matter will be known.

Second, an often-overlooked caveat for investigators is "do your job." In other words, fulfill your duty in an objective, professional, and thorough manner and you will have nothing major to worry about. Our justice system does not expect absolute perfection. If it did, we would all be in a world of trouble. It expects reasonable perfection. Reasonable perfection sounds like an oxymoron. It is not. It is simply another way of saying that humans are what we are. We all suffer from the human condition and mistakes are inevitable. Errors and omissions will occur and memories will fail us. It is a fact of life, and defense attorneys will be quick to point out our failings.

In fact, the whole premise behind the adversarial justice system is the notion that defense attorneys must seize upon mistakes and attempt to hammer holes in the small chinks that reveal themselves in the armor of our case. The result, at least in theory, is that investigators should strive to minimize the glaring errors and obvious mistakes that tend to insinuate themselves into any investigation. Defense attorneys keep us on our toes—they force us to do our jobs.

In truth, it is not the investigator's admission of minor mistakes that loses cases; rather, cases are lost when the defense attorney is able to successfully attack the credibility and veracity of the witness. Nothing is more effective in losing a case than catching an investigator in a fabrication. Whether it's an intentional fabrication resulting from some malicious purpose, or an innocent fabrication that is the result of a faulty memory coupled with shoddy reporting, witness fabrication, especially professional witnesses like investigators, instantly destroys the credibility of the entire prosecution.

A habit of scanty reporting leads an investigator to rely too heavily on fragile recall. These powers will inevitably fail, and when they do, human nature urges us to "fill in the blanks." Sometimes the answer is accurate, but more often it is not. Avoid placing yourself in this situation by recording your actions accurately and completely.

So, in sum, the clash between Spartan and lavish reporting may be answered by following these two principles. (1) As an investigator, do your job to the best of your ability according to standard accepted procedure and with no shortcuts; and (2) report your investigative activities as accurately as possible, regardless of where the findings lead—truth is the objective, not conviction of the suspect.

Within that framework, you should construct the narrative of your investigative report in chronological order, detailing the events of your investigation as they unfold. The investigative report is distinguished from the fact narrative that we discussed in Chapter 10 regarding story telling in that it tells a story, not just a story of the event. Instead, it tells the story of your involvement as an investigator.

This section of the book should also contain a master chronology, which, as noted earlier, is invaluable in clarifying the chain of events under investigation. The chronology is an evolving document that expands as new facts are added and old facts are eliminated. It is always in flux, and it helps to clearly anchor the event in a reference system that is familiar to us. (For a fuller discussion of the limitations of anachronistic story telling, see Chapter 10.)

A detailed list of witnesses will appear in this section. With this portion of the section we begin to realize the full power of the casebook system. Each witness is assigned a unique identifying number, such as (W1), and gets its own individually tabbed section. Included behind each tab should be the full identification of the witness, including address, phone number, and the full contact information that might become necessary in order to locate the witness quickly. It might also be helpful to include a photograph of the witness, especially in the event the witness suddenly becomes "difficult to locate," and canvassing needs to begin.

Then each witness's anticipated testimony should be summarized and included with that witness's entry. This facilitates recall of what each witness can bring to the case. Similarly, an exact listing of each piece of evidence or proposition to which the witness will testify is kept. For example, our medical examiner in the JoAnn and Frank hypothetical, Dr. Jones, would be listed as witness W1, with an attendant summary of her involvement. Following that summary, we would compile a list of propositions that Dr. Jones will be responsible for substantiating. Each entry in this fact list will correspond to an entry on our key list (and subsequently on our inference model).

If the witness provides physical evidence, such as a document or other tangible item, that item will be listed here in the witness section, and you will file the item in the evidence section of the casebook. (A detailed explanation of how the evidence section is organized follows this section.)

Finally, any unfavorable information about this witness must be included. Information that reflects upon the witnesses' credibility such as prior arrests, previous misconduct, or perhaps inducements to testify is important. By listing this information here, the investigator can assess the potential weight that the witness's testimony can be expected to have on the jury in light of potential defense impeachment.

Following the witness portion of the investigative section is a serialized listing of all the evidence collected to this point, with a reference to its location within the inference model. For example, we will list the suicide note in the hypothetical with a corresponding reference to node 40. In addition, this item of evidence will have a reference to which witness will authenticate and testify regarding its importance. In this case, the responding officer who discovered the note would testify to its discovery; therefore, his corresponding witness number would appear in the evidence list next to the note.

Other witnesses, however, may need to testify regarding this item. Crime lab technicians tested the blood, and handwriting experts analyzed the signature. Although each of those witnesses would have individual documents from which they would testify—a lab report and a written analysis report, respectively—they will also testify to the note itself. Therefore, each of these witnesses will also be listed adjacent to the evidentiary item.

Finally, this section will contain a detailed listing, by number, of each item in our key list. Every proposition that appears in our model will be restated in this section, with a reference to every evidentiary item that will be used to establish the proposition, as well as every witness from whom the proposition was developed.

In the hypothetical, proposition no. 35 (the handgun was missing two rounds) would be accompanied by the reference entry for the physical evidence (the gun) as well as a reference to the witness entry for the responding officer.

By using these three portions of the investigative section, the investigator can move seamlessly from model to witness to evidence and back without losing his mind. If we want to better understand proposition no. 35 in our model, we simply look up no. 35 in our key list section and find out what it stands for, who provided us with the information, and what physical evidence supports it. In this case, the responding officer and a handgun would all be revealed. From here, we can delve further into the system by looking up the witness using the witness number and finding out the entirety of the witness's testimony and all pertinent facts surrounding his involvement.[4]

As we will discover momentarily, we can also trace the evidence necessary to prove, or resulting from, this proposition in our key list. Our relatively simple and straightforward filing system effectively manages our navigation among its components.

The Evidentiary Section

The last section of the book, the evidentiary section, can take on a number of forms. For smaller cases, it is possible that nothing more than photocopies of papers will comprise the entirety of the section. Conversely, in larger cases, it is possible that this section of the book will itself be an index to folders within a file box or filing cabinet.

As evidence is collected, it must be assigned a unique number within the case. Whether the item is a document or a gun, it is imperative that we be able to discretely reference each item by a unique number.

There are probably as many acceptable ways of identifying evidentiary items as there are investigators. Whatever system you choose, it may be helpful to include within the numbering system some way of immediately recognizing the tangible quality of the evidence. For example, it could be helpful, from an organization standpoint, to be able to immediately recognize that the particular item in question is a piece of narcotics evidence as opposed to a document. With that in mind, an alpha character followed by a serial number may be helpful. For example, the alpha character "D" could be used to designate all documentary evidence such as bank records or other documents. A "W" might be used to preface the serial number for all weapons and so forth. The specificity with which you assign prefixes to the serial number is entirely within your discretion, provided you maintain both consistency and uniqueness.

Often, the evidence in economic crime cases consists solely of documentary evidence. Documentary evidence offers a unique opportunity for cross-referencing. Within the confines of the rules of evidence, each document should be uniquely numbered, and working copies of these documents must be made in order to preserve the original "best evidence" for introduction in court. Numbering of documentary evidence should consist of individually serializing each page within compound documents.

Although this recommendation may at first blush appear rather obsessive, internal references to specific pages within questioned documents may be made in the investigative report's story narrative and probable cause documents with one simple succinct number. This greatly simplifies complex masses of documentary evidence and makes it easy to locate the item within the evidentiary section.

At this point, we would like to briefly comment on Bates® numbers— the multi-digit numbers that appear at the bottom of most legal documents in the law firm setting. So named for the fact that, originally, they were hand stamped on each document using an auto-incrementing "Bates®" brand self-inking stamp, they uniquely identify each document in a legal file. Bates® numbers can be an efficient method of marking and serializing a large mass of evidence in a relatively short period of time.

We have had great success using this system in complex cases where large numbers of documents have been seized during a search warrant. In this situation, careful planning and division of labor offer tremendous efficiency in collecting and organizing your case.

If you are faced with the task of executing a search warrant, or perhaps collecting documents under a subpoena or request for production, a Bates®-type self-inking stamp is a powerful tool. First, as with all search warrant executions, it is imperative that one individual on the search team be tasked with the sole and limited responsibility of recording the collection of evidence. Commonly called the "scribe," this member of the team should set up camp in a central location at the search site with his stamp and recording method at the ready.[5] As the members of the search team collect documents, they bring them to the scribe who records the location of recovery and the name of the search team member who recovered them, and immediately serializes the document using the stamp. In this manner, each document is instantly marked for later reference, and orderly collection of evidence is ensured.

A little pre-planning can further refine this method of collection. When planning the raid or collection event, draw a diagram of the collection sight. Artistic ability and scale are not necessary. All that is important is that you accurately depict the layout of the site. Floor-plan-type sketches are ideal for this task. Once the sketch has been made, assign an alpha character to each room (if your organization system utilizes letters as designators for different types of evidence, you may need to select another method of identifying each area, depending on the overall design of your identification method) or area to be searched. The granularity of the sketch (how finely you wish to divide the search space) is entirely up to you. Critical search missions could perhaps even benefit from an over-grid of the entire scene and assignment of a unique identifier to each individual grid square.

As the search proceeds, each member of the search team is tasked with individual responsibility for a certain area. All evidence recovered from that area is designated using the letter assigned to that portion of the floor plan or grid. For example, when searching an office suite where the CEO's office is identified by the letter "A," a corporate resolution recovered from the top drawer of his filing cabinet would be listed as having been recovered from "first drawer of filing cabinet location 'A'." This shorthand notation can both save time and limit frustration as the investigative team encounters large volumes of evidence. In addition, computer software can be used to locate all items in location "A" quickly.

Regardless of the method you employ to collect the evidence, it is practically worthless unless you can quickly locate it when you need to. This is where the casebook system offers assistance. Each item of evidence is identified by serial number.[6] As such, it is filed either in the pages of our casebook or in our supplemental filing system (file boxes or filing cabinet) by numerical order—or alphanumeric depending on the labeling system you chose.

As you proceed through your inference model, or the investigative section of the casebook, locating discrete items of evidence instantly is a simple task. If you examine a node on the inference model that points you to a proposition in the key list, the key list will point you to the serial number of the evidentiary item.

Working in reverse order, from evidentiary item to casebook, the serial number of the item corresponds to an entry in the investigative section of the casebook. This entry in turn corresponds to both a witness number/name and key list proposition number. As you can see, working from either end of the system is a simple task because of its robust cross-reference capability.

CLOSING THE BOOK ON THE CASEBOOK SYSTEM

As we have repeated throughout this text, the key to successfully mounting an investigation into a complex economic crime, at the heart of which is a large volume of evidence, is careful planning and strong organization. In the absence of either one, you will achieve less-than-optimum results.

In keeping with this mantra, we have exposed the reader to some powerful concepts for creating an organizational strategy. As we said earlier, what we have introduced, and explicated to one degree or another, are not a series of silver bullets guaranteed to create order from chaos. Instead, they are just what we have purported them to be—concepts. The key ingredient in all the ideas presented here is a reference system and flexibility. Without flexibility you are faced with creating a new system each time the fact pattern you encounter changes slightly from the scenario for which the organizational scheme was designed. Creation is a slow process that is to be avoided unless absolutely necessary. Adaptation is a much better path.

With that in mind, we urge you to ruminate upon the ideas that we have offered. You are welcome to borrow, discard, or massage any of them into what will be effective for your particular needs. You may use all, some, or none, and we encourage you to think critically about what their strengths are but, more importantly, what their limitations are. By understanding the limitations of the systems, you can navigate around them or mitigate them in the planning stages of your investigation.

As we move on to the next chapter, we hope to build on our notion of a coherent filing system and offer you some insights into how to effectively integrate the investigative tools we have discussed thus far, the investigative inference, and the casebook organization system with your role as a witness.

In truth, whether your investigative skills are being tested as a criminal investigator, as a civil investigator, or perhaps as a member of an audit team who uncovered a complex embezzlement scheme, you will eventually be tasked with conveying what you have discovered to some very interested third parties. In this role, you will be required to act both as a professor, teaching your audience about the concepts learned in the first part of this text relating to accounting, and as a salesman, convincing your audience that your version of the facts is more plausible than that of the opposition. Balancing the demands of both of these tasks is often difficult, but if you have done your homework and carefully charted your progress using our investigative inference model, both tasks will become decidedly more manageable.

In the next chapter, the techniques of investigation meet the demands of presentation. It is here that the investigative inference model often earns its salary. This is true in part because the demonstrative quality of the chart itself often makes vague arguments clear and confusing propositions more logically intuitive. It can be used as a teaching tool and will help you persuade the jury to make the baby-steps necessary to link complex chains of inferences into a compelling argument that leads to one inescapable conclusion—guilt.

NOTES

1. T. Anderson and W. Twining, *Analysis of Evidence: How to Do Things with Facts Based on Wigmore's Science of Judicial Proof* (Evanston, IL: Northwestern University Press, 1991), pp. 266–267.

2. Although in reality the terms *casebook* and *trial book* are often used interchangeably, we will reserve the use of the term *trial book* for those times when we are making reference to its use by lawyers. The term *casebook* will be reserved for those times when we are referring to its application to investigations.

3. The authors claim neither to have invented the notion of the casebook nor to have revolutionized it as a method of organization. Our sole contribution to the field is in applying it to the area of the investigative art.

4. We would like to point out that an entry in the book must appear for the suspect and the victim. In our case, both JoAnn and Frank would be listed in the investigative section with all pertinent information surrounding their involvement.

5. An equally effective, if not far superior, method of organizing collection efforts involves the use of a laptop computer, bar code scanner, and self-adhesive bar code labels. Using the labels, a database program, and the scanner, the scribe can instantly identify, record, and catalog every item of evidence with instant reporting capability. This setup offers the added ability to produce an instant property list and warrant return for deposit at the scene.

6. Because we are discussing economic crimes, we are dealing primarily with documentary evidence. However, as an investigator you will undoubtedly encounter a mixture of other types of physical evidence— evidence that is often cumbersome and bulky. In that case, since the actual evidence must be secured in an evidence facility anyway, a simple photograph or Polaroid can stand in for the actual item. For example, in our hypothetical, a Polaroid of the actual gun can represent the murder weapon in our filing system.

14

TESTIFYING IN FINANCIAL CRIME CASES

INTRODUCTION

Although conducting the investigation is a substantial task in and of itself, it is only part of your responsibility as an investigator. In addition, you must testify to your findings. In many cases, your role as witness will require substantially less time commitment than your role as investigator. In fact, the more time and effort you have expended on creating a strong case, the smaller the probability is that you will end up in court at all.

If you do your job as an investigator well, the opposing side will have a much greater incentive to avoid the uncertainty of litigation altogether and will be inclined to accept, or offer, a suitable settlement. Whether this settlement is in the form of a monetary award or a plea bargain, the end result is the same—pre-trial intervention.

From a litigation perspective, the lawyer's job is ultimately to avoid trial. As paradoxical as this might sound in light of customary legal-fee structures, it is in reality the ultimate goal. The reason for this is simple. Regardless of the perceived strength of a case, all lawyers familiar with litigation recognize that, once the case enters the courtroom, the question of win-lose often becomes a game of chance. It was Louis Pasteur who said, "Chance favors the prepared mind." As true as this may be in theory, in practice the element of chance often dictates taking a more predictable course of action.[1]

Largely uncontrollable variables such as individual juror predisposition, judicial bias, and even the skill and acumen of opposing counsel make *all* trips before the bar of justice a veritable crapshoot. Therefore, given the opportunity to avoid the uncertainty of trial—regardless of personal conviction about the "righteousness of their cause"—most attorneys will opt for pre-trial settlement. The adage about the bird-in-the-hand versus the bird-in-the-bush rings true in this context as well.

As an investigator, your role in avoiding the cost and uncertainty of trial cannot be overestimated. After all, it is largely based on your efforts that the attorneys will make their decisions regarding fight or flight. Assuming that you have done a thorough job during the investigation, it is imperative that you follow through and finish strong. Finishing strong includes being a prepared and effective witness.

In this chapter, we hope to offer some clarification regarding your role as a witness, both expert and otherwise, that will help you, as investigator, prepare for the "big show." In addition, we hope to offer you some tips that you can incorporate into your investigative routine that will make your role as a witness easier.

THE ROLE OF THE PROFESSIONAL WITNESS

Neutrality

First and foremost, the professional witness[2] must testify from a position of neutrality. It is not your job to influence the jury through emotion: rather, it is your job to influence the jury through facts. Victims and other eyewitnesses may be used strategically to play upon the heartstrings of the jury. You however, must appear as a disinterested reporter of facts and results.[3]

Much as you are responsible for objectivity and truthfulness during the investigation phase, so you have a duty to accurately and faithfully report your findings that transcends any personal biases you may have concerning the case at hand.

This task may in fact be more difficult than it sounds. As the person who has become intimately familiar with every detail of the case, it is difficult to remain objective and report your conclusions regarding the guilt or innocence of the defendant in a detached and professional manner. Nonetheless, as hard as it may be, the integrity of the justice system requires it—your own personal integrity requires it as well.

How can you accomplish this difficult task? At the risk of oversimplifying, we would like you to internalize one thing above all else: do not make the outcome of the case personal.

As veterans of both the investigative and testimonial trenches, we recognize that some cases will make this task nearly impossible. After all, there are just some cases where justice *must* be done, and the path to justice is clear. Admittedly, in financial crime cases these occasions may be rare. The painfully disfigured victims, the conspicuously absent loved-ones, and the heinously evil villains are often relegated to the more glamorous (arguably) "persons" crimes or torts. However, there will be occasions when you become personally involved during your investigation. Notwithstanding your burning desire to see the defendant behind bars (or lighten his wallet as the case may be), visibly personal concern over the outcome will, in the long run, damage both your reputation and your ability to offer effective testimony. Leave the zealous advocacy to the attorneys.

Education

Disinterested neutrality does not necessarily mean disinterested monotony. Financial crime evidence often tends to be highly technical and somewhat complicated. Add to this the fact that debits and credits are not nearly as "sexy" as eyewitness testimony about a robbery, and you have a recipe for boredom. Be that as it may, it is your job, as a professional witness in financial cases, to capture the attention of the jury. If you do not, your message, and probably your case as well, will be lost.

Therefore, it is important to approach your role as a professional witness in financially focused cases as that of a teacher. As such, you must educate the jury about not only the facts of the case, but often the underlying principles behind the investigative analysis. Juries are invariably an admixture of laypersons with varying experiences and skill levels in terms of financial matters. It is not only possible, but also likely, that the level of financial knowledge among the jurors will range from bookkeepers and accountants to those among us who can barely balance a checkbook. For this reason, as you approach your job of testifying, you should be constantly aware of the diversity of your audience.

As you prepare and deliver your presentation to the jurors, keep in mind the characteristics of most successful teachers. Keeping those characteristics in mind, you will find that not only is your message well received, but also that you will establish a rapport with your audience. Aside from the practical aspect of preventing boredom and keeping their attention, rapport building offers you the chance to subliminally develop credibility. And, as we all know, credibility is the key to persuasive testimony.

Credibility

Think back to a particular professor or instructor whom you regard as the most influential in your life (academically or otherwise). Invariably, there are feelings of admiration as well as respect. Underlying those feelings however, is probably a sense of credibility. This is the person of unquestionable authority—not because his position of explicit authority demanded it, but because his expertise and personality earned it. This implicit authority should be the goal of every professional witness.

No doubt, the prosecutor or attorney for whom you are testifying will inform both the judge and the jury of your expertise in the subject matter about which you will testify. In that sense, you will be given explicit authority—much like a teacher's position in the classroom. The students recognize that, in order to attain that position, a teacher must achieve certain levels of education and professionalism. Notwithstanding that, most students have experienced the situation where the explicit authority conferred by the teacher's position evaporated upon his speaking word one.

Whether it was due to a lack of facility in the subject matter or a personality characteristic that made him unbelievable, this teacher became uneffective in his role. Because he was ineffective, learning was nonexistent and probably so too was discipline. In the courtroom, discipline is not a problem; after all, the courthouse equivalent of being sent to the principal's office could involve a night in the local lock-up. On the other hand, a learning deficit in the courtroom is a serious problem.

Communication

As we have said, learning is the product of a teacher's knowledge of the subject matter combined with his ability to communicate his message. In turn, communication is strongly influenced by personality characteristics—a caustic and condescending attitude will block a free flow of ideas. It is our hope that after completing this text you will be well on your way to proficiency in both areas. The preceding chapters are designed to help you with the knowledge portion, and this chapter, we hope, will introduce you to the need to develop effective communications skills.

Knowledge can be broken down further into two additional components: subject matter knowledge and practical application. Subject matter knowledge will be gained by studying the principles and concepts in this text as well as further exploration in an autodidactic mode. Practical application, however, is entirely dependent on your efforts as an investigator. We can offer you a solid foundation in both the principles of accounting as they apply to financial crime investigation and some techniques for effectively pursuing such investigations. We cannot give you facility in your individual case.

Practical application is entirely about knowing your individual case. A doctorate-level knowledge of accounting will not help you testify if you do not have a working knowledge of the facts of your case. For that reason, preparation is key to effectively educating the jury. You must know your case inside and out. Failure to know the intimate details will end up costing you credibility in front of the jury and will ultimately detract from your message. Assuming that you have developed both subject matter knowledge and practical knowledge about the case, we will move on to how you communicate that knowledge to the jury.

An effective professional witness is in reality very similar to a professional educator—both must convey an often complicated and dull subject to a somewhat captive audience. In order to achieve this goal, both must have knowledge of their subject as well as the capacity to translate this subject matter knowledge into learning. As a professional witness, you may find it helpful to recall an educator with whom you are familiar that possesses both traits. If you can visualize how this model of education would convey the subject about which you are speaking, perhaps the process of jury education will become more natural.

COMMUNICATING YOUR KNOWLEDGE

There is an overabundance of literature dedicated to the topic of "how to testify," so we will not add to the glut of information by adding our own list of the "top ten" keys to testifying. In addition, we will not overburden the reader any more than necessary with discussions of how to behave or how not to react. More eloquent texts are currently available that do far more justice to that area of discussion than we could hope to in a single chapter.

Instead, we would like to offer a set of principles as guidance. These principles fall generally into three categories—demeanor, appearance, and performance—and are really what amounts to common sense. And as most of us have discovered through years of real-life experiences, common sense is anything but. That is why we will concentrate on effective witness testimony.

Demeanor

Demeanor refers to how you relate to the jury. Along with aspects such as presenting a professional approach and conveying a sense of an appropriate seriousness regarding the situation, demeanor includes treating the jury with respect.

Although your education and experience in the subject matter is likely superior to that of the jury, it is imperative that you avoid conveying a sense of superiority. This advice may sound very basic, but it is startling how easily professional witnesses forget to treat the jury as equals. If you "talk down" to the jury, or treat them as though the concepts that you are discussing are well beyond their comprehension, you will risk alienating them. No one likes to feel alienated, and doing so will prevent you from being as effective a witness as you have the potential to be.

Even though the subject you are discussing, whether it is net worth analysis or link matrix analysis, may be somewhat complex, the concepts are obviously of great importance to the success of your case. Therefore, it is imperative that you temper your explanations with respect. You must strike a balance between talking down to the jury and talking over their heads. Such a balance is neither easy to find nor always in the same place. As you move through your career, again, try and keep in mind the definition of the educator who was most influential in your life and strive to filter your explanations through that prism.

Appearance

Appearance is an area where once again common sense is key. Dressing appropriately is such a simple goal, yet many professional witnesses misapprehend the bigger purpose behind this rule. Continuing the comparison of your role as a professional witness with that of an educator, we see that the underlying importance of appearance once again makes sense.

Persuasive authority derives not only from explicit badges of authority but from conduct that implies authority. This is evidenced in the admonition that police officer witnesses should always wear their uniform during court appearances. For nonuniformed officers and those professional witnesses in the private sector, the choice of attire is often more complex.

Generally speaking, conservative business attire is appropriate. A conservative suit with a single-colored shirt, set off with a simple-print tie, should be standard issue in any professional witness's clothing arsenal. Choices in gray, blue, and black all work well for professional witnesses in the financial arena. Either single-breasted or double-breasted, given the individual's build, is a fine choice, as are choices between two- or three-button jackets. At the bare minimum, a professional witness should wear a conservative blazer.

You should avoid loud shirts with wild or busy prints. Regardless of your own personal fashion sense, these shirts tend to be distracting and mar the overall impression made by the witness.

Your choice of tie is often a much more personal one. Here, unlike the suit, there is probably a little more room for leeway, but do not overdo it. Ties commonly referred to as "power ties"—usually red, burgundy, or diagonally striped red and blue—are good choices, as are ties with a simple design or conservative polka dots.

Lest you mistake our point here, let me emphasize that these recommendations have nothing to do with "fashion." What we want to do is point out that your appearance will create an impression on the jury. This impression can be a powerful subliminal motivator and to the extent that you are aware of it, you can control its impact.

The courtroom, and more importantly the witness box, is not a place to make a fashion statement. If you feel as though you could have just stepped off the cover of the most recent edition of *Gentlemen's Quarterly*®, your choice of outfit is probably a bit too daring. A good rule-of-thumb is this: if you feel you look too conservative, you are probably dressed just right.

To those of our readers whose idea of "classic" movies encompasses such favorites as *Saturday Night Fever*, we suggest you make a trek to your local video store and pick up a copy of something from the late 1940s and 1950s. Two great examples of the indomitable style exuded by Bogart and Grant are *Casablanca* and *An Affair to Remember*, respectively. Both are sure to entertain, with the added benefit of introducing you to the power of simple conservative attire.

Although our suggestions have been partially tongue-in-cheek, the underlying premise is not. Conservativeness is an inextricably intertwined element of credibility—especially in the area of financial matters. If you doubt the truth of this statement, we suggest you look no further than Wall Street or your local large CPA firm. Most people's mental image of a financial professional conforms to the stereotype of the gray or blue suit, perhaps pinstripe, with a starched white shirt and wingtip shoes.

Anything else connotes an irresponsibility that most people would rather not associate with someone to whom they entrust their fortunes. It is inarguably both an antiquated and an inaccurate stereotype. However, as a professional witness your responsibility is not to change people's stereotypical perceptions. Rather, it is to recognize where they exist, negotiate around them, and persuade people that you are a credible expert. In this case, conservative is as conservative does.

In other fields of expertise, such emphasis on attire might not be nearly as important. For example, if we were discussing a dress code for an accident reconstructionist, there would probably be very little emphasis on attire beyond an exhortation to dress in a professional manner. Their role in the courtroom drama is different, however, from that of the financial expert.

Your role in the eyes of the jury is that of an expert in the area of financial matters, whether you are an actual CPA or merely a highly trained and experienced investigator. The jury must see you as a consummate professional whose opinion is to be given the highest regard. As a practical matter, you can rest assured that the financial professional that the opposition will hire will conform to the jury's stereotypical expectations of a financial professional—even if you don't.

Hand-in-hand with attire goes grooming; our personal grooming habits are a large component of how others perceive us. To that end, a professional witness would do well to visit the barber regularly and maintain a neat and business-like appearance. As with clothing choice, hairstyles are a very personal matter. While we do not propose to tell the reader how to select a hairstyle, we will offer you a few words of advice for choosing from among your options. Outlandish hairstyles suggest unorthodoxy. This in turn detracts from witness credibility in a conservative area such as financial matters.

Similarly, unwashed (or infrequently washed) hair suggests a lack of discipline and poor attention to detail—neither of which you want the jury to infer from your appearance. Undoubtedly, some jurors will perceive a witness groomed in such a manner as being eccentric and perhaps even avant-garde—after all it worked for Einstein. Whether or not this is true is immaterial. The truth of the matter is that a courtroom battle between experts is won and lost based solely on the jury's perception of their credibility.

Because credibility and stereotypes play an unavoidable role in the outcome of the case, you must acknowledge them and work within them if you want to win, even if you do not agree with the stereotypes. It is as true inside the walls of the courtroom as it is in life that "you don't get a second chance to make a first appearance." The difference is, in life someone's freedom rarely hangs on the balance of your first impression.

Performance

Some would argue that performance is an inappropriate topic in courtroom considerations. We disagree, as do many lawyers who have enrolled in college courses and workshops in theater and performance. While the idea of the lawyer as actor seems inherently unethical, you cannot escape the fact that a trial is largely a performance.[4]

In this sense, lawyers are both the directors and actors within this intricate three-act play performed for a captive audience of jurors. Highly successful lawyers try and choreograph the entire process down to the exact phrasing of their closing arguments. From choice of costume to arrangement of witnesses, every litigation-professional stages an elaborate production with one goal in mind—to tell a compelling story. In the end, the critics of this little micro-drama are the jurors who offer their "two thumbs up" in the form of a guilty or not guilty verdict.[5]

Obviously, dishonesty and distortion of the truth are inappropriate within this "theater." The appropriateness of showmanship and staging, however, do not appear to be as clear. If, as we have intimated in earlier chapters, story and theme represent a powerful tool in legal case preparation, why then should the natural extension of this principle not be equally powerful? In short, it is.

As you are preparing your case, you are ultimately scripting a story (see Chapter 10 for more on the concept of story, theme, and theory). Although your involvement in scripting this mini-drama ends with presentation to the prosecuting attorney, your role in its production and staging does not.

Once you have completed the investigation and the attorneys take over, you have merely shifted from playwright to actor. The implication of this transition is often lost not only on investigators but also on the attorneys who are running the show. We suggest you remain cognizant of the role that performance plays in presenting the case to the jury.

We should note that performance in no way implies embellishment. In fact, there is very little room for "improvisation" in the legal arena. Therefore, lest the reader think we advocate playing fast and loose with the facts of the case, we should reiterate that truth, honesty, and integrity are the most important principles in the legal process. To the extent that you can be unwaveringly faithful to them, you should think of how your performance will influence the audience.

Although we do not necessarily think a professional witness should take acting lessons, we do think you can benefit from adhering to some of the principles common to great performances. The first and foremost is rehearsal.

Rehearsal

A great actor would never think of stepping on stage without knowing his lines. You should feel the same way. Although memorizing a speech word for word is ill advised, knowing exactly what you are going to say will give you a level of comfort and familiarity with your own words that will convey confidence and credibility to the jury.

A witness's performance consists of essentially two stages: direct examination and cross-examination. There is no reason why a professional witness in an important case cannot be fully prepared for the questions that you will need to answer on direct examination. For that matter, even those questions that you will face on cross-examination are relatively predictable.

Body Language

If you appear fidgety, unfocused, and unconvincing, your value as a witness will be negligible. Your tone of voice, choice of words, and extemporaneous movements all feed into the message that you convey. If your body posture or body language overshadows your words, the audience will naturally gravitate toward the more compelling of the two. Distracting movements or poor posture conveys a subliminal message to your audience. Which message the audience receives is up to you.

Similarly, eye contact, or lack of it, makes a very real statement about honesty and can either enhance or obscure the importance of your message. As a witness, you should constantly maintain eye contact with the jury. As a cautionary note, there is a vast difference between maintaining nonthreatening eye contact and staring in an obsessive stalker-like manner. Finding a balance between the two comes through practice and experience.

In evaluating and modifying your body language, the first tenet of presentation proves invaluable. As you are rehearsing what you are going to say, you should also rehearse how you are going to say it. This includes not only the body mechanics of your delivery, but also the other nonverbal communications channels such as diction, volume, and emphasis.

Although the words convey the message, how you deliver them injects meaning and shapes their impact. Dry, monotonous delivery is boring, and the jury will soon tune you out. On the other hand, an enthusiastic, inflected delivery with emotion (not overemotion or advocacy) will entrance and capture the jury's imagination and will leave them wanting more. There is no better way to step down from the witness box than feeling as though the jury had lost track of time. In the same way that story tellers strive for a suspension of disbelief, the professional witness should try to suspend time while he is on the stand. The last thing you want a juror to think about is the time. Instead, capture their attention through your delivery. If you do that, they will receive your entire message, and your time on the stand, besides being highly productive, will have a powerful, persuasive effect on them.

In sum, paying close attention to *how* you testify in addition to content will enhance your value as a professional witness. You can greatly increase your effectiveness as a persuader by paying particular attention to your demeanor, appearance, and performance while on the stand. As we have said, a trial is really a form of performance. As such, how well you play your part influences the critic's opinion of the production. In this case, the critics—the jurors—will weigh in by casting a vote for your version of the performance or that of the opposition. You can tip the scales in favor of your side by knowing your lines; carefully rehearsing your part, and remaining cognizant of the overall impact your part has on the "bigger picture."

THE ROLE OF THE FINANCIAL CRIME EXPERT IN LITIGATION

The expert witness plays an important role in many stages of the litigation process. It is helpful when thinking about the role of the expert to view the lawyers and everyone who assists them as members of a litigation team. As the captain of the team, the lawyer generally plans and carries out the offensive (or defensive) strategy in order to reach the goal. But, as with any team, his job is made easier by recruiting other individuals that possess skills in areas of team weakness. No lawyer can be expected to be an expert in all areas. In fact, the only area in which a lawyer may be expected to possess superior knowledge or skill is in the area of litigation. For all other areas, prudence dictates that the lawyer call on outside experts for assistance.

The assistance can come in many forms, the most visible being that of a trial witness. However, the expert can play a number of other, nontestimonial roles during the course of a complex case, notably:

- *Case evaluation and strategy*—Prior to filing the actual complaint, it may be beneficial for the attorney to consult with an expert in the field to assess both the potential for success and the nature of the complaint.[6] Even though the lawyer is the expert in case strategy, his ability to plan the course of litigation is limited by his knowledge of the field in which the case falls. An expert's valuable experience in a specialized field such as accounting and fraud can assist the lawyer in predicting outcomes, shaping complaints, and testing hypotheses about causation. In addition, the expert's specialized skills can aid in selecting additional helpful witnesses.[7]

  Even though an expert is qualified in a particular area, she may not be qualified within a subspecialty of that area. For example, a financial expert in the area of business loss valuation may not necessarily be competent in the area of stock manipulations or Securities and Exchange Commission (SEC) regulations. As a member of a "fraternity of experts," you will be able to guide the lawyer in the process of selecting additional witnesses for the litigation team.

- *Education*—Lawyers need to know a little bit about everything, but the depth of their knowledge in specific technical areas is usually limited. Often, a great deal can be discovered about a case, or the potential for a case, by consulting with an expert in a tutorial capacity.

244

In this capacity, the expert witness is still an educator. But instead of educating the jury, she is educating the attorney. The expert witness can provide the attorney with a strong working knowledge about the subject matter of the case. In the financial case, lawyers often consult with experts regarding items such as the standard of care for accountants, whether the tenets of generally accepted accounting practice (GAAP) have been followed, and other specific technical issues in the area of finance.

- *Exhibits*—When dealing with complicated issues or large amounts of evidence, it may be helpful to create demonstrative exhibits. These exhibits are merely visual aids that the lawyer can use to help witnesses educate the jury about their version of the case. Graphic summaries of transactions, or visual representations of the flow of money, help the jury grasp the often-convoluted processes or schemes used by the defendant to conceal a theft. The expert can be of great assistance in preparing these exhibits. Regardless of who will be using them to testify, the expert can facilitate their creation by lending her specialized knowledge of the subject matter.

As you can see, the role of the experts is both varied and indispensable. Generally, the duties they perform can be divided into two categories—preparatory and testimonial. These categories are not mutually exclusive, and often an expert plays a part in both areas.[8]

The Testimonial Expert

As we intimated earlier, the role of testimonial expert is often the most visible and so is probably the one most people are familiar with. When lawyers speak of a case being "a battle of the experts," they are referring to the fact that both parties will present expert testimony (obviously of opposing opinion) regarding a pivotal aspect of the case. Some battles focus on causation issues, while others might center solely on damage issues. Either way, a battle of the experts boils down to which party's expert offers the more compelling explanation of the facts.

Although we do not wish to downplay the importance of expert assistance in the preparatory area, we will be focusing for the remainder of this chapter on your role as a testimonial expert—a role that may be broken down into the subcategories of pre-trial testimony and trial testimony.

Discovery

Pre-Trial

In every trial, the pre-trial process proceeds through what is referred to as a discovery phase—the part of the case where both sides endeavor to learn as much about the opponent's case as possible. To the layperson, the process of discovery is both confusing and a bit intimidating. It is confusing in the sense that providing your opponent with your game plan ahead of time seems to run counter to the notion of adversarial combat. It is intimidating in the sense that many times the opposition uses the discovery process to probe for weaknesses and gauge the most likely spot for a frontal assault. This probing maneuver is usually aggressive and often seems overbearing to the uninitiated witness.

As an expert witness, it is important that you understand the need for, and the reasons behind, the process. If you understand it, you may be less intimidated, and as a result you will be a more confident and effective witness. Hopefully, we can dispel any concerns you may have regarding your role and participation in the discovery process.

Even though the trial process is basically an adversarial one, the underlying goal is to determine the truth. Therefore, our system of dispute resolution tries to make the battle as even as possible. Our rules are in place to try and ensure that the winner is the winner because he made the best case for his version of the truth—not because he was better at keeping his battle plan a secret. If it were any other way, the attorney more practiced in the art of surprise and ambush would usually win whether or not his case was stronger. To a large degree, this is the goal that our modern rules of pre-trial discovery seeks to reach. Full disclosure by each side is believed to promote fairness of adjudication on the merits.[9]

As for the intimidating nature of the discovery process, this is an adversarial system. By definition, one side must win by weakening the opponent. Discovery—especially deposition practice—is the first shot at locating weaknesses and gauging an opponent's overall strategy. Once a weakness has been found, resources can be marshaled to exploit it. Because the lawyer is probing for weakness, the deposition often becomes a very stressful event. This is essentially a chance for opposing counsel to test your mettle and find out if you will be a viable target while on the stand.[10]

Ultimately, the deposition process is a discovery process. Consequently, the scope of the questions and the manner in which the lawyer may ask them are wildly different from what is seen in the courtroom. There are very few questions that an opposing lawyer cannot ask in the deposition. Even if certain evidence is irrelevant to trial, witnesses in deposition must answer them.[11] This greatly expands the scope of the deposition.

This is not to say that a deposition is a free-for-all; it is not. In fact, all state courts and the federal courts have very specific rules governing allowable conduct in the discovery process. These rules cover such issues as when opposing counsel must produce information about their case, what must be produced, when and by whom depositions may be taken—and retaken in some cases—and penalties for slow or uncooperative behavior. Although each state's rules of procedure differ slightly, most are patterned after the Federal Rules of Civil Procedure.

There are also rules governing pre-trial discovery in the criminal system. Although they are similar and seek to achieve the same goal, the different nature of the criminal process makes discovery rules in that area slightly different from those in the civil arena.

If this were a legal text directed at lawyers preparing expert witnesses for trial, it would be appropriate at this juncture for us to address some of the very specific legal issues surrounding the use of experts in a testimonial capacity. If you are interested in learning more about the legal niceties of the rules of discovery, we recommend you start by reading the Federal Rules of Evidence and the Federal Rules of Civil/Criminal Procedure. From there, read the particular rules of the state in which you wish to serve as an expert witness, paying close attention to the similarities to, and differences from, the federal rules.

We find that the best source of information on a legal topic is the actual rules themselves. However, if you are still feeling unprepared, visit a local law library or courthouse (which usually houses a library containing a fair selection of basic legal texts) and find a general text on the rules of discovery. If your efforts fail to give you the level of comfort you desire, we suggest you consider enrolling in your nearest law school, since the learning bug has obviously bitten you.

We will introduce you to some very basic notions here. Though not specific to any particular venue or jurisdiction, they are fairly universally applicable. If you keep these in the back of your mind as you prepare to serve as an expert witness, the process should be less confusing and intimidating.

What Is an Expert?

There are essentially two species of witnesses: the expert and the lay witness. Legally, the distinction between expert and lay witness makes a crucial difference in the role that each may play.

Depending on the complexity of your case and the nature of the financial crime, you may find yourself serving as both expert and lay witness. The most significant difference between the two is the nature of the testimony each may render. Generally, a witness's testimony is limited to matters on which he possesses personal knowledge.[12] Generally, people may only testify to what they have deduced based on use of their five senses—what they have witnessed or personally observed. For example, a lay witness would be quite well qualified—assuming she is competent—to testify to the description of a vehicle or the color of the defendant's shirt. She would not be allowed to testify to the defendant's mental state or to give her opinion about his motivation.[13]

By contrast, expert witnesses may testify to matters beyond their personal observation. They may testify to their opinion regarding certain matters that will help the jury determine the ultimate fact in issue. The subject matter to which they may testify is limited to the area in which they have some superior skill, education, or ability. For example, a Certified Public Accountant (CPA) would likely be qualified, based on her education and experience, to testify regarding auditing methods that comprise the Generally Accepted Auditing Standards (GAAS). But it is not likely that she would be qualified to testify regarding the mental state of the defendant at the time he made entries into the accounting records. It is the notion of "qualification" that gives rise to many of the issues about which lawyers in the trial context argue; these issues are largely resolved based on reference to the rules of evidence.[14]

Generally speaking, you must overcome two hurdles when trying to qualify as a testimonial expert; one involves the individual qualifications of the witness, and the other centers on the actual field in which the expert wishes to qualify.

Individual Qualification

A witness may qualify as an expert in a particular field when her knowledge, skill, experience, training, or education, or a combination thereof, gives her special knowledge above and beyond that possessed by ordinary members of the public. There are no hard-and-fast rules regulating how much or what type of experience and education qualifies a witness as an expert. Each individual case will be evaluated on its own merits, and the judge will make the determination of whether or not the witness qualifies as an expert.[15] Usually, expert qualification is based on one or more of the following criteria:

- Advanced education: bachelor's, master's, or doctorate degree
- Advanced independent study, including documentation of
  - Books read
  - Research conducted
  - Journals read
- Extensive personal experience such as derived from years in a specialized field like:
  - Law enforcement
  - Fire science
- Authorship in refereed or respected books and journals
- Recognition within a particular industry
- Professional certification or designation
  - CPA
  - CFE

As an expert or potential expert witness, it is incumbent upon you to maintain an accurate and thorough resume. Your resume should reflect both professional accomplishments and independent learning pursuits in the area for which you wish to be qualified. In addition, you must maintain both a listing and a copy of all articles, books, and papers that you have written, both published and unpublished. In particular, you should also remain aware of any papers or articles that you have written that might advocate a position adverse to that which you anticipate rendering in court.[16]

It is imperative that you maintain currency in all areas related to your area of expertise. You can accomplish this by frequently reading the most relevant journals and scholarly publications in your field. For the financial witness, this includes such publications as *The Journal of Forensic Accounting*, *The CPA Journal*, *Practical Accountant*, *The Journal of Accounting*, *The Journal of Accountancy*, and many others. Maintaining currency will help to ensure that your opinion (once you are qualified to render it) is not easily discredited by more current research in the field. Not only is testifying to outdated information a serious blow to credibility, but it is a personally embarrassing situation.

Field Qualification

In overcoming the second hurdle, an expert witness may face an attack on the field in which she practices. These challenges to the legitimacy of the field of study, called *Daubert* challenges after the Supreme Court decision of *Daubert v. Merrill Dow Pharmaceuticals, Inc.*, 509 U.S. 579 (1993), scrutinize the underlying basis for the scientific principles upon which the expert's opinion is based. *Daubert* challenges are often more difficult than individual qualification. They are an attack on the credibility of the *field* in which the expert intends to testify. Sometimes the battle is characterized as a battle between real science and junk science, but the focus is usually on the methods and procedures used in the particular field of endeavor.[17]

Although rules 702 and 703 of the Federal Rules of Evidence do not explicitly require that the field of endeavor fall within a traditional scientific or technical venue, it is easier to qualify as an expert in those fields (provided the individual qualifications are attained). For example, medicine, psychology, and engineering are universally accepted as fields of endeavor from which expert testimony can be rendered. Conversely, other areas, or highly specialized areas within each recognized area, are open for more vigorous challenges. Areas such as "new age" medicine and other holistic forms of treatment are usually strongly attacked through the mechanisms of *Daubert* because of their less conventional origin and methodologies.[18]

In general, since the rendition of the Supreme Court's decision in *Daubert*, the test for admissibility under Rule 702 focuses on the concept of "scientific knowledge." Although the Court refused to elucidate a definitive checklist or test, it did discuss several factors it considered relevant to determining when an area of endeavor was reliable enough to warrant introduction into evidence. The Court intimated that the following factors were pertinent to the inquiry:

- Whether the theories and techniques employed have been tested.
- Whether the theories have been subjected to peer review and publication.

- Whether the techniques employed have a known error rate.
- Whether they are subject to standards governing their application.
- Whether the theories and techniques enjoy widespread acceptance.

Further, the Court made it clear that, far from a checklist, the procedure must be a flexible one that focuses "solely" on principles and methodology, not on the conclusions that are generated.

This definition clearly narrows the field from which expert testimony may derive. However, this should not prove cumbersome for the expert in the area of financial crimes unless the techniques you employ are so far outside the scope of GAAP or GAAS that they are not within the taxonomy of the science.

For a substantial period following *Daubert*, there was some confusion regarding its application. Some practitioners believed that the application of the Supreme Court's *Daubert* opinion was limited to decidedly "scientific" pursuits such as medicine or engineering or accounting, while others argued that *all* expert testimony was subject to the *Daubert* challenge.

This question was finally answered in 1999. In *Kumho Tire Co v. Carmichael* 526 U.S. 137 (1999), the Supreme Court examined the question of whether or not a tire expert who based his opinion solely on technical skill and experience, not scientific methodology, was subject to the *Daubert* challenge.[19]

The Eleventh Circuit ruled that the Supreme Court's holding applied only to scientific principles and not to other specialized knowledge. However, the Supreme Court granted *certiorari* and held that *Daubert* is a doctrine of flexibility that applies to assist the trial court in its gatekeeping function of admitting only relevant evidence in cases of both scientific and technical knowledge as well as areas of other specialized knowledge. Finally, the Supreme Court's position was clear—all areas of specialized knowledge are subject to attack under the *Daubert* principles.[20]

As we stated, for the expert witness seeking to testify to conventional areas in the financial crime arena, *Daubert* should be little inconvenience. However, it is important that you remain aware of the burdens that the attorney for whom you work will face when attempting to get you onto the stand. These considerations should help guide your choice of methods and procedures as you go about the task of evaluating or investigating the case at hand. If they do not, your efforts, regardless of how well meaning they were, may never see the inside of a courtroom.

SUMMARY

The investigative efforts you inject into a particular case, though immeasurably important, are of little significance if you cannot put them in front of the jury effectively. This idea of "putting the evidence before the jury" is more than simply taking the stand and reciting a litany of investigative activity. Instead, it is a complex process of capturing both the attention and imagination of the jury and selling them a compelling story.

The process is a complicated tapestry of threads requiring a coordinated effort by the lawyer, the investigator, and all the support staff at both their disposals. As an investigator, it is paramount that you remain aware of your role, how it intertwines with the role of the lawyer for whom you work and with the other members of the litigation team. Remember that testimony—credible testimony—is the end goal. In order to get there, many technical hurdles must be overcome, only some of which are beyond your control. Once you are there, the impact your testimony has on the finder-of-fact is entirely within your control. You can influence the outcome significantly by applying common sense coupled with what you have hopefully gained from this chapter.

NOTES

1. A. Partington, ed., *The Oxford Dictionary of Quotations* (New York: Oxford University Press, 1992), p. 509.
2. We would like to clarify our use of the term *professional witness*. Although the term might connote a "hired gun" who sells his testimony, regardless of ethical concerns, to the highest bidder, that is not the way in which it is being used. We use the term here merely to distinguish between a witness for whom testimony on a regular basis is one facet of his or her job from a witness who is called to testify as a matter of happenstance or coincidence. We will use the terms *professional* and expert interchangeably; however, you should keep in mind that the term expert has a very distinct legal meaning that will become more clear later in the chapter.
3. R. A Gardner, *Testifying in Court* (Cresskill, NJ: Creative Therapeutics, 1995), pp. 111–112.

4. "Learning Acting Techniques for a Real-life Courtroom Drama," *The Washington Post*, July 22, 1991.
5. "Bringing Drama to the Courtroom," *The Christian Science Monitor*, September 20, 1991.
6. Z. Telpner and M. Mostek, *Expert Witnessing in Forensic Accounting: A Handbook for Lawyers and Accountants* (Boca Raton, FL: CRC Press, 2003), pp. 1–6.
7. Ibid., p. 3.
8. Ibid., pp. 15–22.
9. R.L. Weil, M.J. Wagner, and P.B. Frank, "The Role of the Financial Expert in Litigation Services," in R.L. Weil, M.J. Wagner, and P.B. Frank, eds., *Litigation Services Handbook: The Role of the Financial Expert*, 3rd ed. (New York: John Wiley & Sons, 2001), pp. 9–14.
10. Ibid.
11. Relevance in the context of a deposition has a much broader meaning than at trial. Generally speaking, a question is allowable in a deposition, unless it deals with attorney-client privilege or attorney work-product, as long as it is reasonably expected to result in uncovering new information about the case.
12. C.W. Gerdts III and C.E. Dixon, "The Federal Law Governing Expert Witness Testimony" in Weil, Wagner, and Frank, eds. *Litigation Services Handbook*, pp. 1–6. See also Rule 701, Federal Rules of Evidence reprinted in Appendix B.
13. Ibid.
14. As we have mentioned, the laws regulating the admissibility of evidence and expert qualifications vary from state to state: therefore, we will address these issues using the Federal Rules of Evidence, Sections 701 through 706, which have been reprinted in the Appendix.
15. Telpner and Mostek, *Expert Witnessing in Forensic Accounting*, pp. 22–26.
16. Ibid., pp. 7–14.
17. Weil, Wagner, and Frank, "The Role of the Financial Expert in Litigation Services," pp. 20–21.
18. Ibid. See also *Daubert v. Merrill Dow Pharmaceuticals, Inc.* (1993) 509 U.S. 579.
19. *Kumho Tire Company, Ltd., et al., v. Carmichael, etc., et al.* (1999) 526 U.S. 137.
20. Ibid.

SUGGESTED READINGS

Brinig, B.P., and E. Gladson. *Developing and Managing a Litigation Services Practice.* New York: Harcourt Professional Publishing, 2000.

Bronstein, D.A. *Law for the Expert Witness.* Boca Raton, FL: CRC Press, 1999.

Dessem, R.L. *Pretrial Litigation: Law, Policy and Practice*, 3rd. ed. St. Paul, Minn.: West Publishing, 2001.

Frye v. United States (1923) 293 F. 1013 (D.C. Cir.).

General Electric Co. v. Joiner (1997) 522 U.S. 136.

Graham, M.H. "The Expert Witness Predicament: Determining 'Reliable' under the Gatekeeping Test of *Daubert, Kumho,* and Proposed Amended Rule 702 of the Federal Rules of Evidence." *University of Miami Law Review*, 54, no. 2 (2000): 317–400.

Haydock, R.S., and D.F. Herr. *Fundamentals of Pretrial Litigation.* Saint Paul, MN: West, 1985.

Mauet, T.A. *Pretrial.* New York: Aspen Law & Business, 2002.

Rodgers, P.A., R.R. Gaughan, and M.J. Trout,. *Expert Economic Testimony: Reference Guide for Judges and Attorneys.* New York: Lawyers & Judges Publishing Co., 1998.

Schum, D.A. "Probability and the Processes of Discovery, Proof, and Choice." *Boston Univ. Law Review*, 66 (1986): 825–876.

Yeschke, C.L. *The Art of Investigative Interviewing: A Human Approach to Testimonial Evidence.* Boston, MA: Butterworth-Heinemann, 2003.

KEY LIST

#1   JoAnn murdered Frank.

#2   Frank is dead.

#3   Frank was murdered.

#4   JoAnn did it.

#5   Autopsy report—detailing Frank's death.

#6   Dr. Jones's testimony "Frank is dead."

#7   Frank died of a gunshot wound.

#8   Frank was shot.

#9   Frank's death was suicide.

#10 Landlady discovered body in bathroom.

#11 Body was in bathroom.

#12 Landlady's testimony.

#13 Frank was killed in the bathroom.

#14 Frank was killed with a gun.

#15 Witness no. 1 saw JoAnn enter the apartment at 4:00 P.M. on day of murder.

#16 Witness's testimony to JoAnn entering apartment.

#17 Witness no. 2 heard a gunshot in the area at about 5:10 P.M.

#18 Witness's testimony to gunshot.

#19 Witness no. 3 saw a woman matching JoAnn's description leave Frank's apartment around 5:30 P.M.

#20 Witness no. 3's testimony.

#21 JoAnn was at Frank's apartment at 5:10 P.M.

#22 Frank died at 5:10 P.M.

#23 People who have strong motives act on them.

#24 Jealousy is a strong motive.

#25 JoAnn was jealous.

#26 Frank was cheating on JoAnn.

#27 Witness no. 4's testimony about Frank's cheating and plans to break it off with JoAnn.

#28 Frank was planning to break up with JoAnn.

#29 Responding officer located body in bathroom.

#30 Body was not moved after death.

#31 Frank was killed with a gun.

#32 The cause of death was a bullet wound.

#33 A .38 caliber handgun was found 3 feet from the body.

#34 The gun had two discharged rounds in the chamber.

#35 One bullet was recovered from the ceiling.

#36 Frank had no GSR on his hands.

#37 Frank had one bullet wound to the right temple.

#38 The responding officer found the gun.

#39 Testimony of the responding officer.

#40 A Suicide note was found by the responding officer.

#41 The note was typed.

#42 The note was covered in blood.

#43 The note was signed with Frank's name.

#44 People who commit suicide often fire one test round.

#45 The gunshot wound was self-inflicted.

#46 The blood on the note is Frank's.

#47 Forensic expert's testimony regarding blood evidence.

#48 Handwriting is Frank's.

#49 Document Examiner's testimony.

#50 Frank was killed in the apartment.

#51 The bathroom is in the apartment.

Key List

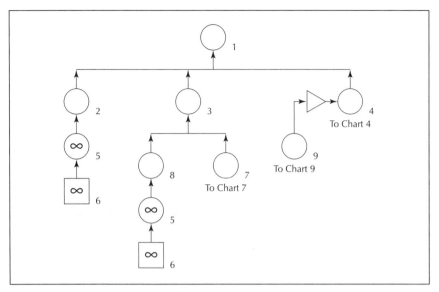

Exhibit A.1 Master Chart

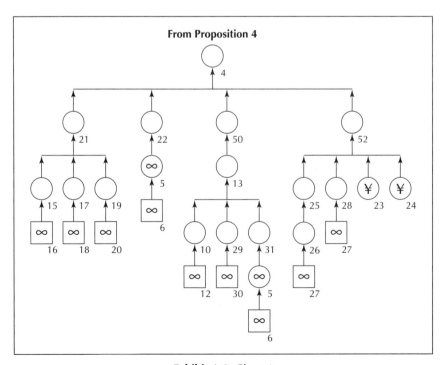

Exhibit A.2 Chart 4

Appendix A

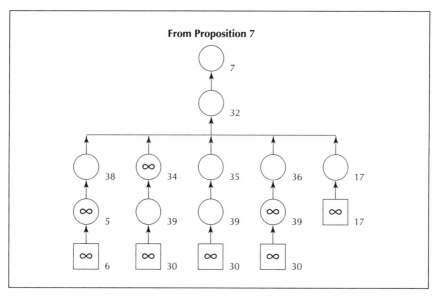

Exhibit A.3 Chart 7

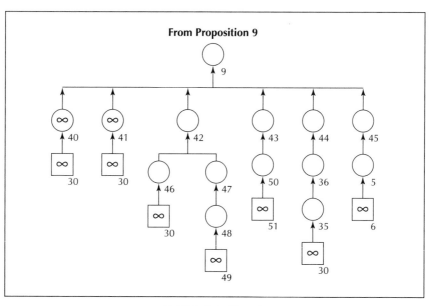

Exhibit A.4 Chart 9

FEDERAL RULES OF EVIDENCE

ARTICLE VII. OPINIONS AND EXPERT TESTIMONY

Rule 701. Opinion Testimony by Lay Witnesses

If the witness is not testifying as an expert, the witness's testimony in the form of opinions or inferences is limited to those opinions or inferences which are (a) rationally based on the perception of the witness, and (b) helpful to a clear understanding of the witness's testimony or the determination of a fact in issue, and (c) not based on scientific, technical, or other specialized knowledge within the scope of Rule 702.

(Pub. L. 93-595, § 1, Jan. 2, 1975, 88 Stat. 1937; Mar. 2, 1987, eff. Oct. 1, 1987; Apr. 17, 2000, eff. Dec. 1, 2000.)

Notes of Advisory Committee on Proposed Rules

The rule retains the traditional objective of putting the trier of fact in possession of an accurate reproduction of the event.

Limitation (a) is the familiar requirement of first-hand knowledge or observation.

Limitation (b) is phrased in terms of requiring testimony to be helpful in resolving issues. Witnesses often find difficulty in expressing themselves in language which is not that of an opinion or conclusion. While the courts have made concessions in certain recurring situations, necessity as a standard for permitting opinions and conclusions has proved too elusive and too unadaptable to particular situations for purposes of satisfactory judicial administration. McCormick § 11. Moreover, the practical impossibility of determining by rule what is a "fact," demonstrated by a century of litigation of the question of what is a fact for purposes of pleading under the Field Code, extends into evidence also. 7 Wigmore § 1919. The rule assumes that the natural characteristics of the adversary system will generally lead to an acceptable result, since the detailed account carries more conviction than the broad assertion, and a lawyer can be expected to display his witness to the best advantage. If he fails to do so, cross-examination and argument will point up the weakness. See Ladd, Expert Testimony, 5 Vand.L.Rev. 414, 415-417 (1952). If, despite these considerations, attempts are made to introduce meaningless assertions which amount to little more than choosing up sides, exclusion for lack of helpfulness is called for by the rule.

Appendix B

The language of the rule is substantially that of Uniform Rule 56(1). Similar provisions are California Evidence Code § 800; Kansas Code of Civil Procedure § 60-456(a); New Jersey Evidence Rule 56(1).

Notes of Advisory Committee on Rules—1987 Amendment

The amendments are technical. No substantive change is intended.

Committee Notes on Rules—2000 Amendment

Rule 701 has been amended to eliminate the risk that the reliability requirements set forth in Rule 702 will be evaded through the simple expedient of proffering an expert in lay witness clothing. Under the amendment, a witness's testimony must be scrutinized under the rules regulating expert opinion to the extent that the witness is providing testimony based on scientific, technical, or other specialized knowledge within the scope of Rule 702. See generally Asplundh Mfg. Div. v. Benton Harbor Eng'g, 57 F.3d 1190 (3d Cir. 1995). By channeling testimony that is actually expert testimony to Rule 702, the amendment also ensures that a party will not evade the expert witness disclosure requirements set forth in Fed.R.Civ.P. 26 and Fed.R.Crim.P. 16 by simply calling an expert witness in the guise of a layperson. See Joseph, Emerging Expert Issues Under the 1993 Disclosure Amendments to the Federal Rules of Civil Procedure, 164 F.R.D. 97, 108 (1996) (noting that "there is no good reason to allow what is essentially surprise expert testimony," and that "the Court should be vigilant to preclude manipulative conduct designed to thwart the expert disclosure and discovery process"). See also United States v. Figueroa-Lopez, 125 F.3d 1241, 1246 (9th Cir. 1997) (law enforcement agents testifying that the defendant's conduct was consistent with that of a drug trafficker could not testify as lay witnesses; to permit such testimony under Rule 701 "subverts the requirements of Federal Rule of Criminal Procedure 16(a)(1)(E)").

The amendment does not distinguish between expert and lay witnesses, but rather between expert and lay testimony. Certainly it is possible for the same witness to provide both lay and expert testimony in a single case. See, e.g., United States v. Figueroa-Lopez, 125 F.3d 1241, 1246 (9th Cir. 1997) (law enforcement agents could testify that the defendant was acting suspiciously, without being qualified as experts; however, the rules on experts were applicable where the agents testified on the basis of extensive experience that the defendant was using code words to refer to drug quantities and prices). The amendment makes clear that any part of a witness's testimony that is based upon scientific, technical, or other specialized knowledge within the scope of Rule 702 is governed by the standards of Rule 702 and the corresponding disclosure requirements of the Civil and Criminal Rules.

The amendment is not intended to affect the "prototypical example[s] of the type of evidence contemplated by the adoption of Rule 701 relat[ing] to the appearance of persons or things, identity, the manner of conduct, competency of a person, degrees of light or darkness, sound, size, weight, distance, and an endless number of items that cannot be described factually in words apart from inferences." Asplundh Mfg. Div. v. Benton Harbor Eng'g, 57 F.3d 1190, 1196 (3d Cir. 1995).

For example, most courts have permitted the owner or officer of a business to testify to the value or projected profits of the business, without the necessity of qualifying the witness as an accountant, appraiser, or similar expert. See, e.g., Lightning Lube, Inc. v. Witco

Corp. 4 F.3d 1153 (3d Cir. 1993) (no abuse of discretion in permitting the plaintiff's owner to give lay opinion testimony as to damages, as it was based on his knowledge and participation in the day-to-day affairs of the business). Such opinion testimony is admitted not because of experience, training or specialized knowledge within the realm of an expert, but because of the particularized knowledge that the witness has by virtue of his or her position in the business. The amendment does not purport to change this analysis. Similarly, courts have permitted lay witnesses to testify that a substance appeared to be a narcotic, so long as a foundation of familiarity with the substance is established. See, e.g., United States v. Westbrook, 896 F.2d 330 (8th Cir. 1990) (two lay witnesses who were heavy amphetamine users were properly permitted to testify that a substance was amphetamine; but it was error to permit another witness to make such an identification where she had no experience with amphetamines). Such testimony is not based on specialized knowledge within the scope of Rule 702, but rather is based upon a layperson's personal knowledge. If, however, that witness were to describe how a narcotic was manufactured, or to describe the intricate workings of a narcotic distribution network, then the witness would have to qualify as an expert under Rule 702. United States v. Figueroa-Lopez, supra.

The amendment incorporates the distinctions set forth in State v. Brown, 836 S.W.2d 530, 549 (1992), a case involving former Tennessee Rule of Evidence 701, a rule that precluded lay witness testimony based on "special knowledge." In Brown, the court declared that the distinction between lay and expert witness testimony is that lay testimony "results from a process of reasoning familiar in everyday life," while expert testimony "results from a process of reasoning which can be mastered only by specialists in the field." The court in Brown noted that a lay witness with experience could testify that a substance appeared to be blood, but that a witness would have to qualify as an expert before he could testify that bruising around the eyes is indicative of skull trauma. That is the kind of distinction made by the amendment to this Rule.

GAP Report—Proposed Amendment to Rule 701. The Committee made the following changes to the published draft of the proposed amendment to Evidence Rule 701:

1. The words "within the scope of Rule 702" were added at the end of the proposed amendment, to emphasize that the Rule does not require witnesses to qualify as experts unless their testimony is of the type traditionally considered within the purview of Rule 702. The Committee Note was amended to accord with this textual change.

2. The Committee Note was revised to provide further examples of the kind of testimony that could and could not be proffered under the limitation imposed by the proposed amendment.

Rule 702. Testimony by Experts

If scientific, technical, or other specialized knowledge will assist the trier of fact to understand the evidence or to determine a fact in issue, a witness qualified as an expert by knowledge, skill, experience, training, or education, may testify thereto in the form of an opinion or otherwise, if (1) the testimony is based upon sufficient facts or data, (2) the testimony is the product of reliable principles and methods, and (3) the witness has applied the principles and methods reliably to the facts of the case.

(Pub. L. 93-595, § 1, Jan. 2, 1975, 88 Stat. 1937; Apr. 17, 2000, eff. Dec. 1, 2000.)

Notes of Advisory Committee on Proposed Rules

An intelligent evaluation of facts is often difficult or impossible without the application of some scientific, technical, or other specialized knowledge. The most common source of this knowledge is the expert witness, although there are other techniques for supplying it.

Most of the literature assumes that experts testify only in the form of opinions. The assumption is logically unfounded. The rule accordingly recognizes that an expert on the stand may give a dissertation or exposition of scientific or other principles relevant to the case, leaving the trier of fact to apply them to the facts. Since much of the criticism of expert testimony has centered upon the hypothetical question, it seems wise to recognize that opinions are not indispensable and to encourage the use of expert testimony in non-opinion form when counsel believes the trier can itself draw the requisite inference. The use of opinions is not abolished by the rule, however. It will continue to be permissible for the experts to take the further step of suggesting the inference which should be drawn from applying the specialized knowledge to the facts. See Rules 703 to 705.

Whether the situation is a proper one for the use of expert testimony is to be determined on the basis of assisting the trier. "There is no more certain test for determining when experts may be used than the common sense inquiry whether the untrained layman would be qualified to determine intelligently and to the best possible degree the particular issue without enlightenment from those having a specialized understanding of the subject involved in the dispute." Ladd, Expert Testimony, 5 Vand.L.Rev. 414, 418 (1952). When opinions are excluded, it is because they are unhelpful and therefore superfluous and a waste of time. 7 Wigmore § 1918.

The rule is broadly phrased. The fields of knowledge which may be drawn upon are not limited merely to the "scientific" and "technical" but extend to all "specialized" knowledge. Similarly, the expert is viewed, not in a narrow sense, but as a person qualified by "knowledge, skill, experience, training or education." Thus within the scope of the rule are not only experts in the strictest sense of the word, e.g., physicians, physicists, and architects, but also the large group sometimes called "skilled" witnesses, such as bankers or landowners testifying to land values.

Committee Notes on Rules—2000 Amendment

Rule 702 has been amended in response to Daubert v. Merrill Dow Pharmaceuticals, Inc., 509 U.S. 579 (1993), and to the many cases applying Daubert, including Kumho Tire Co. v. Carmichael, 119 S.Ct. 1167 (1999). In Daubert the Court charged trial judges with the responsibility of acting as gatekeepers to exclude unreliable expert testimony, and the Court in Kumho clarified that this gatekeeper function applies to all expert testimony, not just testimony based in science. See also Kumho, 119 S.Ct. at 1178 (citing the Committee Note to the proposed amendment to Rule 702, which had been released for public comment before the date of the Kumho decision). The amendment affirms the trial court's role as gatekeeper and provides some general standards that the trial court must use to assess the reliability and helpfulness of proffered expert testimony. Consistently with Kumho, the Rule as amended provides that all types of expert testimony present questions of admissibility for the trial court in deciding whether the evidence is reliable and helpful. Consequently, the admissibility of all expert testimony is governed by the principles of Rule 104(a). Under that Rule, the proponent has the burden of establishing that the pertinent admissibility requirements are met by a preponderance of the evidence. See Bourjaily v. United States, 483 U.S. 171 (1987).

Daubert set forth a non-exclusive checklist for trial courts to use in assessing the reliability of scientific expert testimony. The specific factors explicated by the Daubert Court are (1) whether the expert's technique or theory can be or has been tested—that is, whether the expert's theory can be challenged in some objective sense, or whether it is instead simply a subjective, conclusory approach that cannot reasonably be assessed for reliability; (2) whether the technique or theory has been subject to peer review and publication; (3) the known or potential rate of error of the technique or theory when applied; (4) the existence and maintenance of standards and controls; and (5) whether the technique or theory has been generally accepted in the scientific community. The Court in Kumho held that these factors might also be applicable in assessing the reliability of nonscientific expert testimony, depending upon "the particular circumstances of the particular case at issue." 119 S.Ct. at 1175.

No attempt has been made to "codify" these specific factors. Daubert itself emphasized that the factors were neither exclusive nor dispositive. Other cases have recognized that not all of the specific Daubert factors can apply to every type of expert testimony. In addition to Kumho, 119 S.Ct. at 1175, see Tyus v. Urban Search Management, 102 F.3d 256 (7th Cir. 1996) (noting that the factors mentioned by the Court in Daubert do not neatly apply to expert testimony from a sociologist). See also Kannankeril v. Terminix Int'l, Inc., 128 F.3d 802, 809 (3d Cir. 1997) (holding that lack of peer review or publication was not dispositive where the expert's opinion was supported by "widely accepted scientific knowledge"). The standards set forth in the amendment are broad enough to require consideration of any or all of the specific Daubert factors where appropriate.

Courts both before and after Daubert have found other factors relevant in determining whether expert testimony is sufficiently reliable to be considered by the trier of fact. These factors include:

(1) Whether experts are "proposing to testify about matters growing naturally and directly out of research they have conducted independent of the litigation, or whether they have developed their opinions expressly for purposes of testifying." Daubert v. Merrill Dow Pharmaceuticals, Inc., 43 F.3d 1311, 1317 (9th Cir. 1995).

(2) Whether the expert has unjustifiably extrapolated from an accepted premise to an unfounded conclusion. See General Elec. Co. v. Joiner, 522 U.S. 136, 146 (1997) (noting that in some cases a trial court "may conclude that there is simply too great an analytical gap between the data and the opinion proffered").

(3) Whether the expert has adequately accounted for obvious alternative explanations. See Claar v. Burlington N.R.R., 29 F.3d 499 (9th Cir. 1994) (testimony excluded where the expert failed to consider other obvious causes for the plaintiff's condition). Compare Ambrosini v. Labarraque, 101 F.3d 129 (D.C.Cir. 1996) (the possibility of some uneliminated causes presents a question of weight, so long as

Appendix B

the most obvious causes have been considered and reasonably ruled out by the expert).

(4) Whether the expert "is being as careful as he would be in his regular professional work outside his paid litigation consulting." Sheehan v. Daily Racing Form, Inc., 104 F.3d 940, 942 (7th Cir. 1997). See Kumho Tire Co. v. Carmichael, 119 S.Ct. 1167, 1176 (1999) (Daubert requires the trial court to assure itself that the expert "employs in the courtroom the same level of intellectual rigor that characterizes the practice of an expert in the relevant field").

(5) Whether the field of expertise claimed by the expert is known to reach reliable results for the type of opinion the expert would give. See Kumho Tire Co. v. Carmichael, 119 S.Ct. 1167, 1175 (1999) (Daubert's general acceptance factor does not "help show that an expert's testimony is reliable where the discipline itself lacks reliability, as, for example, do theories grounded in any so-called generally accepted principles of astrology or necromancy."); Moore v. Ashland Chemical, Inc., 151 F.3d 269 (5th Cir. 1998) (en banc) (clinical doctor was properly precluded from testifying to the toxicological cause of the plaintiff's respiratory problem, where the opinion was not sufficiently grounded in scientific methodology); Sterling v. Velsicol Chem. Corp., 855 F.2d 1188 (6th Cir. 1988) (rejecting testimony based on "clinical ecology" as unfounded and unreliable).

All of these factors remain relevant to the determination of the reliability of expert testimony under the Rule as amended. Other factors may also be relevant. See Kumho, 119 S.Ct. 1167, 1176 ("[W]e conclude that the trial judge must have considerable leeway in deciding in a particular case how to go about determining whether particular expert testimony is reliable."). Yet no single factor is necessarily dispositive of the reliability of a particular expert's testimony. See, e.g., Heller v. Shaw Industries, Inc., 167 F.3d 146, 155 (3d Cir. 1999) ("not only must each stage of the expert's testimony be reliable, but each stage must be evaluated practically and flexibly without bright-line exclusionary (or inclusionary) rules."); Daubert v. Merrill Dow Pharmaceuticals, Inc., 43 F.3d 1311, 1317, n.5 (9th Cir. 1995) (noting that some expert disciplines "have the courtroom as a principal theatre of operations" and as to these disciplines "the fact that the expert has developed an expertise principally for purposes of litigation will obviously not be a substantial consideration.").

A review of the caselaw after Daubert shows that the rejection of expert testimony is the exception rather than the rule. Daubert did not work a "seachange over federal evidence law," and "the trial court's role as gatekeeper is not intended to serve as a replacement for the adversary system." United States v. 14.38 Acres of Land Situated in Leflore County, Mississippi, 80 F.3d 1074, 1078 (5th Cir. 1996). As the Court in Daubert stated: "Vigorous cross-examination, presentation of contrary evidence, and careful instruction on the burden of proof are the traditional and appropriate means of attacking shaky but admissible evidence." 509 U.S. at 595. Likewise, this amendment is not intended to provide an excuse for an automatic challenge to the testimony of every expert. See Kumho Tire Co. v. Carmichael, 119 S.Ct. 1167, 1176 (1999) (noting that the trial judge has the discretion "both to avoid unnecessary 'reliability' proceedings in ordinary cases where the reliability of an expert's methods is properly taken for granted, and to require appropriate proceedings in the less usual or more complex cases where cause for questioning the expert's reliability arises.").

264

When a trial court, applying this amendment, rules that an expert's testimony is reliable, this does not necessarily mean that contradictory expert testimony is unreliable. The amendment is broad enough to permit testimony that is the product of competing principles or methods in the same field of expertise. See, e.g., Heller v. Shaw Industries, Inc., 167 F.3d 146, 160 (3d Cir. 1999) (expert testimony cannot be excluded simply because the expert uses one test rather than another, when both tests are accepted in the field and both reach reliable results). As the court stated in In re Paoli R.R. Yard PCB Litigation, 35 F.3d 717, 744 (3d Cir. 1994), proponents "do not have to demonstrate to the judge by a preponderance of the evidence that the assessments of their experts are correct, they only have to demonstrate by a preponderance of evidence that their opinions are reliable. . . . The evidentiary requirement of reliability is lower than the merits standard of correctness." See also Daubert v. Merrill Dow Pharmaceuticals, Inc., 43 F.3d 1311, 1318 (9th Cir. 1995) (scientific experts might be permitted to testify if they could show that the methods they used were also employed by "a recognized minority of scientists in their field."); Ruiz-Troche v. Pepsi Cola, 161 F.3d 77, 85 (1st Cir. 1998) ("Daubert neither requires nor empowers trial courts to determine which of several competing scientific theories has the best provenance.").

The Court in Daubert declared that the "focus, of course, must be solely on principles and methodology, not on the conclusions they generate." 509 U.S. at 595. Yet as the Court later recognized, "conclusions and methodology are not entirely distinct from one another." General Elec. Co. v. Joiner, 522 U.S. 136, 146 (1997). Under the amendment, as under Daubert, when an expert purports to apply principles and methods in accordance with professional standards, and yet reaches a conclusion that other experts in the field would not reach, the trial court may fairly suspect that the principles and methods have not been faithfully applied. See Lust v. Merrill Dow Pharmaceuticals, Inc., 89 F.3d 594, 598 (9th Cir. 1996). The amendment specifically provides that the trial court must scrutinize not only the principles and methods used by the expert, but also whether those principles and methods have been properly applied to the facts of the case. As the court noted in In re Paoli R.R. Yard PCB Litig., 35 F.3d 717, 745 (3d Cir. 1994), "any step that renders the analysis unreliable . . . renders the expert's testimony inadmissible. This is true whether the step completely changes a reliable methodology or merely misapplies that methodology."

If the expert purports to apply principles and methods to the facts of the case, it is important that this application be conducted reliably. Yet it might also be important in some cases for an expert to educate the factfinder about general principles, without ever attempting to apply these principles to the specific facts of the case. For example, experts might instruct the factfinder on the principles of thermodynamics, or bloodclotting, or on how financial markets respond to corporate reports, without ever knowing about or trying to tie their testimony into the facts of the case. The amendment does not alter the venerable practice of using expert testimony to educate the factfinder on general principles. For this kind of generalized testimony, Rule 702 simply requires that: (1) the expert be qualified; (2) the testimony address a subject matter on which the factfinder can be assisted by an expert; (3) the testimony be reliable; and (4) the testimony "fit" the facts of the case.

As stated earlier, the amendment does not distinguish between scientific and other forms of expert testimony. The trial court's gatekeeping function applies to testimony by any expert. See Kumho Tire Co. v. Carmichael, 119 S.Ct. 1167, 1171 (1999) ("We conclude that Daubert's general holding—setting forth the trial judge's general 'gatekeeping' obligation—applies not only to testimony based on 'scientific' knowledge, but also to testimony based on 'technical' and 'other specialized' knowledge."). While the relevant factors for determining reliability will vary from expertise to expertise, the amendment rejects the premise that an expert's testimony should be treated more permissively simply because it is outside the realm of science. An opinion from an expert who is not a scientist should receive the same degree of scrutiny for reliability as an opinion from an expert who purports to be a scientist. See Watkins v. Telsmith, Inc., 121 F.3d 984, 991 (5th Cir. 1997) ("[I]t seems exactly backwards that experts who purport to rely on general engineering principles and practical experience might escape screening by the district court simply by stating that their conclusions were not reached by any particular method or technique."). Some types of expert testimony will be more objectively verifiable, and subject to the expectations of falsifiability, peer review, and publication, than others. Some types of expert testimony will not rely on anything like a scientific method, and so will have to be evaluated by reference to other standard principles attendant to the particular area of expertise. The trial judge in all cases of proffered expert testimony must find that it is properly grounded, well-reasoned, and not speculative before it can be admitted. The expert's testimony must be grounded in an accepted body of learning or experience in the expert's field, and the expert must explain how the conclusion is so grounded. See, e.g., American College of Trial Lawyers, Standards and Procedures for Determining the Admissibility of Expert Testimony after Daubert, 157 F.R.D. 571, 579 (1994) ("[W]hether the testimony concerns economic principles, accounting standards, property valuation or other nonscientific subjects, it should be evaluated by reference to the 'knowledge and experience' of that particular field.").

The amendment requires that the testimony must be the product of reliable principles and methods that are reliably applied to the facts of the case. While the terms "principles" and "methods" may convey a certain impression when applied to scientific knowledge, they remain relevant when applied to testimony based on technical or other specialized knowledge. For example, when a law enforcement agent testifies regarding the use of code words in a drug transaction, the principle used by the agent is that participants in such transactions regularly use code words to conceal the nature of their activities. The method used by the agent is the application of extensive experience to analyze the meaning of the conversations. So long as the principles and methods are reliable and applied reliably to the facts of the case, this type of testimony should be admitted.

Nothing in this amendment is intended to suggest that experience alone—or experience in conjunction with other knowledge, skill, training or education—may not provide a sufficient foundation for expert testimony. To the contrary, the text of Rule 702 expressly contemplates that an expert may be qualified on the basis of experience. In certain fields, experience is the predominant, if not sole, basis for a great deal of reliable expert testimony. See, e.g., United States v. Jones, 107 F.3d 1147 (6th Cir. 1997) (no abuse of discretion in admitting the testimony of a handwriting examiner who had years of practical experience and extensive training, and who explained his methodology in detail); Tassin v. Sears Roebuck, 946 F.Supp. 1241, 1248 (M.D.La. 1996) (design engineer's testimony can be admissible when the expert's opinions "are based on facts, a reasonable investigation, and traditional technical/mechanical expertise, and he provides a reasonable link between the information and procedures he uses and the conclusions he reaches"). See also Kumho Tire Co. v. Carmichael, 119 S.Ct. 1167, 1178 (1999) (stating that "no one denies that an expert might draw a conclusion from a set of observations based on extensive and specialized experience.").

If the witness is relying solely or primarily on experience, then the witness must explain how that experience leads to the conclusion reached, why that experience is a sufficient basis for the opinion, and how that experience is reliably applied to the facts. The trial court's gatekeeping function requires more than simply "taking the expert's word for it." See Daubert v. Merrill Dow Pharmaceuticals, Inc., 43 F.3d 1311, 1319 (9th Cir. 1995) ("We've been presented with only the experts' qualifications, their conclusions and their assurances of reliability. Under Daubert, that's not enough."). The more subjective and controversial the expert's inquiry, the more likely the testimony should be excluded as unreliable. See O'Conner v. Commonwealth Edison Co., 13 F.3d 1090 (7th Cir. 1994) (expert testimony based on a completely subjective methodology held properly excluded). See also Kumho Tire Co. v. Carmichael, 119 S.Ct. 1167, 1176 (1999) ("[I]t will at times be useful to ask even of a witness whose expertise is based purely on experience, say, a perfume tester able to distinguish among 140 odors at a sniff, whether his preparation is of a kind that others in the field would recognize as acceptable.").

Subpart (1) of Rule 702 calls for a quantitative rather than qualitative analysis. The amendment requires that expert testimony be based on sufficient underlying "facts or data." The term "data" is intended to encompass the reliable opinions of other experts. See the original Advisory Committee Note to Rule 703. The language "facts or data" is broad enough to allow an expert to rely on hypothetical facts that are supported by the evidence. Id.

When facts are in dispute, experts sometimes reach different conclusions based on competing versions of the facts. The emphasis in the amendment on "sufficient facts or data" is not intended to authorize a trial court to exclude an expert's testimony on the ground that the court believes one version of the facts and not the other.

There has been some confusion over the relationship between Rules 702 and 703. The amendment makes clear that the sufficiency of the basis of an expert's testimony is to be decided under Rule 702. Rule 702 sets forth the overarching requirement of reliability, and an analysis of the sufficiency of the expert's basis cannot be divorced from the ultimate reliability of the expert's opinion. In contrast, the "reasonable reliance" requirement of Rule 703 is a relatively narrow inquiry. When an expert relies on inadmissible information, Rule 703 requires the trial court to determine whether that information is of a type reasonably relied on by other experts in the field. If so, the expert can rely on the information in reaching an opinion. However, the question whether the expert is relying on a sufficient basis of information—whether admissible information or not—is governed by the requirements of Rule 702.

The amendment makes no attempt to set forth procedural requirements for exercising the trial court's gatekeeping function over expert testimony. See Daniel J. Capra, The Daubert Puzzle, 38 Ga.L.Rev. 699, 766 (1998) ("Trial courts should be allowed substantial discretion in dealing with Daubert questions; any attempt to codify procedures will likely give rise to unnecessary changes in practice and create difficult questions for appellate review."). Courts have shown considerable ingenuity and flexibility in considering challenges to expert testimony under Daubert, and it is contemplated that this will continue under the amended Rule. See, e.g., Cortes-Irizarry v. Corporacion Insular, 111 F.3d 184 (1st Cir. 1997) (discussing the application of Daubert in ruling on a motion for summary judgment); In re Paoli R.R. Yard PCB Litig., 35 F.3d 717, 736, 739 (3d Cir. 1994) (discussing the use of in limine hearings); Claar v. Burlington N.R.R., 29 F.3d 499, 502-05 (9th Cir. 1994) (discussing the trial court's technique of ordering experts to submit serial affidavits explaining the reasoning and methods underlying their conclusions).

The amendment continues the practice of the original Rule in referring to a qualified witness as an "expert." This was done to provide continuity and to minimize change. The use of the term "expert" in the Rule does not, however, mean that a jury should actually be informed that a qualified witness is testifying as an "expert." Indeed, there is much to be said for a practice that prohibits the use of the term "expert" by both the parties and the court at trial. Such a practice "ensures that trial courts do not inadvertently put their stamp of authority" on a witness's opinion, and protects against the jury's being "overwhelmed by the so-called 'experts'." Hon. Charles Richey, Proposals to Eliminate the Prejudicial Effect of the Use of the Word ``Expert'' Under the Federal Rules of Evidence in Criminal and Civil Jury Trials, 154 F.R.D. 537, 559 (1994) (setting forth limiting instructions and a standing order employed to prohibit the use of the term "expert" in jury trials).

GAP Report—Proposed Amendment to Rule 702. The Committee made the following changes to the published draft of the proposed amendment to Evidence Rule 702:

1. The word "reliable" was deleted from Subpart (1) of the proposed amendment, in order to avoid an overlap with Evidence Rule 703, and to clarify that an expert opinion need not be excluded simply because it is based on hypothetical facts. The Committee Note was amended to accord with this textual change.

2. The Committee Note was amended throughout to include pertinent references to the Supreme Court's decision in Kumho Tire Co. v. Carmichael, which was rendered after the proposed amendment was released for public comment. Other citations were updated as well.

3. The Committee Note was revised to emphasize that the amendment is not intended to limit the right to jury trial, nor to permit a challenge to the testimony of every expert, nor to preclude the testimony of experience-based experts, nor to prohibit testimony based on competing methodologies within a field of expertise.

4. Language was added to the Committee Note to clarify that no single factor is necessarily dispositive of the reliability inquiry mandated by Evidence Rule 702.

Rule 703. Bases of Opinion Testimony by Experts

The facts or data in the particular case upon which an expert bases an opinion or inference may be those perceived by or made known to the expert at or before the hearing. If of a type reasonably relied upon by experts in the particular field in forming opinions or inferences upon the subject, the facts or data need not be admissible in evidence in order for the opinion or inference to be admitted. Facts or data that are otherwise inadmissible shall not be disclosed to the jury by the proponent of the opinion or inference unless the court determines that their probative value in assisting the jury to evaluate the expert's opinion substantially outweighs their prejudicial effect.

(Pub. L. 93-595, § 1, Jan. 2, 1975, 88 Stat. 1937; Mar. 2, 1987, eff. Oct. 1, 1987; Apr. 17, 2000, eff. Dec. 1, 2000.)

Federal Rules of Evidence

Notes of Advisory Committee on Proposed Rules

Facts or data upon which expert opinions are based may, under the rule, be derived from three possible sources. The first is the firsthand observation of the witness, with opinions based thereon traditionally allowed. A treating physician affords an example. Rheingold, The Basis of Medical Testimony, 15 Vand.L.Rev. 473, 489 (1962). Whether he must first relate his observations is treated in Rule 705. The second source, presentation at the trial, also reflects existing practice. The technique may be the familiar hypothetical question or having the expert attend the trial and hear the testimony establishing the facts. Problems of determining what testimony the expert relied upon, when the latter technique is employed and the testimony is in conflict, may be resolved by resort to Rule 705. The third source contemplated by the rule consists of presentation of data to the expert outside of court and other than by his own perception. In this respect the rule is designed to broaden the basis for expert opinions beyond that current in many jurisdictions and to bring the judicial practice into line with the practice of the experts themselves when not in court. Thus a physician in his own practice bases his diagnosis on information from numerous sources and of considerable variety, including statements by patients and relatives, reports and opinions from nurses, technicians and other doctors, hospital records, and X rays. Most of them are admissible in evidence, but only with the expenditure of substantial time in producing and examining various authenticating witnesses. The physician makes life-and-death decisions in reliance upon them. His validation, expertly performed and subject to cross-examination, ought to suffice for judicial purposes. Rheingold, supra, at 531; McCormick § 15. A similar provision is California Evidence Code § 801(b).

The rule also offers a more satisfactory basis for ruling upon the admissibility of public opinion poll evidence. Attention is directed to the validity of the techniques employed rather than to relatively fruitless inquiries whether hearsay is involved. See Judge Feinberg's careful analysis in Zippo Mfg. Co. v. Rogers Imports, Inc., 216 F.Supp. 670 (S.D.N.Y. 1963). See also Blum et al, The Art of Opinion Research: A Lawyer's Appraisal of an Emerging Service, 24 U.Chi.L.Rev. 1 (1956); Bonynge, Trademark Surveys and Techniques and Their Use in Litigation, 48 A.B.A.J. 329 (1962); Zeisel, The Uniqueness of Survey Evidence, 45 Cornell L.Q. 322 (1960); Annot., 76 A.L.R.2d 919.

If it be feared that enlargement of permissible data may tend to break down the rules of exclusion unduly, notice should be taken that the rule requires that the facts or data "be of a type reasonably relied upon by experts in the particular field." The language would not warrant admitting in evidence the opinion of an "accidentologist" as to the point of impact in an automobile collision based on statements of bystanders, since this requirement is not satisfied. See Comment, Cal.Law Rev.Comm'n, Recommendation Proposing an Evidence Code 148-150 (1965).

Notes of Advisory Committee on Rules—1987 Amendment

The amendment is technical. No substantive change is intended.

Committee Notes on Rules—2000 Amendment

Rule 703 has been amended to emphasize that when an expert reasonably relies on inadmissible information to form an opinion or inference, the underlying information is not admissible simply because the opinion or inference is admitted. Courts have reached different results on how to treat inadmissible information when it is reasonably relied upon by an expert in forming an opinion or drawing an inference. Compare United States v. Rollins, 862 F.2d 1282 (7th Cir. 1988) (admitting, as part of the basis of an FBI agent's expert opinion on the meaning of code language, the hearsay statements of an informant), with United States v. 0.59 Acres of Land, 109 F.3d 1493 (9th Cir. 1997) (error to admit hearsay offered as the basis of an expert opinion, without a limiting instruction). Commentators have also taken differing views. See, e.g., Ronald Carlson, Policing the Bases of Modern Expert Testimony, 39 Vand.L.Rev. 577 (1986) (advocating limits on the jury's consideration of otherwise inadmissible evidence used as the basis for an expert opinion); Paul Rice, Inadmissible Evidence as a Basis for Expert Testimony: A Response to Professor Carlson, 40 Vand.L.Rev. 583 (1987) (advocating unrestricted use of information reasonably relied upon by an expert).

When information is reasonably relied upon by an expert and yet is admissible only for the purpose of assisting the jury in evaluating an expert's opinion, a trial court applying this Rule must consider the information's probative value in assisting the jury to weigh the expert's opinion on the one hand, and the risk of prejudice resulting from the jury's potential misuse of the information for substantive purposes on the other. The information may be disclosed to the jury, upon objection, only if the trial court finds that the probative value of the information in assisting the jury to evaluate the expert's opinion substantially outweighs its prejudicial effect. If the otherwise inadmissible information is admitted under this balancing test, the trial judge must give a limiting instruction upon request, informing the jury that the underlying information must not be used for substantive purposes. See Rule 105. In determining the appropriate course, the trial court should consider the probable effectiveness or lack of effectiveness of a limiting instruction under the particular circumstances.

The amendment governs only the disclosure to the jury of information that is reasonably relied on by an expert, when that information is not admissible for substantive purposes. It is not intended to affect the admissibility of an expert's testimony. Nor does the amendment prevent an expert from relying on information that is inadmissible for substantive purposes.

Nothing in this Rule restricts the presentation of underlying expert facts or data when offered by an adverse party. See Rule 705. Of course, an adversary's attack on an expert's basis will often open the door to a proponent's rebuttal with information that was reasonably relied upon by the expert, even if that information would not have been discloseable initially under the balancing test provided by this amendment. Moreover, in some circumstances the proponent might wish to disclose information that is relied upon by the expert in order to "remove the sting" from the opponent's anticipated attack, and thereby prevent the jury from drawing an unfair negative inference. The trial court should take this consideration into account in applying the balancing test provided by this amendment.

This amendment covers facts or data that cannot be admitted for any purpose other than to assist the jury to evaluate the expert's opinion. The balancing test provided in this amendment is not applicable to facts or data that are admissible for any other purpose but have not yet been offered for such a purpose at the time the expert testifies.

The amendment provides a presumption against disclosure to the jury of information used as the basis of an expert's opinion and not admissible for any substantive purpose, when that information is offered by the proponent of the expert. In a multi-party case, where one party proffers an expert whose testimony is also beneficial to other parties, each such party should be deemed a "proponent" within the meaning of the amendment.

GAP Report—Proposed Amendment to Rule 703. The Committee made the following changes to the published draft of the proposed amendment to Evidence Rule 703:

1. A minor stylistic change was made in the text, in accordance with the suggestion of the Style Subcommittee of the Standing Committee on Rules of Practice and Procedure.
2. The words "in assisting the jury to evaluate the expert's opinion" were added to the text, to specify the proper purpose for offering the otherwise inadmissible information relied on by an expert. The Committee Note was revised to accord with this change in the text.
3. Stylistic changes were made to the Committee Note.
4. The Committee Note was revised to emphasize that the balancing test set forth in the proposal should be used to determine whether an expert's basis may be disclosed to the jury either (1) in rebuttal or (2) on direct examination to "remove the sting" of an opponent's anticipated attack on an expert's basis.

Rule 704. Opinion on Ultimate Issue

(a) Except as provided in subdivision (b), testimony in the form of an opinion or inference otherwise admissible is not objectionable because it embraces an ultimate issue to be decided by the trier of fact.

(b) No expert witness testifying with respect to the mental state or condition of a defendant in a criminal case may state an opinion or inference as to whether the defendant did or did not have the mental state or condition constituting an element of the crime charged or of a defense thereto. Such ultimate issues are matters for the trier of fact alone.

(Pub. L. 93-595, § 1, Jan. 2, 1975, 88 Stat. 1937; Pub. L. 98-473, title II, § 406, Oct. 12, 1984, 98 Stat. 2067.)

Notes of Advisory Committee on Proposed Rules

The basic approach to opinions, lay and expert, in these rules is to admit them when helpful to the trier of fact. In order to render this approach fully effective and to allay any doubt on the subject, the so-called "ultimate issue" rule is specifically abolished by the instant rule.

The older cases often contained strictures against allowing witnesses to express opinions upon ultimate issues, as a particular aspect of the rule against opinions. The rule was unduly restrictive, difficult of application, and generally served only to deprive the trier of fact of useful information. 7 Wigmore § 1920, 1921; McCormick § 12. The basis usually assigned for the rule, to prevent the witness from "usurping the province of the jury," is aptly characterized as "empty rhetoric." 7 Wigmore § 1920, p. 17. Efforts to meet the felt needs of particular situations led to odd verbal circumlocutions which were said not to violate the rule. Thus a witness could express his estimate of the criminal responsibility of an accused in terms of sanity or insanity, but not in terms of ability to tell right from wrong or other more modern standard. And in cases of medical causation, witnesses were sometimes required to couch their opinions in cautious phrases of "might or could," rather than "did," though the result was to deprive many opinions of the positiveness to which they were entitled, accompanied by the hazard of a ruling of insufficiency to support a verdict. In other instances the rule was simply disregarded, and, as concessions to need, opinions were allowed upon such matters as intoxication, speed, handwriting, and value, although more precise coincidence with an ultimate issue would scarcely be possible.

Many modern decisions illustrate the trend to abandon the rule completely. People v. Wilson, 25 Cal.2d 341, 153 P.2d 720 (1944), whether abortion necessary to save life of patient; Clifford-Jacobs Forging Co. v. Industrial Comm., 19 Ill.2d 236, 166 N.E.2d 582 (1960), medical causation; Dowling v. L. H. Shattuck, Inc., 91 N.H. 234, 17 A.2d 529 (1941), proper method of shoring ditch; Schweiger v. Solbeck, 191 Or. 454, 230 P.2d 195 (1951), cause of landslide. In each instance the opinion was allowed.

The abolition of the ultimate issue rule does not lower the bars so as to admit all opinions. Under Rules 701 and 702, opinions must be helpful to the trier of fact, and Rule 403 provides for exclusion of evidence which wastes time. These provisions afford ample assurances against the admission of opinions which would merely tell the jury what result to reach, somewhat in the manner of the oath-helpers of an earlier day. They also stand ready to exclude opinions phrased in terms of inadequately explored legal criteria. Thus the question, "Did T have capacity to make a will?" would be excluded, while the question, "Did T have sufficient mental capacity to know the nature and extent of his property and the natural objects of his bounty and to formulate a rational scheme of distribution?" would be allowed. McCormick § 12.

For similar provisions see Uniform Rule 56(4); California Evidence Code § 805; Kansas Code of Civil Procedures § 60-456(d); New Jersey Evidence Rule 56(3).

Amendment by Public Law

1984—Pub. L. 98-473 designated existing provisions as subd. (a), inserted "Except as provided in subdivision (b)", and added subd. (b).

Rule 705. Disclosure of Facts or Data Underlying Expert Opinion

The expert may testify in terms of opinion or inference and give reasons therefor without first testifying to the underlying facts or data, unless the court requires otherwise. The expert may in any event be required to disclose the underlying facts or data on cross-examination.

(Pub. L. 93-595, § 1, Jan. 2, 1975, 88 Stat. 1938; Mar. 2, 1987, eff. Oct. 1, 1987; Apr. 22, 1993, eff. Dec. 1, 1993.)

Notes of Advisory Committee on Proposed Rules

The hypothetical question has been the target of a great deal of criticism as encouraging partisan bias, affording an opportunity for summing up in the middle of the case, and as complex and time consuming. Ladd, Expert Testimony, 5 Vand.L.Rev. 414, 426-427 (1952). While the rule allows counsel to make disclosure of the underlying facts or data as a preliminary to the giving of an expert opinion, if he chooses, the instances in which he is required to do so are reduced. This is true whether the expert bases his opinion on data furnished him at secondhand or observed by him at firsthand.

The elimination of the requirement of preliminary disclosure at the trial of underlying facts or data has a long background of support. In 1937 the Commissioners on Uniform State Laws incorporated a provision to this effect in the Model Expert Testimony Act, which furnished the basis for Uniform Rules 57 and 58. Rule 4515, N.Y. CPLR (McKinney 1963), provides:

"Unless the court orders otherwise, questions calling for the opinion of an expert witness need not be hypothetical in form, and the witness may state his opinion and reasons without first specifying the data upon which it is based. Upon cross-examination, he may be required to specify the data * * *,"

See also California Evidence Code § 802; Kansas Code of Civil Procedure § 60-456, 60-457; New Jersey Evidence Rules 57, 58.

If the objection is made that leaving it to the cross-examiner to bring out the supporting data is essentially unfair, the answer is that he is under no compulsion to bring out any facts or data except those unfavorable to the opinion. The answer assumes that the cross-examiner has the advance knowledge which is essential for effective cross-examination. This advance knowledge has been afforded, though imperfectly, by the traditional foundation requirement. Rule 26(b)(4) of the Rules of Civil Procedure, as revised, provides for substantial discovery in this area, obviating in large measure the obstacles which have been raised in some instances to discovery of findings, underlying data, and even the identity of the experts. Friedenthal, Discovery and Use of an Adverse Party's Expert Information, 14 Stan.L.Rev. 455 (1962).

These safeguards are reinforced by the discretionary power of the judge to require preliminary disclosure in any event.

Notes of Advisory Committee on Rules—1987 Amendment

The amendment is technical. No substantive change is intended.

Notes of Advisory Committee on Rules—1993 Amendment

This rule, which relates to the manner of presenting testimony at trial, is revised to avoid an arguable conflict with revised Rules 26(a)(2)(B) and 26(e)(1) of the Federal Rules of Civil Procedure or with revised Rule 16 of the Federal Rules of Criminal Procedure, which require disclosure in advance of trial of the basis and reasons for an expert's opinions.

If a serious question is raised under Rule 702 or 703 as to the admissibility of expert testimony, disclosure of the underlying facts or data on which opinions are based may, of course, be needed by the court before deciding whether, and to what extent, the person should be allowed to testify. This rule does not preclude such an inquiry.

Rule 706. Court Appointed Experts

(a) Appointment.—The court may on its own motion or on the motion of any party enter an order to show cause why expert witnesses should not be appointed, and may request the parties to submit nominations. The court may appoint any expert witnesses agreed upon by the parties, and may appoint expert witnesses of its own selection. An expert witness shall not be appointed by the court unless the witness consents to act. A witness so appointed shall be informed of the witness's duties by the court in writing, a copy of which shall be filed with the clerk, or at a conference in which the parties shall have opportunity to participate. A witness so appointed shall advise the parties of the witness's findings, if any; the witness's deposition may be taken by any party; and the witness may be called to testify by the court or any party. The witness shall be subject to cross-examination by each party, including a party calling the witness.

(b) Compensation.—Expert witnesses so appointed are entitled to reasonable compensation in whatever sum the court may allow. The compensation thus fixed is payable from funds which may be provided by law in criminal cases and civil actions and proceedings involving just compensation under the fifth amendment. In other civil actions and proceedings the compensation shall be paid by the parties in such proportion and at such time as the court directs, and thereafter charged in like manner as other costs.

(c) Disclosure of appointment.—In the exercise of its discretion, the court may authorize disclosure to the jury of the fact that the court appointed the expert witness.

(d) Parties' experts of own selection.—Nothing in this rule limits the parties in calling expert witnesses of their own selection.

(Pub. L. 93-595, § 1, Jan. 2, 1975, 88 Stat. 1938; Mar. 2, 1987, eff. Oct. 1, 1987.)

Notes of Advisory Committee on Proposed Rules

The practice of shopping for experts, the venality of some experts, and the reluctance of many reputable experts to involve themselves in litigation, have been matters of deep concern. Though the contention is made that court appointed experts acquire an aura of infallibility to which they are not entitled. Levy, Impartial Medical Testimony—Revisited, 34 Temple L.Q. 416 (1961), the trend is increasingly to provide for their use. While experience indicates that actual appointment is a relatively infrequent occurrence, the assumption may be made that the availability of the procedure in itself decreases the need for resorting to it. The ever-present possibility that the judge may appoint an expert in a given case must inevitably exert a sobering effect on the expert witness of a party and upon the person utilizing his services.

The inherent power of a trial judge to appoint an expert of his own choosing is virtually unquestioned. Scott v. Spanjer Bros., Inc., 298 F.2d 928 (2d Cir. 1962); Danville Tobacco Assn. v. Bryant-Buckner Associates, Inc., 333 F.2d 202 (4th Cir. 1964); Sink, The Unused Power of a Federal Judge to Call His Own Expert Witnesses, 29 S.Cal.L.Rev. 195 (1956); 2 Wigmore § 563, 9 Id. § 2484; Annot., 95 A.L.R.2d 383. Hence the problem becomes largely one of detail.

The New York plan is well known and is described in Report by Special Committee of the Association of the Bar of the City of New York: Impartial Medical Testimony (1956). On recommendation of the Section of Judicial Administration, local adoption of an impartial medical plan was endorsed by the American Bar Association. 82 A.B.A.Rep. 184-185 (1957). Descriptions and analyses of plans in effect in various parts of the country are found in Van Dusen, A United States District Judge's View of the Impartial Medical Expert System, 322 F.R.D. 498 (1963); Wick and Kightlinger, Impartial Medical Testimony Under the Federal Civil Rules: A Tale of Three Doctors, 34 Ins. Counsel J. 115 (1967); and numerous articles collected in Klein, Judicial Administration and the Legal Profession 393 (1963). Statutes and rules include California Evidence Code § 730-733; Illinois Supreme Court Rule 215(d), Ill.Rev.Stat.1969, c. 110A, § 215(d); Burns Indiana Stats. 1956, § 9-1702; Wisconsin Stats.Annot.1958, § 957.27.

In the federal practice, a comprehensive scheme for court appointed experts was initiated with the adoption of Rule 28 of the Federal Rules of Criminal Procedure in 1946. The Judicial Conference of the United States in 1953 considered court appointed experts in civil cases, but only with respect to whether they should be compensated from public funds, a proposal which was rejected. Report of the Judicial Conference of the United States 23 (1953). The present rule expands the practice to include civil cases.

Subdivision (a) is based on Rule 28 of the Federal Rules of Criminal Procedure, with a few changes, mainly in the interest of clarity. Language has been added to provide specifically for the appointment either on motion of a party or on the judge's own motion. A provision subjecting the court appointed expert to deposition procedures has been incorporated. The rule has been revised to make definite the right of any party, including the party calling him, to cross-examine.

Subdivision (b) combines the present provision for compensation in criminal cases with what seems to be a fair and feasible handling of civil cases, originally found in the Model Act and carried from there into Uniform Rule 60. See also California Evidence Code § 730-731. The special provision for Fifth Amendment compensation cases is designed to guard against reducing constitutionally guaranteed just compensation by requiring the recipient to pay costs. See Rule 71A(l) of the Rules of Civil Procedure.

Subdivision (c) seems to be essential if the use of court appointed experts is to be fully effective. Uniform Rule 61 so provides.

Subdivision (d) is in essence the last sentence of Rule 28(a) of the Federal Rules of Criminal Procedure.

Notes of Advisory Committee on Rules—1987 Amendment

The amendments are technical. No substantive change is intended.

GLOSSARY

Alternative Remittance Systems Sometimes referred to as parallel banking systems, ARSs function alongside and transparent to the legitimate banking system. The Black Market Peso Exchange, Hawala system, and the Asian Chit system are all examples of ARSs. Using ARSs, individuals can transfer large sums of cash among countries without leaving a paper trail.

Antecedent Phrase The subject phrase of the major premise of a syllogism.

ARS *See* Alternative Remittance Systems.

Bank Secrecy Act, the The foundation of U.S. money-laundering laws. Passed in 1970, it creates "paper trail" requirements for banks, making the tracking and recovery of illegal proceeds easier for law enforcement.

Bates Numbers Multi-digit numbers frequently used in filing systems in law offices. They are called Bates numbers because Bates® brand self-inking stamps were used to serialize each page of legal documents.

Bayesian Network An inference network based on the theory of Thomas Bayes, an eighteenth-century minister, that allows scientists to combine test data with prior hypotheses and observations to arrive at new probabilistic predictions of cause and effect.

Bearer Shares A form of corporate ownership characterized by possession of unregistered stock certificates. There is no written record identifying actual corporate shareholders. As a result, corporate ownership in this form is popular among money launderers. This form of corporate ownership is largely illegal in most developed nations. However, some LDCs still permit incorporation by bearer share.

Casebook System An organizational tool of value in complex investigations. The casebook system is based on the trial book concept in legal practice and acts as a central repository for everything related to the current investigation. It facilitates retrieval of information.

CBCA Criteria Based Content Analysis. A method of evaluating written statements based on proven psychological tendencies and variations between truthful written statements and fabrications. This technique has been the subject of considerable study and controversy in its use in assessing alleged abuse victims' statements to police.

CEO Chief Executive Officer.

CFO Chief Financial Officer.

Circumstantial Evidence Evidence that indirectly proves the ultimate fact in question. Circumstantial evidence consists of evidence that builds up a series of inferences leading up to the final conclusion that a fact occurred.

CMIR *See* Currency and Monetary Instrument Report.

Cogency The probative force, weight, or impact a particular piece of evidence will have.

Cognitive Interview A form of interview technique based on the principles of cognitive interviewing developed in the late 1980s by Dr. R. Edward Geiselman and his colleagues. CI is essentially a systematized approach to exploiting recognized models of human information encoding and retrieval.

Comptroller Usually a high-ranking officer of a company whose primary responsibility is fiscal oversight. Often a CPA or CFO.

Concatenate Inferences A chain of inferences.

Confabulation Refers to a spurious memory constructed wholly within the subject's mind. For example, reporting that the suspect carried a gun when in fact he did not would be a confabulation. Confabulations may or may not be intentional.

Consequent Phrase The predicate of the major premise of a syllogism.

Consigliere Term used to refer to an advisor or counselor within an Italian organized crime family. From the Latin *consiglio*.

Context Reconstruction A cognitive interview technique in which the subject is asked to mentally re-create the environment in which the memory was encoded. For example, the subject is instructed to picture the room in which the crime happened.

Correspondent Bank A banking arrangement whereby one bank provides services to another to move funds, exchange currencies, and carry out other financial transactions. Correspondent banking has been identified as a gateway for money laundering because the bank-to-bank transactions are unregulated and untraceable.

CPA Certified Public Accountant.

Cryptography Refers to the encryption and deciphering of secret messages using code. Often found in relation to computer information and used by criminals to protect valuable data relevant to their criminal activity. Can be a significant hurdle to investigative efforts.

CTR *See* Currency Transaction Report.

Currency and Monetary Instrument Report Must be filed by anyone entering or leaving the United States with currency or monetary instruments in excess of $10,000.

Currency Transaction Report A report required to be filed when a financial institution receives or dispenses more than $10,000 in currency.

Glossary

Cyber-Laundering A relatively new term used to describe money-laundering activity that is perpetrated or facilitated by using high-tech means such as smart cards, E-cash, or Internet banking.

***Daubert* Challenge** Refers to an opposition challenge to expert witness testimony in a particular area on the grounds that the area of study is not a recognized field of study.

Decryption The reverse process of encryption whereby an encrypted message is decoded into plain text, rendering it readable.

Deductive Reasoning A form of logic that reasons from the general to the specific, often referred to as "top-down" reasoning.

Deposition A court-compelled interview conducted by counsel for either side in a dispute. The purpose of deposition information is discovery of relevant information about the case. As such, the rules of evidence regarding testimony are relaxed. Deposition is a key part of an expert witness's role in a case.

Direct Evidence Refers to evidence that directly proves the ultimate fact in issue with no intervening inferential steps. Comes in the form of eyewitness testimony that actually saw, heard, or touched some thing or event.

Discovery The pre-trial process of investigation centering around producing and obtaining information about the opposition's case.

Due Diligence Procedures a financial institution must undertake to prevent the use of its services for criminal purposes such as money laundering

EFT *See* Electronic Funds Transfer.

Electronic Funds Transfer A transfer of money between banks or other financial entities where no actual money is exchanged but merely an electronic reconciliation from one account to another takes place.

Encryption The act of encoding a plain-text message, rendering it unintelligible without the proper code.

Evidence Probative Value The inferential weight that a particular piece of evidence is expected to have on the finder-of-fact.

Evidence Type Refers to the extrinsic quality of the evidence; for example, fingerprints, documentary evidence.

Ex Post Facto A constitutional prohibition against exacting punishments not in existence at the time a crime was committed.

Exculpatory Tending to acquit, vindicate, or prove innocent.

FATF *See* Financial Action Task Force

Federal Rules of Civil Procedure The federal rules that dictate allowable and prohibited conduct in pre-trial, trial, and post-trial activity. In particular, expert witness opinions and reports are subject to strict regulation under the federal rules.

Federal Rules of Evidence The federal rules governing admissibility of evidence, including qualification of expert witnesses.

Financial Action Task Force An international anti-money-laundering alliance established in 1987 by the G-7 nations. The FATF issues annual advisories and bulletins regarding non-cooperating nations and money-laundering activities.

Foreign Bank Account Form Required to be filed by anyone controlling more than $10,000 in a foreign bank account during any single year.

Form 8300 IRS form required when any person in business receives cash payments in exchange for goods or services exceeding $10,000 in a single transaction or a series of related transactions.

Free Report A cognitive interview technique that encourages the subject to relate any information regardless of perceived importance in a free-narrative form.

Frye **Challenge** A challenge to testimony of an expert witness on the grounds that the area of expertise is not a legitimate area of science. This challenge is most often used in state court. The federal equivalent is *Daubert*.

GAAP Generally Accepted Accounting Practice. The methods and practices accepted as legitimate within the accounting industry.

GAAS Generally Accepted Auditing Standards. The methods and practices generally acceptable within the auditing profession.

Generalization An assumption made by a large segment of the population. Often based on common sense, generalizations may be referred to as implicit inferences. For example, the statement "dropped objects fall" is a generalization about the nature of gravity.

GSR Gun shot residue. The trace particles of powder and metal deposited on a person's hands or clothing when firing a gun.

Haven Nation Countries, often LDCs, whose legislation, geographic location, and non-cooperation with international anti-money-laundering efforts make them a favored location for money-laundering activity.

IMF *See* International Monetary Fund.

Inculpatory Network A graphic representation of a complex probabilistic reasoning problem.

Information Technology Security The policy and procedure an entity has in place to protect its information and technology assets from theft or conversion.

Integration The third step of the money-laundering process. In this stage the money is reintroduced into the economy using methods that give the appearance of legitimate income. Often, shell and high-volume cash businesses will serve as fronts for this stage of the wash cycle.

International Monetary Fund An international organization headquartered in Washington, D.C., whose purpose is to monitor monetary and trade conditions throughout the world. The IMF oversees member countries' monetary policies and exchange rates. Today virtually every country in the world is a member.

Investigative Inference Model A chart model of an inference network that depicts the inferential steps necessary to link a suspect to a crime. The chart allows the investigator to track and analyze the logical steps necessary to develop probable cause for arrest.

ITSEC *See* Information Technology Security.

Key List A numerical list of facts, testimony, and propositions on which the investigative inference model is based. The key list contains an entry for every fact, evidentiary item, and generalization made about the investigation. It is from the key list that each node on the Investigative Inference Model is defined.

Kinesic Mirroring An NLP interview technique that involves the interviewer gradually and imperceptibly adopting the gestures, body posture, and subtle movements of the subject in order to develop a rapport.

Know Your Customer A policy enforced by financial institutions that requires employees to make every effort to know their clients personally. It is believed that this initiative helps bank personnel identify suspicious activities and trends.

La Cosa Nostra Italian for "this thing of ours." Commonly used to refer to Italian organized crime.

Language Matching An NLP interview technique where the interviewer relates to the subject through similar linguistic cues and sensory retrieval methods.

Lapping A fraud scheme involving manipulation of accounts receivable, most often by an AR clerk. Income payments are used to replace money previously stolen by the suspect until incoming payments run out.

Layering The second step in the money-laundering process. In this stage, large sums of money are moved within the financial system through a series of transactions. Correspondent banking and OFCs often play a key role in this stage.

LCN *See* La Cosa Nostra.

LDC *See* Less Developed Countries.

Less Developed Countries Countries formerly referred to as Third World nations. These countries often become OFCs in order to attract foreign investment of capital in their economy. As a result, they are often viewed as haven nations and the weak link in money-laundering investigations.

Linguistic Cues Cues into a person's representational system.

Markov Models Inference networks that assist in solving complex probabilistic problems.

Master Chronology The case depicted as a timeline of events.

Memory Error As opposed to confabulations, memory errors are inaccuracies in an otherwise legitimate memory. For example, reporting that the suspect's shirt was blue when in fact it was red would be a memory error.

Mixed Mass of Evidence Evidence whose composition is largely heterogeneous and voluminous. Often encountered in complicated cases and financial crimes involving multiple suspects.

Money Laundering A three-step process by which the proceeds of illegal activity are concealed and disguised as legitimate income.

NCCT *See* Non-Cooperative Countries and Territories.

NeuroLinguistic Programming A communications model developed by Dr. John Grinder at U.C. Santa Cruz, premised on the foundation that all communication originates from sensory sources, auditory, visual, kinesic, gustatory, or olfactory.

NLP *See* NeuroLingistic Programming.

Node An individual item of evidence, testimony, or proposition leading up to the ultimate conclusion in the Investigative Inference model. Each node is depicted on the chart using a single symbol identified by the key list number.

Non-Cooperative Countries and Territories Countries whose non-cooperation in international anti-money-laundering efforts makes them attractive locations for money-laundering activity. Annually, the FATF issues a list of NCCTs and monitors their activities.

OCE *See* Organized Criminal Enterprise.

OFC *See* Offshore Financial Center.

Offshore Finance The provision of financial services by banks and other agents to nonresidents.

Offshore Financial Center A place that hosts financial activities that are separated from major regulating units by geography and legislation. Although OFCs serve a legitimate purpose in the world of global finance, the existence of strict bank secrecy laws in the host countries makes OFCs attractive for money laundering.

Organized Criminal Enterprise An association of two or more entities whose acknowledged purpose is to profit from illegal activity.

Paralanguage Matching An NLP interview technique in which the interviewer adopts speech patterns such as volume, cadence, and tone, similar to the subject.

Parallel Banking Systems *See* Hawala.

Penultimate Probanda The one or more facts immediately below the ultimate probandum that must be proven in order to support the logical conclusion that the ultimate probandum is true. In a murder investigation, the penultimate probanda would be that (1) the B, the victim, is dead, (2) he did not die of natural causes, and (3) A in fact killed him.

Placement A term used in money laundering to describe the first step in the process where large sums of cash are introduced into the financial system for later legitimization.

Postmortem Latin for done or occurring after death. Commonly used to describe the examination done by a forensic pathologist to determine the cause and time of death.

Presentment The act of presenting a completed investigation to a prosecuting authority. Often this authority is a state or district attorney or grand jury; however, this act may also refer to initiation of a civil suit by a private attorney.

Proactive A method of criminal investigation based on officer-/investigator-initiated action. In the proactive investigation, law enforcement activity often occurs prior to reported criminal activity.

Probandum A fact needing to be proven.

Probative Value *See* Evidence Probative Value.

Public/Private Key Encryption A robust system of encryption using a complex set of key pairs that provides highly secure protection.

Reactive A method of criminal investigation based on victim- /witness-initiated action. In the reactive investigation, law enforcement activity often occurs after a crime has been committed or reported by the victim or witness.

Registered Shares Shares of stock signifying corporate ownership interest that are registered and often serialized to facilitate immediate identification of true corporate ownership. The standard form of corporate ownership in most developed nations.

Relevance As related to evidence, it is the tendency to either prove or disprove a fact in question.

Representational System A person's method of encoding, storing, and accessing information that follows a sensory model of sight, sound, touch, taste, and smell.

RICO Racketeering Influence Corrupt Organization.

SAR *See* Suspicious Activity Report.

Schema Theory A theory of memory and cognition that explains human memory in terms of a hierarchy of slots where new memories are encoded based on a script of familiar events.

SEC Securities and Exchange Commission—the governmental authority responsible for overseeing and regulating the sale of public securities.

Second Retrieval A cognitive interview technique that attempts to elicit missed information by asking the subject to make a second attempt at remembering the data.

Shell Banks Banks created in offshore financial centers that exist in name only for the purpose of facilitating money-laundering activity. Shell banks are often used to establish correspondent banking relationships with legitimate domestic banks in order to wire-transfer funds into haven nations.

Shell Corporation A legal entity created in name only. The use of shell corporations is common in layering and integration stages of money laundering because tracing true ownership of the corporation can often be difficult.

Smurfing A term used to describe a money-laundering placement strategy. In a smurfing operation, large sums of illegal profits are divided among many street-level runners for deposit into separate accounts. The transactions are structured to avoid the CTR reporting requirements.

Stare Decisis Latin for let the decision stand. A legal concept on which the common law system of legal adjudication of disputes is based, in which current disputes are decided largely based on previous cases.

Story of the Case A narrative account of the events in chronological order. Story is important in the investigativ`e context because it arranges the events of the case into a cohesive purposeful whole.

Structured Interview The predecessor of the cognitive interview.

Subpoena A legal document used to compel a party to either produce documents and records or appear and answer questions.

Suspicious Activity Report Report filed by bank when any employee has reason to suspect a person of money laundering, regardless of transaction size.

Syllogism A deductive scheme of formal argument that consists of a major premise, a minor premise, and a conclusion.

Theme of the Case A framework on which to hang the case. It is the underlying force showing why the defendant is wrong morally.

Theory of the Case A logical statement that defines the case as a whole. A statement that may be expressed as a series of concise syllogisms.

Ultimate Probandum That fact which is the ultimate fact in issue. For example, in a murder investigation, the ultimate probandum would be the fact that person A murdered person B.

INDEX

Index

Index

Index

Index

Index

Index

Index

ONE WEEK LOAN